FISCAL FEDERALISM IN UNITARY STATES

ZEI Studies in European Economics and Law

edited by:

Jürgen von Hagen and Christian Koenig
Center for European Integration Studies (ZEI)
University of Bonn
Walter Flex Strasse 3
D-53113 Bonn
Germany

Volume I
REGIONAL ASPECTS OF MONETARY POLICY IN EUROPE
edited by Jürgen von Hagen and Christopher J. Waller

Volume II
INSTITUTIONS, POLITICS AND FISCAL POLICY
edited by Rolf R. Strauch and Jürgen von Hagen

Volume III
EMPIRICAL STUDIES OF ENVIRONMENTAL POLICIES IN EUROPE
edited by John W. Maxwell and Jürgen von Hagen

Volume IV
REGIONALISM IN EUROPE:
Geometries and Strategies After 2000
edited by Jürgen von Hagen and Mika Widgren

Volume V
POLITICAL ECONOMY OF TRANSITION AND DEVELOPMENT:
Institutions, Politics and Policies
edited by Nauro F. Campos and Jan Fidrmuc

Volume VI
FISCAL FEDERALISM IN UNITARY STATES
edited by Per Molander

FISCAL FEDERALISM IN UNITARY STATES

edited by

Per Molander

SPRINGER SCIENCE+BUSINESS MEDIA, LLC

Library of Congress Cataloging-in-Publication

Fiscal Federalism in Unitary States / editor, Per Molander
ISBN 978-1-4020-7561-2 ISBN 978-1-4615-0503-7 (eBook)
DOI 10.1007/978-1-4615-0503-7

Printed on acid-free paper.

TABLE OF CONTENTS

PREFACE

Per Molander

Mapsec, Stockholm

In February 2000, the SNS Constitutional Project – a multi-year effort to investigate alternatives for constitutional reform in Sweden – hosted a workshop on fiscal federalism at Johannesberg Manor north of Stockholm. Professor Dennis C. Mueller was instrumental in bringing together a group of scholars from Canada, the US and the European continent, and the common task was to discuss the relevance of the theory of fiscal federalism to the problems of multi-level democracies. The contributions to the workshop were published in a special issue of the *Journal of Constitutional and Political Economy* (Vol. 12, No.2, June 2001).

In a second phase of the project, an extended group of experts were invited to investigate more in depth the problems specific to unitary states with a well-developed local autonomy, such as the Nordic countries. Within this project, two more workshops have been organised, one in Sweden and the second at the Center for European Integration Studies (ZEI) in Bonn.

The present volume summarises the findings of this group of scholars. The complex of power division and fiscal relations is illuminated from a range of perspectives – economic, legal, and democratic. Although the theory of fiscal federalism was originally developed as a tool of analysis for truly federal states, we believe that perspectives and results from this literature are relevant also to the study of unitary states – increasingly so, given the process of decentralisation of political power that currently sweeps across industrialised countries as well as transition and developing countries.

Economic support from the SNS Constitutional Project and the ZEI in Bonn is gratefully acknowledged. The conclusions and recommendations put forward are at the responsibility of each author or group of authors.

Per Molander

1

INTRODUCTION - PROBLEMS OF MULTI-LEVEL DEMOCRACIES

Per Molander

Mapsec, Stockholm

INTRODUCTION

"Only a few years ago the inhabitants of Gothenburg were faced with just two ballot forms, one for the Riksdag (the national parliament) and one for the municipality," Olof Petersson writes in his contribution to this book. "Today the people of Gothenburg are represented by politicians at six levels: the European Parliament, Västra Götaland (the county council), the Gothenburg region (indirectly elected), Gothenburg (the municipality), and the neighbourhood council (also indirectly elected)[1]. How will popular will be realised in what is far from a transparent system?"

The public sector is organised in several levels in all countries except the very smallest ones. The tasks assumed by the public sector in a modern state are many and multi-faceted, and there is no reason to assume that all these tasks are managed rationally at one and the same level. In general terms thus, a multi-level format appears rational. On the other hand, a quick look shows that the division of powers and the distribution of tasks varies substantially even among countries that are similar in many other respects. This indicates that there is no particular division of powers that represents the highest degree of rationality. Different countries have different political and administrative traditions reflecting different priorities, and this is how it should be. Nonetheless, there may be substantial room for improvement. The six levels that the inhabitants of Gothenburg have to live with are not the result of a careful design of the public-sector hierarchy. There may be something to learn from other countries, and there is a possibility of genuine innovation.

STATE VERSUS LOCAL – A CLASSICAL PROBLEM

Already the presence of two levels in the public sector creates problems. The debate on relations between state and local powers is, not surprisingly, an old one. Countries differ in at least three dimensions: administrative, functional, and financial[2]. In *administrative* respects countries differ by the status that they assign to the local level. Some countries mention municipalities in the constitution (South Africa, Sweden), whereas others do not (the United States, Norway). How easy it is to create or merge municipalities? Is financial autonomy guaranteed by the

[1] Nilsson (red.) (2002).
[2] See Davidsson (forthcoming) with further references.

constitution? Sweden represents an intermediate position in these respects. Chapter 1 of the Swedish constitution establishes that democratic governance is assured *inter alia* via local autonomy. Further, the constitution mentions municipalities and county councils and establishes their right to levy taxes in order to finance their activities. The formation or merging of municipalities is not mentioned however, but is decided by the Government.

The oldest administrative units, the village and the "härad" (approximately the hundred), are pre-Christian. Following the establishment of Christianity, the parish became the basic unit of several functions beside the religious-administrative, for instance poor relief and – much later – basic education. The hundred was as natural a candidate for basic unit at the time of the municipal reform in 1862, but the parish was chosen in exchange for the support of the clergy for the dismantling of the estates-based parliament[3]. After the wave of mergers that was finalised in the mid-1970's, Sweden was in fact back at roughly the territorial division that would have obtained had the hundred instead been chosen as the basic administrative unit.

Also in *functional* respects there are important differences between countries. In some countries, municipalities are entitled to manage only what has been explicitly assigned to them by the state, whereas Sweden and other countries have a more generous definition of the legitimate municipal sphere. The requirement is that the activities be of general interest and that there is link to the area or the members of the municipality. Activities managed by the state, by other municipalities or by county councils are excluded.

That the state assigns certain tasks to the local level is, as we have seen, an old tradition. Poor relief, a partial responsibility for the military infrastructure, smallpox prophylactics, and basic education are early examples of such functions.

When it comes to *financing* finally, the picture is no les varied. A number of countries do guarantee the local power of taxation in the constitution. Other solutions are based upon tax base sharing, transfers from the state to the local level, fees and other revenues. The Nordic countries are characterised by a relatively high degree of local financial autonomy, but even within this group there are variations. In order to judge the degree of autonomy it is of course necessary to take into consideration how much of local activities are in fact prescribed by the state, and to what extent such activities are partly or wholly financed by the state.

Even in the simple case of two levels, there is a third party that complicates the analysis – the citizen. Arguments for or against local autonomy at the very least have to account for the consequences for the citizen of the various alternatives considered. And – as will be clear from the discussion to follow – what is "closest to the citizen" in the sense of being handled at the local level is not necessarily what is best for her.

---

[3] Stjernquist (2000).

ARGUMENTS FOR AND AGAINST LOCAL AUTONOMY

Arguments for and against local autonomy are linked both to ideas about the essence of democracy and to more material aspects on governance such as economic efficiency. One argument for strong local autonomy is that it is claimed to give more *freedom* to the citizens. The individual is in this case the point of departure, and every restriction on individual freedom of actions stemming from memberships in social groups encroaches upon the freedom of the individual. An individual in isolation cannot accomplish much without interacting with others, however, so it is not group membership as such but rather its mandatory character that is seen as problematic. The small-sized municipality would in this perspective be easier to live with than the national state.

A closely related argument is that the municipality can be the basis of a *community* of a different kind than the national state can offer. Ideological arguments of this kind have been used extensively in the debate between liberal and communitarian thinkers[4]. The strength of this argument to some degree depends on what groups it is considered reasonable for a group to interact with. The conditions for a communitarian feeling are obviously not the same in a small agglomeration of a few thousand inhabitants as in the city of Stockholm with 750 000.

Arguments for local autonomy aiming at political institutions tend to concentrate on *closeness* and *participation*. Geographical proximity to decision-makers is then assumed to be translatable into a deeper form of political nearness. That a higher degree of local autonomy leads to higher levels of participation can be correct in the sense that more political posts are assigned to individuals in general elections. The size of the basic administrative unit is obviously an important parameter in this context; in Europe, the average number of citizens per elected official varies from just over 100 (Czech Republic) to more than 5 000 (Greece). But more vital to the function of democracy than whether 1 or 3 per thousand of the population are elected officials is the interaction between these officials and the population as a whole.

Efficiency arguments for local autonomy have also been put forward. Efficiency is a concept with many dimensions. Efficiency in the *macroeconomic* sense would allegedly be reflected in a smaller public sector; the idea is that a number of mechanisms tend to make the public sector larger than what citizens really desire, and that the restraining mechanisms would be stronger the smaller the size of the political unit[5]. No matter whether the first part of the argument is correct or not, it is fairly easy to verify that there is no empirical support for the latter part; there is simply no clear correlation between the degree of local autonomy and the total public expenditure level[6]. By way of illustration, the Nordic countries combine a relatively high degree of local autonomy with a comparatively large public sector.

---

[4] Mulhall and Swift (1992).
[5] Stigler (1957), Brennan and Buchanan (1980).
[6] For some different views on the subject, see contributions by Söderström and by Moesen and Van Rompuy in Prud'homme (ed.) (1991).

But efficiency can also be interpreted in the sense that public service production better *reflect citizen preferences* if decisions are made at the local level. The idea is that the municipalities offer bundles of public services and that citizens can move to the municipality that best corresponds to their demands[7]. The empirical support for this hypothesis is not particularly strong[8]; moving implies high direct costs and can also lead to social costs in the form of lost social networks. A factor of some importance is also that lower tax levels tend to capitalise in the form of higher estate prices, which tends to increase friction. Nonetheless, Dahlberg and Fredriksson[9] have found some empirical support for the idea that mobility in local or regional labour markets is affected by the supply of public services and tax rates, whereas the mobility between regions shows no such effects.

An argument that connects to both closeness and efficiency is that local autonomy permits more of *experimentation* and therefore leads to a more rapid adaptation to new environmental conditions or changed preferences among the citizens. At least in theory, the conditions for variation are greater among decision-makers who see the local electorate as their principal than among regional or local managers within a national administrative structure. But it is an empirical question to what extent this potential variation actually materialises, and if so whether it is compatible with the idea of equal treatment.

Another argument related to efficiency is that local decision-makers know local conditions of production better. This was in fact one of the main arguments presented for the transition from ear-marked to general state transfers in Sweden in the early 1990's. Again, there seems to exist little empirical support for this argument. The transition from ear-marked to general state subsidies in principle liberates resources that could be used for tax reductions, but this sort of transition often turns out to have less noticeable effects than theory prescribes and the resources tend to stick in the municipal sector (the so-called "fly-paper effect")[10].

Adaptation to local conditions is of course possible also within national administrations such as the National Road Administration, provided that local managers are given appropriate freedom of action. Whether such adaptation actually occurs is an open questions, given that conditions of loyalty differ between national and local administrations.

Arguments against extensive local autonomy can be summoned areas as arguments in favour. Basic *human rights* of the kind that are enumerated in the constitution must be guaranteed by the national level. The protection of minorities can then (but need not) become stronger. In order to protect single individuals from abuse or assaults the state is prepared to intervene even into the nuclear family. On the other hand, history provides numerous examples of attacks on minorities that have been led from the national level, so it is difficult to draw any clear-cut conclusions in this respect.

[7] Tiebout (1956).
[8] Rubinfeld (1986).
[9] Dahlberg and Fredriksson (2001).
[10] Oulasvirta (1997). An example where conditions do have effects on behaviour is described in Bergström, Dahlberg and Johansson (1998).

Among these basic rights most people would be prepared to include access to services such as basic education and health care, services for which the state must accordingly guarantee minimal access. This requires either full state responsibility for the production or delegation of responsibilities combined with inspections and a right to intervene against deviations from the national norm.

The goal of *equalising* conditions of living may also come into conflict with far-reaching local autonomy. If public services to a great extent are defined and financed locally, there is of course also a substantial risk that the supply in certain areas will not meet nationally defined standards. This can be countered via different types of equalisation systems. The level of ambition and the design of these systems depend on the choice of tax bases, general transfers and other factors.

Against the communitarian ideology stands the idea that the nation is the traditional unit that can serve as a basis for political identity, and that ties of solidarity consequently should be defined at the national rather than the local level. A certain cultural homogeneity across the nation would then be beneficial.

Efficiency arguments can also be mustered against local autonomy. Extensive financial freedom threatens the capacity of the national government to maintain macro-economic stability[11]. Stabilisation in the event of economic shocks can also be difficult to accomplish at the local or regional level.

The existence of *economies of scale* in administration, public purchase etc. is an argument against too small units of administration. This was one of the main arguments for the mergers of the 1960's and the 1970's. The growth of public-sector engagement required economic and administrative competences considered to be beyond the reach of a small municipality.

Similar arguments are valid for the function of economic control. Many – perhaps most – issues are simply too complicated for the average citizen to have the necessary competence and time to assume the role of controller. Professional audit, qualified economic journalism etc. are necessary ingredients in the control process and are more easily supplied in large municipalities or at the national level.

ORGANISATION OF THE BOOK

Against the background of the many trade-off problems characterising state-local relationships, it should come as no surprise that there is substantial variation between countries, and that hybrid solutions are common within one and the same country. Such hybrids are often marred by internal contradictions and often lead to friction between the levels. The overall aim of the present book is to investigate whether there is room for changes that may contribute to reducing this kind of friction – for example by improving accountability, by changing the design of horizontal mechanisms of equalisation, or by strengthening the budget process.

---

[11] Ter-Minassian and Craig (1997).

The economic theory of multi-level democracy, the theory of fiscal federalism, has been developed primarily with formally federal states in mind[12]. The main application is by consequence a federal structure, in between a unitary state and a confederation. In relation to a fully unitary state, this represents some degree of decentralisation of political power. Starting instead from a group of autonomous states, the term of "federalism" will by contrast refer to a process of centralisation; this is how it is currently used in the discussion about the future development of the European Union.

The Nordic countries are of course not federal states, but they exhibit relatively far-reaching local autonomy by international comparison. The institutional problems that appear in such structures remind of what one finds in traditional federal states, which makes it natural to investigate to what extent existing methods and results from the theory of fiscal federalism are applicable in this context.

The report is published within the framework of the SNS Constitutional Project, and the perspective is basically constitutional. The question underlying the different analyses is *if*, and if so *how*, the relationship between the state and the local level should be regulated in the constitution in other ways than at present.

In chapter 2, Robin Boadway and Eva Mörk survey the division of powers between the state and the local level in an economic perspective. Which tasks are appropriately handled at the local level, and which are more naturally managed by the state? What are the consequences for the distribution of financial powers and the need for equalisation of economic resource bases?

Chapter 3, written by Jürgen von Hagen and Matz Dahlberg, concentrates on the financial freedom of action at the local level. In what way does the freedom of municipalities interact with the state's responsibility for maintaining financial stability? Is there a risk that municipalities behave irresponsibly, knowing that the state will in the last instance take care of acute financial problems in the future? Experiences from abroad indicate that this might be the case.

In the following chapter Howard Chernick analyses the ambitious Swedish system of equalisation. Ever since its introduction in the early 1990's, the system has been criticised for various reasons – for violating the constitution, for reducing or eliminating incentives to economic growth, for stimulating over-consumption of public services, etc. Chernick analyses some of these issues against the background of experiences from other countries.

In chapter 5, Clayton Gillette analyses the state-local relationship from a legal perspective. The chapter uses American experiences to illuminate how conflicts concerning the use of state transfers and local autonomy in other respects can be handled.

The three following chapters widen the perspective from the state-local perspective. Olof Petersson treats some of the complications that follow with EU membership for the classical discourse on democratic governance and local autonomy. Dennis

[12] See classical text such as Musgrave (1959) and Oates (1972); further, Oates (1999) and Boadway (2001).

Mueller and Emil Uddhammar widen the perspective even further to include the trade-off between public and private. They argue not only for a redistribution of tasks between the state and the local level but also for a much stronger role for benefit taxes and for private financing of public services via fees.

The final chapter collects some of the observations from the previous, and further presents a handful of theses on the problems of multi-level democracies, stressing the main concerns from a constitutional perspective.

REFERENCES

Bergström, P., Dahlberg, M., Johansson, E. (1998) "The Effects of Grants and Wages on Municipal Labour Demand", WP IFAU, Uppsala; under review for being published in *Journal of Labour Economics*.

Boadway, R. (2001) "Inter-Governmental Fiscal Relations: The Facilitator of Fiscal Decentralization", *Journal of Constitutional Political Economy* 12, 93-121.

Brennan, G., Buchanan, J. (1980) *The Power to Tax: Analytical Foundations of a Fiscal Constitution*. Cambridge University Press, Cambridge.

Dahlberg, M., Fredriksson, P. (2001) *Migration and Local Public Services*. Working Paper, Nationalekonomiska institutionen, Uppsala Universitet.

Davidsson, L. (forthcoming) *Modeller för lokal självstyrelse. Normativa och empiriska lösningar på den vertikala maktdelningens problem*. (Models for local autonomy. Normative and empirical solutions of the problem of vertical division of powers). To be published within the SNS Constitutional Project.

Mulhall, S., Swift, A. (1992) *Liberals and Communitarians*. Sec. ed. (1996). Blackwell, Malden, Mass.

Musgrave, R.A. (1959) *The Theory of Public Finance*. McGraw-Hill, New York.

Nilsson, L. (red.) (2002) *Flernivådemokrati i förändring* (Multi-level democracy in a process of change). SOM-rapport 27, University of Göteborg.

Oates, W.E. (1972) *Fiscal Federalism*. Harcourt Brace Jovanovich, New York.

Oates, W.E. (1999) "An Essay on Fiscal Federalism", *Journal of Economic Literature*, vol. XXXVII (September 1999), 1120-1149.

Oulasvirta, L. (1997) "Real and Perceived Effects of Changing the Grant System from Specific to General Grants", *Public Choice* 91, 397-416.

Prud'homme, R. (ed.) (1991) *Public Finance with Several Levels of Government*. Foundation Journal of Public Finance, The Hague.

Rubinfeld, D.L. (1987) "The Economics of the Local Public Sector", chapter 11 in *Handbook of Public Economics*, vol. II (eds. Auerbach and Feldstein). Elsevier/North-Holland, New York.

Stigler, G. (1957) "Tenable Range of Functions of Local Government", in *Federal Expenditure Policy for Economic Growth and Stability*. Joint Economics Committee, Washington D.C.

Stjernquist, N. (2000) *Den kommunala självstyrelsen – i backspegeln och bortom nästa vägkrök*. (Local autonomy – looking backwards and forwards) Svenska Kommunförbundet, Stockholm.

Ter-Minassian, T., Craig, J. (1997) "Control of Subnational Government Borrowing", i Ter-Minassian, T. (ed.), *Fiscal Federalism in Theory and Practice*. International Monetary Fund, Washington D.C.

Tiebout, C. (1956) "A Pure Theory of Local Expenditure", *Journal of Political Economy* 64, 416-24.

2

DIVISION OF POWERS*

Robin Boadway and Eva Mörk

Queen's University, Canada

Uppsala University and Institute for Labour Market Policy Evaluation, Uppsala

INTRODUCTION

One of the main tasks when organizing a fiscal federalism structure in a country is to find the appropriate division of powers between different levels of government. In this chapter we discuss some principles of fiscal assignments and possible mechanisms for assigning functions. In addition, we study the Swedish case, investigating the present division of power and identifying potential problems with this division. Finally, we conclude our analysis by presenting some implications for constitutional design.

PRINCIPLES OF FISCAL ASSIGNMENT

Governments take a variety of economic decisions, including both budgetary decisions involving expenditures and taxation, and regulatory decisions that can affect economic activity without having direct budgetary consequences. In virtually all countries, there is more than one level of government, with the lower levels exercising varying degrees of responsibility for these economic decisions. The literatures on fiscal federalism and local public finance have devoted, and continue to devote, considerable attention to the so-called *assignment problem*—what powers each level of government should have over various types of decisions and responsibilities.[1] The literature suggests some general principles governing the types of responsibilities that each level should have, as well as some more particular arguments concerning the case for decentralizing expenditure, taxation and regulatory decisions.

---

* Comments from Sören Blomquist, Howard Chernick, Matz Dahlberg, Per Molander, Clas Olsson and participants at the SNS workshops are gratefully acknowledged.

[1] The original literature on fiscal federalism goes back to Musgrave (1959) and Oates (1972), both of whom dealt with the assignment problem. For a survey of the more current literature, see Boadway (2001). The theory of local public goods owes much to Tiebout (1956). Some of the consequences of the Tiebout model for local public finance are recounted in Wildasin (1986).

General Principles

At the broadest level, government intervention is rationalized by efficiency, equity and stabilization considerations. The efficiency rationale is based on the notion of market failures, especially those arising from the free-rider problem and from some forms of scale economies. The provision of public goods is the archetypical type of public intervention motivated by the free-rider problem, and governments are also involved in providing or regulating various forms of infrastructure that combine economies of scale and common benefits (e.g., transportation networks). There seems to be relatively little controversy in principle about the assignment of such functions. Those public goods and elements of infrastructure that provide benefits throughout the nation might be provided by the state, while those whose benefits are more local might be provided locally.[2] In this way, the mix of public goods provided can better reflect the preferences of local citizens. This is the branch that is called "allocation" in the words of Oates (1972), following Musgrave's (1959) classic classification of government functions into allocation, distribution and stabilization.

Likewise, the assignment of the stabilization function is relatively non-controversial, although the proper role of government in stabilization can be. The need for stabilization arises because of fluctuations in economic aggregates, including GDP, unemployment, inflation and, where relevant, the exchange rate. To the extent that these fluctuations are correlated across the nation, it is natural that monetary and fiscal policies that might be used to address them be at the state level. There may be regionally specific idiosyncratic fluctuations that regional governments might play a role in countering. But, even here, the state government might be in a better position to provide some form of interregional insurance to help insulate regions from the adverse effects of regional shocks.

The most difficult responsibility to assign is that for redistribution. The extent to which governments should redistribute and the forms it should take are controversial. Redistributive goals are multifaceted, including such broad national objectives as equality of opportunity, income equality, and economic security. These involve a wide range of instruments that include not just the tax-transfer system but also various forms of public services, in-kind transfers and social insurance. Indeed, a substantial proportion of the modern government budget is devoted to redistributive objectives, and many of the policy instruments used are in the hands of lower levels of government. It is worth mentioning that governments not only redistribute from rich to poor in either a monetary form or using public services, but also that they may distribute resources across life for the same individual or take the role of insurance provider against risks (e.g. the risk of losing

[2] In what follows, we refer to the national government as the state government and the sub-national governments as local governments. We focus on the case where there are two levels of government, although similar principles apply when there is also an intermediate level, such as the regional or provincial.

your job).[3] Moreover, social insurance objectives might be addressed by redistributing on the basis of non-income characteristics, such as ill health, family circumstances or disability.

Much of what governments at all levels do has redistributive consequences. This problem is further compounded by the fact that citizens in different regions have different preferences for redistribution. The inevitable result is that the Musgravian dictum that redistribution ought to be assigned to the state level of government is difficulty to apply.[4] But given that local citizens care about the well being of not only their closest neighbors but also the whole population, redistribution might be too limited if left to local governments. Thus, redistribution is inevitably a shared responsibility, and the issue then becomes one of deciding what overriding influence the central government ought to exercise over lower government decision-making, and how that influence ought to be implemented. This issue will have a bearing on any set of recommendations for the division of powers.

Before moving on to more detailed principles of assignment, two other general issues might be raised, namely, whether one takes a 'top-down' or a 'bottom-up' perspective on the distribution of powers, and the question of accountability. The top-down and bottom-up approaches to the division of powers differ in what might be considered the default option. Under a top-down approach, one imagines starting from a unitary or centralized state and asking what powers ought to be decentralized to local governments. From this perspective, one can think of decentralization as arising from an inability of the state government to perform all functions satisfactorily. Presumably the onus is on making the case for decentralizing functions, and where the case is not made, the function remains at the center. The bottom-up approach takes the opposite point of view. Functions that are better performed at the center are moved up from the local to the state level. This is equivalent to the principle of subsidiarity, which entails making a case for centralization. One can imagine the two approaches converging if an exhaustive list of functions can be spelled out. However, a more likely consequence is that not all powers can be assigned explicitly, especially those in future areas of government intervention that are not foreseen. A bottom-up approach might take as a default position that unassigned powers—so-called *residual powers*—lie with the local governments, while a top-down approach might take the opposite approach. This has obvious importance for the long-run development of the nation, and its ability to respond to changes in environment.

There is obviously more than economic considerations to the choice between a top-down and bottom-up approach. The top-down approach might be more appropriate in a nation in which all residents share a sense of common community or

[3] In Söderström *et al.* (1999) it is stated that if one divides the expenditures of the Swedish welfare state across the three different branches of distribution, one finds that approximately 60 percent consists of redistribution across life, 30 percent consists of risk insurance and as little as 10 percent is redistribution to genuinely weak groups.

[4] McLure (2001) has recently argued for tax and expenditure assignment to sub-national governments in federations being based on the benefit principle. This would be a way of minimizing the redistributive consequences of lower government decisions. However, this is far from the practice in actual federations, and conflicts with other well-established principles of decentralization.

citizenship, and have an expectation about some form of common consensus and equal treatment in the provision of government services. The bottom-up approach is better suited to the confederation of separate nations or political communities in which each one maintains some sense of individual identity. In practice, the reality may lie somewhere between the bottom-up and top-down approaches. In many federations, citizens may share a sense of community both with the nation as a whole, but also with their own community. The assignment of powers then reflects a compromise between these two communities.

The second important general principle is that of accountability of government to its citizens. The effective functioning of democratic decision-making requires that political decision–makers be fully accountable for their decisions. This requires that there be a clean and transparent line of accountability for decisions taken and for the responsibility for decision-making. A desirable feature of the division of responsibilities is that it be clear which level of government is responsible for which decisions. If citizens have a grievance with respect to the quality of a particular service, they ought to know whose responsibility it is to address that grievance. If responsibilities for particular services are shared, which will inevitably be the case to some extent, it is important to be as clear as possible which level is responsible for which types of decisions. This applies also to the financing of fiscal choices. If one level is responsible for providing a service, but not for financing it, accountability necessarily becomes blurred.

As well as deciding who is responsible for providing a service, one also has to decide who is responsible for financing it, and who is responsible for determining the quality and level of services. Each of these has implications for the efficiency, equity and, especially, accountability, and these implications may well be conflicting. Full decentralization would imply that local governments are responsible for provision, financing and service levels. This would presumably lead to clear accountability, but it might well violate efficiency and equity. Both would be compromised if different localities have different tax capacities and needs, which is almost certainly to be the case. As well, as mentioned, efficiency will be compromised if spillover effects exist, and equity will be violated if the service fulfils some redistributive objective. Moreover, if localities are left with the responsibility to finance their local expenditures entirely, this will inevitably lead to fiscal externalities arising on the tax side: tax competition, and tax distortion affecting the efficiency of national markets for products and factors of production. The implication in each case is that the state government has a legitimate role to play, but it must be clear to the citizens which role the state plays and which the local governments. This question is related to the bailout problems discussed by Jürgen von Hagen and Matz Dahlberg in chapter three. If the municipalities are not capable of financing their local expenditures, there is the potential that the state government will intervene and bail them out. The municipalities hence, in some aspect, face soft budget constraints, which may induce them to take actions that increase the possibility of future bailouts. The risk of bailouts is particularly large if the services that municipalities supply are services over which there exist national objectives. In this case, the state government will be reluctant simply to let the municipalities work out their own financial problems for fear that the quality of services will suffer.

Particular Arguments for Decentralized Assignment

There are a number of arguments that have been made for assigning various types of functions to sub-national governments. What follows is a catalogue of them.

Catering to Local Preferences

The traditional Musgrave-Oates-Tiebout argument for local provision of public goods and services was that local governments would be better able to design public programs to suit local preferences, needs and priorities than the state government. The presumption is that the latter would tend to provide uniform levels of public service across all localities. This argument relies on it being desirable to have differentiated levels of public services across localities. In the case where such services provide benefits solely to local residents and serve no broader national purpose, presumably that is the case. It might be more of an issue where public programs are designed in part to attract business and skilled persons from other localities, or where part of the purpose of the program is to serve some national objective such as one of the redistribution goals mentioned above.

Information Advantages

The effectiveness of some public programs depends on having detailed information about the local clients that the programs are designed to serve. For example, targeted transfers, social insurance and in-kind transfers depend on being able to identify characteristics of the target population, such as need, skills, health status, labor market participation, and so on. These are necessarily monitored by agencies close to the persons being served by the program. This inevitably involves some decentralization of decision-making, if only to the local agencies that are in charge of administering the program. It might be argued that these agencies will be more effective if they are the responsibility of the local rather than state government. The local government may be in a better position to monitor the agency, and to deal with its employees. As well, local responsibility reduces the number of layers of bureaucracy. Of course, the strength of this argument may be lessened to the extent that local programs are required to conform to national standards.

Accountability

The lines of accountability might also be clearer if decision-making about the public services provided to local residents are the responsibility of local governments. If there is some local dissatisfaction with the quality of a service, it may be much easier to hold a local government accountable, and to expect remedial action, than if the service is the responsibility of the state government. In the latter case, the local representative to the state parliament may be in a sense accountable, but may not really have the authority to change the way in which the state government responds to a local problem. This principle also has some implications for financing responsibilities. Accountability is enhanced to the extent that local expenditure decisions must be financed out of discretionary local sources, which includes the pool of general revenues that the local government controls. Part of this pool can, of course, include fungible funds received as transfers from the state government.

Fiscal Competition

Just as competition in the private sector can induce efficiency in the allocation of resources, so too political competition can induce efficiency in local fiscal behavior. The mobility of the tax base, along with the need to be judged locally on the basis of decisions taken that affect the local community, lead to more vigilant and responsible local governments. For example, fiscal competition can reduce waste and rent-seeking behavior at the local level. As well, in a decentralized setting, citizens can compare the performance of their local government with that of neighboring jurisdictions, a form of so-called *yardstick competition.*

Innovation

Related to this is the fact that fiscal competition can induce local governments to look for ways of providing services in newer and more innovative ways. There will be more opportunities for experimentation as well as for learning from the experiences of other localities. This presumes that the rewards of cost-reduction that come with innovation are not implicitly taxed away by the state government in its inter-governmental transfer scheme. Otherwise, the incentive for cost-reducing innovation will be blunted.

While these arguments for decentralization are compelling, they must be set against some disadvantages that might result from decentralized decision-making, some of which can be addressed by remedial measures. There are three main sorts of potential disadvantages of decentralization.[5]

The first is that fiscal decentralization inevitably gives rise to differences in the capacity of local governments to provide public services. This can arise because of differences in per capita tax capacities across localities and because of differences in need. If different localities have different abilities to raise revenues at given tax rates, different tax rates will be required in order to provide a given level of public services. Similarly, if localities differ in their demographic make-ups, this will give rise to different needs for expenditures per capita in order to provide services that are targeted to particular demographic groups. These differences in fiscal capacity and need, if not corrected by a set of inter-jurisdictional equalization transfers, will provide a purely fiscal incentive for economic activity to migrate to localities with higher fiscal capacities, rather than location being determined solely by productivity. As well, horizontal equity will be violated in the sense that otherwise identical persons residing in different localities will be treated differently by the public sector.

---

[5] This is drawn from Boadway (2001), where it is discussed in more detail.

To the extent that solidarity or community sharing is intended to extend to all citizens of the nation, this violation of equal treatment by the overall public sector ought to be corrected.

The issue of equalization will be taken up by Howard Chernick in chapter four in this book. For our purposes, two caveats should be mentioned. First, the inefficiencies and inequities arising from differential fiscal capacities will not occur to the extent that local governments abide by the benefit principle. In practice, this is unlikely to be the case. As a benchmark, it is often assumed that local taxes are roughly in proportion to income, while important public services are made available to eligible recipients whatever their incomes. In these circumstances, differences in ability to raise revenues lead to net fiscal benefit differentials and the possibility of fiscally induced migration and horizontal inequity. Second, differences in need for public services ought to be distinguished from differences in the cost of providing them. If the costs of providing public services only differ because of differences in wage rates or transport costs, it should not be expected that these should be fully equalized. That is, there is no reason why these localities should be expected to provide comparable levels of public services.

The second potential adverse consequence of fiscal decentralization is that efficiency in the national economy may be compromised by fiscal externalities or spillovers arising from the decisions of local governments. They may compete in tax rates or in the provision of service to business in order to attract economic activity from other localities. Or they may adopt other forms of beggar-thy-neighbor or discriminatory practices, such as preferential procurement or hiring practices, or eligibility restriction on recipients of local public services. Even if they do not adopt strategic practices, the mere fact that they are choosing independent policies in an interdependent world may give rise to distortions in national markets. While it may be difficult to rule out such practices entirely, the state government may have a role to play in inducing localities to behave in a non-discriminatory way or to harmonize the structure of their public tax and expenditure policies. Of course, this should be done so as not to compromise the accountability and autonomy of local governments in their spheres of responsibility.

Third, the policies of local governments may have an important influence on redistributive objectives in which the state government may also have an interest. Thus, public services like health, education and welfare services that are often provided at the local or regional level are often important elements of national redistributive objectives. While it may be efficient to decentralize the provision of these services to local governments for the reasons mentioned above, the state government has an interest in encouraging the localities to design their programs with national objectives in mind. Again, the challenge is to accomplish this without unduly compromising the efficiency and accountability of public service provision.

Implications for the Division of Powers

We can draw some tentative conclusions from these principles about the sorts of functions for which local governments ought to have at least some responsibility. It is useful to distinguish among three categories of functions, which vary according to the extent to which their consequences spillover into other localities. These categories do not constitute watertight compartments. Rather they constitute a conceptual division of a continuum of types of functions. The difficulty of compartmentalizing local functions precisely will in turn affect the extent to which one can, or might want to, specify local functions precisely in a constitution.

The first category involves matters of mainly local interest. These include local public goods and services, as well as local regulation, whose benefits accrue locally. Examples include goods and services like sanitation, parks and recreation, libraries, sewage, local roads, local law enforcement, fire protection, water supply and other local utilities, as well as local by-laws and property regulation. These functions serve largely efficiency purposes, and their primary benefit accrues to local residents. That is not to say that they do not affect non-residents to some extent. Visitors to the locality will certainly benefit from them. Moreover, the quality and mix of services may well influence the location of households and businesses. However, there seems to be no compelling reason why local governments should not have exclusive decision-making authority in these areas. To the extent that one is worried about the use of local policies in ways that compromise the efficiency of the national economy—for example, by using them in beggar-thy-neighbor ways—this might be better addressed by general rules that apply to all governments, and that preclude the use of discriminatory or distortionary policies.

The second broad category includes matters of local interest that have significant spillover benefits to other jurisdictions. These might include matters of public health (e.g., clean water), local environmental issues, major local roads that connect with those of other localities, and so on. Again, these are items that serve mainly efficiency rather than redistributive purposes, and there are compelling reasons for their being local responsibilities. At the same time, since they provide potentially significant spillover benefits to neighboring localities, there is need for some mechanism of coordination to ensure that these spillover benefits are taken into account. This can be a purely financial mechanism (conditional grants) or it can be a more direct form of oversight, such as the setting of standards or the mandating of minimum service levels. These are sometimes referred to as methods of *positive integration*, as opposed to those of *negative integration* that preclude the forms of non-discriminatory behavior discussed above. The danger is that whatever the means of internalizing the externalities, they may interfere too much with local decision-making. Local autonomy is desired both to induce efficient local provision, but also to foster accountability.

The third broad category consists of government services that can most efficiently be provided locally, but that also serve important national functions. The obvious examples of these are education, health and social services, each of which serves some equity function (e.g. equality of opportunity, social insurance, targeted transfers). Since these are mainly services provided to people, the efficiency of their provision can be enhanced by local provision for the reasons outlined above. Of course, the argument might be the other way around. If, for example, local politicians or bureaucrats are less competent than those at the state level, or if they are motivated by something other than the well-being of the users of the public service in question, they may be ineffective at providing the service. Other functions that partly serve national interests might include training and major infrastructure projects. Given that these have a national dimension, the case for some harmonization in terms of service levels and standards is enhanced. Thus, there might be a case for common curriculum standards and classroom sizes in education, a basic list of state-provided health services, and minimum levels of in-kind and targeted transfers provided to the needy, the elderly and to children. If left completely to their own devices, different localities may well provide very different levels of such services, thereby resulting in different standards of redistributive equity across localities. As well, since most of these services are redistributive in nature (net benefits tend to fall with income) there may be a tendency to compete down levels of service in order to attract more desirable households. Thus, although efficiency and accountability suggest local provision, some effective means of harmonizing service levels is desirable.

Presumably, the task of inducing harmonization rests with the state government since it represents national interests. In principle, harmonization could be accomplished by negotiated agreements among the local governments. However, given the large number of such governments and the requirement for unanimity, these agreements would be very difficult to consummate. As in the case of spillovers, the challenge is to find a means of exercising that task without compromising either efficiency in provision or accountability. Local governments must retain an incentive for efficient provision, and must be able to exercise discretion within bounds in order to cater to the special needs of their own citizens. At the same time, the lines of responsibility must be clear enough that citizens know which level of government to hold responsible for which aspects of provision. Having said that, it seems clear that there is some level of joint responsibility for these services that partly serve national objectives.

MECHANISMS FOR ASSIGNING FUNCTIONS

The division of powers, including the assignment of responsibilities to local governments, can be accomplished by a variety of institutional means. It is useful to distinguish two broad approaches. One is to spell out the division of powers between state and local governments in the constitution. The other is to leave it be determined by legislation. In principle, the relevant legislation could be state or local.[6] If the top-down approach to nation-building is appropriate, the powers of local government would be defined by the state government and devolved by state legislation. A bottom-up approach would, instead, rely on local governments to pass on powers to the state level according to some notion of subsidiarity. The two approaches need not be mutually exclusive. The constitution might define a *status quo* from which legislation could reassign responsibilities up or down as appropriate. As well, there may be some constitutional guidelines concerning the types of powers that might be transferred by legislation or restrictions on the

[6] This assumes that local governments have legislative authority. Swedish local governments currently have no such authority: they do not pass laws, which is the exclusive capacity of the central government.

frequency or duration of changing powers. The two broad approaches can vary in terms of flexibility, accountability, and outcomes. Let us consider the two in turn.

Constitutional Division of Powers

Writing the division of powers into a constitution implies some permanency. This means that precisely how the powers are specified is important, as are the procedures that are put in place for dealing with unforeseen changes in circumstances. The division of powers can be specified in more or less detail. At one end, there could be a full list of local and state responsibilities, defined by functional area (sanitation, local roads, sewage, water, etc. for local governments; and defense, foreign affairs, currency, etc. for the state government). At the other extreme, the division of powers could be defined according to more general principles (matters of local versus national interest, principle of subsidiarity, matters dealing with civil and property rights, matters of redistribution, and so on). In either case, it would be virtually impossible for the powers to be either exhaustively defined or mutually exclusive or perfectly well defined. Thus, some mechanism for dealing with ambiguities and unforeseen circumstances would be needed.

The problem of a non-exhaustive definition of powers can be dealt with by assigning the residual power, that is, the responsibility for matters that are not spelled out in the constitution, to one level or the other. As mentioned, the assignment of the residual power is related to whether one takes a top-down or bottom-up approach. Under a top-down approach, one might expect that the residual power should lie with the state government, while under a bottom-up approach, the opposite would hold. The residual power can be made more flexible under either approach by allowing for a power of *delegation*. This power enables one level of government or both to delegate its responsibility to the other. It could apply either to residual powers or to those spelled out in the constitution.

For those powers that are not defined in mutually exclusive ways—either because they cannot be or because there are both local and national interests at stake—powers can be co-occupied. These joint responsibilities might simply be exercised in a joint fashion independently by both levels of government. Alternatively, one level might be made *paramount*. Thus, if there is joint occupancy of a power with state paramountcy, local governments can legislate in the area unless superceded by state legislation, and vice versa for local government paramountcy. Note that co-occupancy of powers with state or local paramountcy can result in an asymmetric division of some powers among local governments. That is, some local governments may end up exercising a power that others do not. While this adds flexibility to the division of powers, it may or may not always be regarded as a good thing.

It might be the case that local governments have legislative jurisdiction, but there is a national interest at stake. In this case, it may be possible for the state government to set out parameters that local legislation must satisfy. Obviously, such powers should be set out with care: otherwise there is the possibility of the state government exercising undue influence over local government behavior, which detracts from accountability.

Finally, there may be disputes over where responsibility lies in cases where powers are not well-defined. On the one hand, powers may appear to be conflicting. For example, care for the elderly might be a local responsibility, while pensions may be a state responsibility, and the dividing line between the two may not be clear. On the other, the power might simply be vaguely defined in light of unforeseen circumstances. An example might be the extent to which lottery revenues or user fees fall within the revenue-raising powers of local governments, or the extent to which criminal activity should be governed by local by-laws as opposed to state criminal laws. In these circumstances, there needs to be a means of settling jurisdictional disputes. The courts might be used to adjudicate constitutional matters. There might also be provision for constitutional reform.

Constitutional reform, of course, has more wide-ranging applicability than simply settling constitutional disputes. It is obviously important to consider the procedures that govern changes in the constitution. On the one hand, one wants the flexibility to address new permanent circumstance. On the other, one does not want the procedure to be too simple for fear that current temporary majorities can use it for their own purpose, or that one level of government can use it to permanently change powers in its favor when that might not be warranted.

Legislative Division of Powers

If legislative powers are not defined by the constitution, they could instead be defined by legislation. Under the top-down approach, the state government would be responsible for setting out the functions of local governments. This is not uncommon in federations in which provincial-level governments determine the powers of municipal governments within their boundaries. In essence, the legislative determination of powers is like using the power of state delegation to assign all local government responsibilities.

This system could be compatible with accountability and autonomy if, once assigned, the powers were reasonably permanent and could be exercised freely and fully by local governments. However, if local governments were beholden to the state legislature for the on-going exercise of their powers, there would be a degree of dependency that would almost certainly compromise the autonomy and accountability of local decision-making. Local governments would be at least partly accountable to the state government as well as to their own constituents, and the full benefits of efficient local government behavior would not be achieved. This suggests that the use of state legislation as a vehicle for assigning local government responsibilities should be exercised with care, vigilance, and control.

The extreme case of local reliance on state legislative authority would be that in which local governments were obliged to implement programs determined by state legislation. In this case, local governments would effectively be administrative agencies of the state government, though with varying degrees of discretion. It may be the case that there would be local input into state legislative decision-making, say, through a second chamber consisting of local representatives, but accountability would be quite indirect in this case.

If local powers were to be defined by state legislation, it might still be possible for the outcome to mimic what might result in a constitution design on top-down principles. For that to be the case, legislated powers would have to have some permanency, and changes in those powers would have to be subject to state legislative rules that were more stringent than simply a legislative vote. The rules for legislating changes in local powers would have to be like rules for constitutional change. Ultimately, there would have to be some built-in constitutional protection that precludes the state legislature from changing the rules of the game at will. Given that, it might be argued that one might as well define local powers constitutionally from the start.

It is somewhat more difficult to imagine the bottom-up approach applying to the case of legislating the division of powers. In this case, it would be local governments that would legislate the powers to be assumed by the state government. Conceptually, one might think of a contractual approach to the division of powers, whereby the division is negotiated between state and local governments. Such a procedure would be difficult to consummate when there are a large number of local governments. Moreover, there might be cases where agreement is not possible, that is, where there is no perception of mutual gains occurring. Nonetheless, the contractual approach might be one that could be used as the guiding principle for dividing powers by other means.

STATE INFLUENCE OVER LOCAL PROGRAMS

As mentioned, the primary objectives of decentralization are to improve the quality and mix of public goods and services provided to local citizens, and to enhance accountability and responsiveness to citizens' needs and preferences. Both objectives can be facilitated by some decentralization of fiscal responsibilities to local governments. At the same time, autonomous decentralized decision-making does not come without cost. Different localities will have different capacities for providing public goods and services. Decisions taken by one community may have spillover costs and benefits to neighboring jurisdictions. And, some public services that can more efficiently be delivered at the local level may serve important national objectives. The state government has a responsibility for matters of national interest. This can include some or all of: i) efficiency in the internal common markets for products and factors; ii) fiscal efficiency and fiscal equity for citizens of the nation no matter where they reside; and iii) national equity, including equality of outcomes, equality of opportunities and social insurance. Given that local fiscal decisions can have an impact on these national objectives, the state may have a legitimate interest in influencing the manner in which local governments exercise particular functions so that the benefits of decentralization can be achieved without compromising national goals. The challenge is to devise means of exercising that influence without reducing local autonomy and accountability.

Some of these matters of national interest might be spelled out in the constitution. There might be certain broad objectives outlined in the constitution to which local programs must conform. The principle of efficiency in the internal common market can be reflected in a common market provision that precludes local governments from discriminating against other local governments or their residents, or from interfering in the free and efficient flow of goods and services, labor, capital and information across local borders. There may also be a bill of rights that might potentially include individual rights, social rights, and/or economic rights. Objectives of redistributive equity might be set out as principles in the constitution to the extent that they reflect a national consensus. There might also be a principle of equalization that recognizes the goal of comparable treatment of citizens no matter where they reside, and that legitimizes the role of equalization payments. Various examples of constitutional provisions of these sorts can be found in federal constitutions in other countries (e.g. Germany, Canada, United States, South Africa). These kinds of principles serve partly to legitimize the role of the state government in exercising oversight or influence over local programs by defining the sorts of principles that can justify intervention.

Broadly speaking, there are two means by which the state government might exercise influence over local governments—direct methods and indirect methods. Direct methods can either be negative or positive. Negative measures are those that essentially prevent localities from taking certain actions. An example of this is the power of *disallowance* whereby a decision that has been enacted locally is disallowed because it contravenes some national objective, such as a proscription on discriminating against residents of other localities. The power of disallowance may reside with the state government or it may reside with the courts. In either case it is a powerful instrument that can potentially restrict the autonomy of local decision-making significantly. It may therefore be desirable to have some safeguards in place for restraining its use.

Positive measures of direct influence are those that require localities to take actions that they might not otherwise do voluntarily. They may be required to deliver certain programs, or they may be required to include certain design features in the programs that they enact. The use of such mandates can also be quite severe, and may be restricted in various ways. For example, mandates might only be allowed where state and local governments co-occupy a certain field. Or, they may be allowed where there are demonstrable national objectives at stake. Moreover, there may be a requirement that mandates be funded by the state government, although that may be difficult to implement with accuracy. The use of positive measures of control can be controversial, and can potentially be extended well into the way in which local governments organize their programs. For example, positive control could influence whether local governments engage in the privatization of local government activities or municipal sellouts. It could also influence the extent to which they are allowed to finance their expenditures by borrowing. Presumably, conflicts would arise, and some means of settling disputes would be required.

Methods of indirect control include those in which the state government influences local decision-making without compulsion. The most important of these might be the use of the spending power, whereby the state government influences local behavior by the use of conditions on grants. (For a discussion of intergovernmental grants in Sweden, see Clayton Gillette's discussion in chapter five). This can occur even in areas of exclusive local legislative responsibility. The spending power is an indirect instrument because local governments are not compelled to accept the grant. But, given the financial incentive it might be very difficult to resist. The spending power is obviously a potentially powerful and intrusive device. To restrain the state government, the ability of the state government to exercise the spending power and limits on that exercise might be spelled out in the constitution. As well, there might have to be full consultation with the localities, and the grant might have to have some persistence and predictability. The constitution might also spell out circumstances in which grants ought to be unconditional. For example, revenue sharing or equalization grants might fit into this category.

Another form of indirect control that is sometimes observed in multi-government nations is state oversight with respect to local fiscal matters. For example, local governments may be made accountable to the state government for the way in which they spend certain types of funds, such as those received from the state government or those obtained by borrowing. Any such accountability to the state government is bound to detract from accountability by local governments to their own constituents.

Finally, given that there will inevitably some amount of influence exercised by the state government over local governments, if only via the spending power, it might be helpful to have in place institutional arrangements that serve to facilitate cooperation between levels of government and make interdependencies fully transparent. Many federations have arms-length advisory or consultative bodies that serve this purpose, Australia being a good example. Among other things, these bodies allow longer-term considerations to be taken into account when state budgets authorizing grants are being formulated. They could also be used as advisory bodies in addressing issues of jurisdictional dispute.

DEFINING SWEDISH LOCAL GOVERNMENT ACTIVITIES

Let us now examine local government activities in Sweden, having the above principles in mind. A good starting point in an examination of the appropriate levels of organizing the various functions of the public sector might be to look at the services for which municipalities and counties are currently responsible. Thereafter we can discuss what characterizes these services with respect to some of the factors we have identified as being important for the division of responsibilities, such as external or spillover effects between localities, the extent to which various local programs serve the national interest, and informational advantages that local governments might have over their state counterpart. On the basis of this discussion, we will be in a position to consider the appropriate assignment of functions to the levels of government.

One of the major arguments for having self-running local governments comes from the seminal paper by Tiebout (1956) where he claimed that sorting into different communities made people announce their preferences for local public goods.

Thereby, an efficient provision of local public goods can be reached. Given the importance of this theoretical model, we will also analyze Tiebout-type migration and the extent to which the mechanisms behind the Tiebout model are valid in Sweden today.

Some Basic Facts about Local Government Activities in Sweden

Local governments in Sweden play a major role in the Swedish welfare state and are responsible for supplying important public services like daycare, schooling, and health care. There are two levels of local governments in Sweden: counties, which are mainly responsible for health care, and municipalities, which are responsible for supplying daycare, schooling and care for the elderly along with many other local public services. There are today 21 counties and 290 municipalities in Sweden. It is worth noting that they do not have a hierarchical relationship. The municipalities are not under the counties' control, but both types of local government are under the control of the central state. There are three types of laws that regulate local government rights and obligations: the constitution, which specifies the right of local self-government as well as common settings for the organization of local governments, and which also states the local governments' right of setting their own taxes; the Municipal Act, which is a state law that plays the role of the municipal constitution stating general regulations; and the "specific laws", which constitute a large number of laws with which the central government imposes activities onto the local governments. For a discussion of these various laws, see Petersson (2001).

Local government activities can be divided into two categories: activities that the municipalities are responsible for by law[7] and activities with which municipalities may involve themselves on voluntary bases. According to Swedish law, the latter group of activities involves "matters of common interest associated with the municipality, or county or its members, and which are not handled by the central state alone, some other municipality, the county or someone else". In the appendix we list these two groups of activities. Local governments have, however, considerable discretion over the activities prescribed by law as well. Typically, the laws only give some minimum level of the service that the municipality must provide, but given that these are fulfilled, the local governments are free to do what they want (as long, of course, the actions of local governments do not break the law). Local governments are free to set their own income tax rates, even though this right has been somewhat restricted over the years. They can also charge user fees for the use of different services. These user fees are not allowed to be higher than the actual cost of the service for which the fee is charged. There are some additional limitations on the amount the municipalities can charge for different services:

---

[7] There is some uncertainty about how large this mandated sector is. Petersson (2001) mentions the figure 80 %, but this can be viewed as an upper limit, since this figure is calculated by looking at the size of the sectors that are partly mandated. But these sectors are not completely regulated and there still exists considerable municipal freedom over them. Murray (1985) on the other hand estimates that about 40 % of local expenditures are obligatory. The truth is probably somewhere in between these two figures.

Education is free of charge, and for some services, such as daycare and care for the elderly, there is a cap on the fees.

As mentioned in footnote 6, Swedish municipalities are not allowed to pass laws. In the social service sector they take decisions regarding social assistance, etc. which involves the "exercise of public authority", but is not really the same as making laws. The municipalities have the following legal powers: i) the taxing-power, ii) the power to charge user fees, iii) the power to pass by-laws regarding local matters such as health, environment and cleaning etc, iv) local planning, v) the right of veto against certain decisions, vi) the right of instruction, that is, the right of designing the internal organization. For a fuller description, see Petersson (2001).

The economic activities of local governments are under the review of accountants of which one or more typically are professionals.

Central State Control of Local Governments

Local governments are hence given a great deal of freedom over their activities. There are, however, some ways that the central government can exercise control over the local governments. First, there are a number of laws and prescriptions giving the constitutional framework for the activities of local governments, as discussed above. Second, there are some detailed prescriptions by central government authorities directed to local governments. Third, the central government may influence local governments by targeted intergovernmental grants. Before 1993, specially targeted grants were common. But after the grant reform in 1993, most grants are unconditional and come in a general or bloc form, and state control of local governments has hence decreased. The central government has chosen not to use its spending power. Lately however, the central state has once again started to give earmarked grants; see for example the discussion of the Wärnersson-money below. Fourth, the central government may order local governments to handle some social planning functions. An example of this is the obligation for local governments to develop an Agenda 21-plan.[8] Fifth, some local government decisions must be submitted to a central government authority before they become effective. Sixth, a local citizen may appeal against a local government decision, in which case the question is handled by an administrative court and with the supreme administrative court as the final court of appeal. Finally, several central government authorities are instructed to supervise local governments. For a more detailed description of the central government control over local governments, see Petersson (2001).

[8] Agenda 21 is the United Nations' program for development and the environment adopted at the Rio conference in 1992. The label Agenda 21 refers to it being a program for the 21st century.

Current Responsibilities of Municipalities and Counties[9]

In this section we will look at local governmental expenditures and divide them into the spending categories described in Table 1.

Table 1: A Definition of Different Municipal Activities

Variable	Description
Political activities	Costs for municipal boards and management support to political parties, auditing and other activities connected to the municipal management.
Infrastructure	Costs for, e.g., physical and technical planning, tourism, road-maintenance, parking lots, parks, rescue services, health and environmental protection and overall defense.
Leisure	Costs for local leisure activities, such as support to clubs, sport centers and youth recreation centers.
Culture	Cost for local culture activities, such as support to cultural associations, educational associations, museums, libraries and the municipal school of music.
Daycare	Costs for daycare centers, after-school recreation centers, family day nurseries, private day nurseries etc.
Schooling	Costs for education including supporting measures such as meals, heath care etc.
Care for elderly	Costs for care for elderly, care for people with disabilities (also younger than 65) and care for mentally retarded.
Individual and family care	Costs for institutional care, non-institutional care and costs for social assistance
Specially targeted contributions	Costs for e.g. refugees and for local public job creation programs.

In Figure 1, we can see how the average municipality divides its budget among the different sectors in Table 1. Schooling and care for the elderly constitute the largest share (more than 60 percent together). Thereafter follow daycare, individual and family care and infrastructure. Finally, we have leisure, culture, specially targeted contributions and politics that made up 1-3 percent of the budget each.

[9] This section has benefited from discussions with Louise Fernstedt and Ulla Åhs at the Swedish Association of Local Authorities, and Bruno-Sigvard Thor at the National Board of Health and Welfare.

Figure 1: Municipal Expenditures

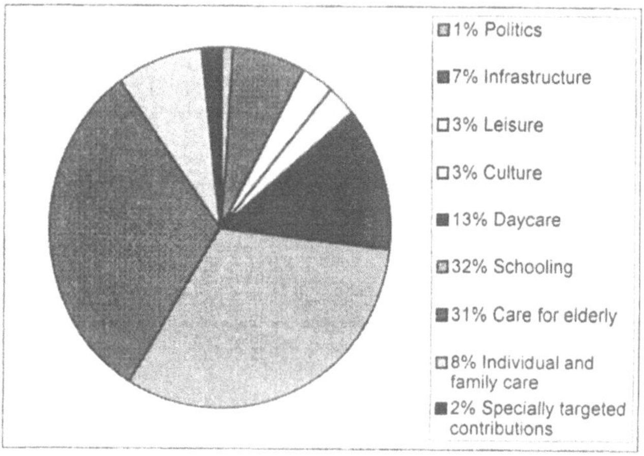

In Figure 2, we have the corresponding budget allocation for the counties. As can be seen from the figure, the single most important service provided by counties is health care. Together with dental care this constitutes 84 percent of the budget.

Figure 2: Counties' Expenditures

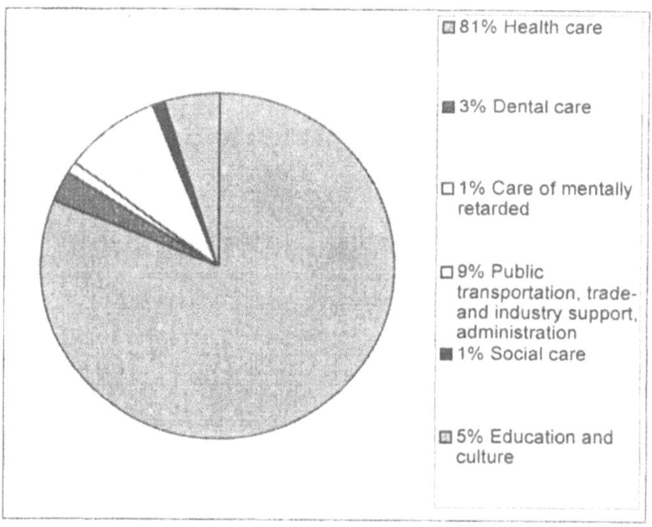

Characterization of Services Supplied by Local Governments

Many of the services that are supplied by local governments are private in nature rather than public. Is there any motivation for supplying them publicly? One mechanism is presented in a number of theoretical papers examining public provision of private goods (see, e.g. Boadway & Marchand, 1995, Boadway, Marchand & Sato, 1998, and Blomquist & Christiansen, 1995, 1998). If the demand for the good provided by the public sector is decreasing in leisure, the provision can help relax the self-selection constraint that limits redistribution, and hence lead to more redistribution being possible. There are of course a number of other arguments for providing private goods publicly. Arguments of equality of opportunity can be raised for example in the case of education and maybe daycare. There are also other equality and equity arguments for providing private services publicly. There might also be social insurance arguments for providing health care publicly. In this section we will not discuss whether it is appropriate to supply these goods and services publicly or not. Instead, we take as starting point that they will be provided publicly and rather discuss the suitable level for this. This differs from the position taken by Mueller & Uddhammar in chapter eight who, among other things, argue for the privatization of some services. In fact, it is universally the case in OECD countries that the state is heavily involved in providing basic education, health and social services. Moreover, lower levels of government are typically given responsibility for their delivery, and to some extent their policy design, albeit with financial assistance from a higher level of government.

Let us consider in turn each of the main categories of local public services in more detail.

Schooling

This is a spending category with a potential national interest. The argument is that everyone should have the same opportunity in life and hence be guaranteed a proper education regardless of where in the country the individual lives. The same is true for children from different family backgrounds. This is also a sector with potential external effects. Thus, there are convincing and widely supported motives for the state's interest in the provision of education. Are there any motives for local provision? Ahlin & Johansson (2001) investigate the preferences for local public schooling by using survey data. In this study preferences are defined by their expenditure levels. These authors find that characteristics like sex, age, family situation and whether one is privately or publicly employed matter for the preferences. Hence, their results indicate that tastes differ among people. This implies that tastes are likely to differ across municipalities with different demographic setups and could motivate local rather than state provision. As well, the usual efficiency arguments for decentralization apply. For example, given that the local governments are responsible for schooling, we might have a case where local governments compete with each other for pupils, which could enhance the efficiency and quality of schooling. A study examining the effects of the reform in

1991 when the responsible for schooling was transferred to the local level would be most interesting.

The organization of schooling, as it stands today, is a clear example of a case where there is a potential problem with accountability. Although the municipalities have been given considerable freedom, especially since the reform in 1991, there still exists quite a lot of central regulation. It is the central state that formulates the School Act, stating the national objectives that the service is to fulfill. The municipalities, in turn, are responsible for the provision of schooling, that is they are responsible for the carrying through the activity in accordance to the School Act, establishing a school plan, budgetary decisions, as well as providing premises and staff. The intention is then that the central government shall evaluate whether the municipalities have managed to fulfill the objectives or not. But this is not the whole story. The School Act not only establishes the national objectives of the education system, but also regulates, sometimes in detail, the work of the headmasters and teachers. Hence, the state regulates the actions of the local schools directly, without involvement of the municipalities. Are the municipalities then responsible for these actions? If the objectives are not fulfilled, who is to blame? There is thus a shared responsibility between the central and the local governments for providing schooling. This mixed responsibility raises obvious questions of accountability.

There is also the problem of financing schooling. The municipalities do not receive any targeted grants to school activities, instead these are part of the lump-sum grant that municipalities receive. However, the amounts were settled in a period when the number of pupils was low, and the municipalities have not been compensated for the increased number of pupils. An exception to this is the recent "Wärnerson-money"[10] where the municipalities get extra money from the state for schooling, which can be used only for increasing the staff. This also means that the freedom the municipalities were given by the grant reform in 1993 has been somewhat restricted lately.

These kinds of tensions always exist whenever both the state and the local government share responsibility for providing a public service. The state responsibility arises because of the idea that education fulfils some objectives that have a national dimension to them. These national objectives have to do with general features of the system such as accessibility for all students to some guaranteed quality of education no matter what their background, as well as maybe some minimal components of the curriculum, class size, and so on. It is not in the state's interest to regulate the details of school provision. The objectives of the state should be achievable using fairly general conditions on bloc grants to local governments, leaving the details of school provision to the latter. Moreover the lines of accountability should be clear. Local governments should first and foremost be accountable to their own citizens rather than to the state government. This argument of course rests on the assumption that the local governments are competent and able to fulfill the general conditions stated by the central government. More research is needed in order to answer this question.

[10] Named after the former Minister of Education.

Care for the Elderly

In 1992, the responsibility for care of the elderly was, to a large extent, transferred from the counties to the municipalities, in "Ädel-reformen". Today, the counties are still responsible for hospital care, including diagnosis and treatment (involving overnight stays), whereas the municipalities are responsible for primary health care for the elderly (for the rest of the population, the counties are responsible for primary health care as well) and for other care, including service flats and help in the home. The accountability problem in this sector is between the municipalities and the counties rather than between the central and local governments. There is an overlap of assignments that the municipalities respectively the counties both can fulfill. In addition, very different types of laws guide these two levels. The social services act, which governs municipal activities, is a law building on municipal obligations and which gives the individual the right of appealing against a municipal decision. The counties, on the other hand, are regulated by a law[11] building on the principle that the responsibility lies with the professionals (doctors and nurses).

The central government has very few formal abilities to influence the municipalities about the running of the care for the elderly. What the central government has done lately is to try to regulate using information, that is, simply informing the local governments what they want them to do, but not being able to impose any punishment if the municipalities do not behave accordingly. In 1997/98 the "National plan for the care for elderly" was established and this nation plan was followed by a "National plan for healthcare". In these documents, the central government informs the municipalities about its intentions and goals with the service in question. In addition to this information, the central government has initiated grant programs, both targeted and general. The central state has then assigned The National Board of Health and Welfare with the task of evaluating whether the municipalities have fulfilled the objectives stated in the national plans. The potential problem with this strategy is that the objectives risk being too general and perhaps too optimistic, given the available funds. The latter of the mentioned national plans builds on a political agreement between the central government and representatives for the local governments. It turns out that this negotiated plan contains more detailed descriptions of the objectives than its predecessor.

The care for elderly-reform in 1991 of course had consequences for municipal economy. Bergström, Dahlberg & Johansson (1999) show, using a dynamic panel data model, that before the reform, municipal labor demand was rather insensitive to the number of old people in the municipality. After the reform, however, the share of the population older than 79 years has a positive significant effect on municipal labor demand. Whether this reform also had consequences on the quality of the care for the elderly is yet unknown. However, the service has clearly become more heterogeneous. Socialstyrelsen (The National Board of Health and Welfare) (2000) has recently attracted attention to the very different fees in different municipalities. They conclude that: i) people with the same need for care pay very different fees in different municipalities; ii) the systems for fees are hard to understand and have, in

---

[11] Lag om yrkesverksamhet på hälso- och sjukvårdens områden, 2001:453.

some cases, absurd consequences; iii) old peoples' protection against high fees is low; and iv) local governments do not respect the laws. Dennis Mueller and Emil Uddhammar discuss care for elderly in their chapter (chapter eight). They argue that because of the risk of a race-to-the-bottom scenario, age care ought to be handled by the central government. This is of course a potential risk with letting municipalities handle care for elderly. However, we believe that the mobility among elderly is rather limited. Lundmark (1995) finds, studying mobility of elderly in Sweden 1972-1992, that it is above all younger and healthier pensioners that move, and that the level of services and economic conditions are rather unimportant for the migration decisions. Of course, it might be the case that the "ÄDEL-reform" in 1992 changed these patterns and an investigation using data after 1992 would be very interesting. The availability of local governments to freely choose fees for elderly care changed in June 2002, when a maximum user fee for care was introduced. There is hence a limit of how much the municipality can charge for care. In addition, there is a lower limit, which states that the municipalities are not allowed to charge any fee for people with an income lower than a set limit.

Daycare

Before deciding the appropriate level of supplying daycare, we must begin by discussing the motives for public provision of daycare, which, like education, is a typical private good. In the theoretical literature, there are at least two motives for why daycare might be supplied by the public sector rather than (or in addition to) the private sector. First, if the local sector supplies daycare, female labor supply can increase, hence yielding a larger taxable income and consequently a large tax income for the local sector, which can be used to finance public services or to lower public taxes. Hence, it is in the interest of the total population to supply subsidized daycare centers. (See Bergstrom & Blomquist, 1996). This puts the discussion of the benefit principle in chapter seven in this book in a little different light. Those benefiting from daycare are hence not only the parents using the daycare service. Since income is the tax base for both local and central taxes, some kind of matching grants may be needed to induce local governments to choose the optimal level of subsidies for daycare. Second, the demand for daycare is decreasing with leisure, making daycare a suitable good to provide publicly in order to release the self-selection constraint, according to the discussion above. One further motivation for supplying daycare publicly has been to improve equality between men and women, giving women the chance to enter the labor market.

One might also look at it from the child's perspective. The question one has to ask is then: Is it in some sense "better" to be at daycare than at home? If this is the case, the supply of daycare might be seen as motivated by an equality of opportunity argument in the sense that a publicly provided daycare ensures that all children, regardless of socioeconomic background, have the same basic goods and services and a chance to lead a full and fruitful life. There is some Swedish evidence of the consequences of daycare on later success in school. Andersson (1989, 1992) studies 130 children in Stockholm and Gothenburg. Controlling for the family situation, socioeconomic status of parents and the education of mothers, he finds weak positive effects on school results of attending daycare. Jonsson (1994) uses data from LNU 1991 and investigates the choice of secondary education of people born between 1965 and 1973. After controlling for parents' education, socioeconomic status and type of community, he as well finds small, but positive and significant effects of number of years in daycare. Söderström et al. (1999) use a considerably larger data set with more background variables collected by the Educational department in Gothenburg. Controlling for the same background characteristics as Andersson and Jonsson, they find positive, but not statistical significant effects, of attending daycare.

Daycare is to a large extent financed by fees that are typically income dependent (i.e. progressive). Lately, there has been a possibility for the local government to impose a maximum fee, in Swedish called "maxtaxa". The idea is that there should be a maximum amount that the local government can charge parents regardless of their income. Hence, there is a limit of the progressivity of the system. This idea comes from the central government, and in order to influence the local governments to impose the maximum fee, the central government has decided to compensate local governments that impose the maximum fee for their economic losses. Whether the municipalities are fully compensated or not is being debated at the moment, but the fact is that all but one municipality have chosen to implement the maximum fee. The maximum fee can be motivated on the benefit principle. The argument is that local government should use the benefit principle when financing their activities and leave redistribution matters to the central government. Otherwise, local governments have an incentive to compete with one another for better-off households leading to a "race to the bottom" in terms of redistribution policy.

Individual and Family Care

The municipalities are responsible for payment of social assistance. Until 1998, the municipalities were free to set their own norms for social assistance (deciding the size and eligibility of the social assistance), even though there existed a recommended norm, set by The National Board of Health and Welfare. The actual norms, however, differed considerably among municipalities. In 1996, barely 45 percent of the municipalities followed the recommended norm. On average the applied norms were 6 percent lower than the recommended norm, but there were municipalities with as much as 33 percent lower norms. In 1998 a central norm ("riksnorm"), which is renewed in the beginning of each year, was established from which the municipalities are not allowed to deviate without some "specific circumstances". Municipal freedom has hence been restricted.

We mentioned above that when the municipalities were free to set their own norms, these differed between municipalities. Does this difference reflect differences in preferences? Not necessarily! There are a number of potential problems, for example the risk of a race to the bottom that has just been mentioned. Uddhammar (1997) studies the migration pattern of receivers of social assistance in 1991. He finds some evidence that these individuals move to municipalities with higher social assistance norms to a larger extent than to municipalities with lower norms. This is the only available Swedish study examining this hypothesis. From American studies (for an overview of these studies, see Brueckner, 2000) we also learn that potential welfare receivers tend to move to regions with more generous welfare benefits, even though this effect is small. However, regions act as if this mechanism is present, and there are hence indications of a race to the bottom, where the chosen welfare benefits are "too low" from the perspective of the society. This might indicate that the responsibility for social assistance ought to be moved to the central level, or at least for the state government to intervene in the setting of national standards. A further motive for this might arise if inhabitants care for poor people in the whole country, not only for poor people in their own region. The level of social assistance might therefore be of national interest rather than, or as well as, of local interest. Given that local administrations have better information about the needs of poor people, it might be the case that it is most efficient to leave the administration at the local level, with the state government providing guidelines or incentives for minimum national standards to be met.

One further problem one might mention is that, as the system is today with social assistance being a local responsibility but unemployment benefits being a central responsibility, there are motives for local governments to get people out of welfare programs and into unemployment programs, since the latter are centrally financed. For a discussion of this subject, see Lundin & Skedinger (2000).

Infrastructure

This is the type of public expenditure that perhaps best fits in under the heading "local public goods". Of course, there are spillover externalities attached to a good or bad infrastructure in a given municipality, but these might not be so large. So there seems to be a strong argument for local responsibility for local infrastructure.

Leisure and Culture

Recreation and cultural activities have potential spillover effects. A person living in one municipality can travel to the neighboring municipality and enjoy the leisure and culture services there. Lundberg (2001a) studies the benefit spillover effects of recreation and culture between Swedish municipalities from 1981-1990. He finds that clusters of municipalities with high expenditure levels are found in the northern part of Sweden, where municipalities are large in area and sparsely populated, and clusters with low expenditures are found in the southern part of Sweden where distances between municipality centers are short. He further finds a negative correlation between recreational and cultural expenditures provided by neighboring municipalities, suggesting that these expenditures are associated with benefit spillovers.

Political Activities

Only one percent of local governments' expenditures goes to this sector, which consists of spending in support of political parties. We are therefore not going to say much about this sector, besides raising the question whether it is suitable that local politicians make the decision regarding support for political parties?

Specially Targeted Contributions

Costs for refugees and local public job creation programs are examples of functions that belong under this category. Labor market policy is typically a central obligation. Lately, however, local governments have started to take more interest in active labor market programs. Since labor market programs typically are central government activities, there might be accountability problems here. The potential advantage of decentralization is that one can take advantage of the knowledge local actors have over local labor market conditions. The potential negative consequences are the following: i) municipal budgets may be favorably affected by shifting person from social assistance to participation in labor market programs; ii) some programs may crowd out regular municipal jobs and subsidize labor; and iii) the programs may serve as means of increasing or maintaining local population. Lundin & Skedinger (2000) discuss what happens when the role of the municipalities were strengthened in the local employment service committees (ESC). They study both a survey as well as register data. In the survey, they find indications that the goals of the municipal members of the ESCs are different than those of the central decision-makers. Their econometric results are the following. They find that decentralization seems to spur local incentives in the form of labor market programs organized by the municipalities, and that targeting outsiders is to some extent more common in municipal projects than in others. They do, however, not find any evidence of a geographical lock-in effect.

Turning to the reception of refugees, this is basically a central state matter but one for which the state engage the municipalities. The local governments agree with the state to accept a given number of refugees and to supply them with some basic services, for example accommodation and training in the Swedish language. In return for this, the municipalities receive a transfer from the central government whose size depends on demographic characteristics of the refugees. Before 1991, the municipalities were compensated on current account, which had some odd incentive effects. If the refugee moves, some of the money is transferred with him or her to the new municipality. There are hence incentives for the municipalities to keep down costs for refugees, since the grants they receive are independent of municipal spending. In addition, there are incentives for the municipalities to try to integrate the refugees into the labor force rather than to support them with social assistance payments. The Swedish Integration Board is responsible for following up the municipalities' introduction programs.

Healthcare

This is a sector where the national objectives of equal treatment may play an important role. Today, the counties run the hospitals and are responsible for primary care (except for the elderly, where the municipalities have been in charge since 1992, as discussed above). The central government has lately been trying to influence the counties using national plans and intergovernmental grants (see above). Regarding accountability problems, we mentioned above that there are some uncertainties of the responsibilities of the counties relative to the municipalities. Do we need both counties and municipalities? A question one might ask is whether the municipalities are too small to run hospitals. This is typically the case; in fact, it might be the case that some counties are too small as well. So letting the municipalities take care of hospital care is probably not a good idea. There are two alternatives to letting the counties run the hospitals, both tested in two of Sweden's neighboring counties. In Finland hospitals are run by municipal confederations, consisting of a number of neighboring municipalities that have united in order to finance and run hospitals. In Norway, on the other hand, the hospitals have been nationalized. Another option is to let the municipalities take responsibility for primary care, but leave hospitals to the counties. This is already the case for care for elderly. As mentioned above, there are some accountability problems connected to this, and this must be held in mind when designing the system for the rest of the population.

What is suitable for Sweden? This is hard to say without any figures on how much health care differs between different counties. If the available services differ too much, there might be the case that the national objectives of e.g. equal treatment are not fulfilled. On the other hand, different service levels might be the result of different preferences across the countries.

An Examination of the Conditions behind Tiebout-type Migration

One of the main arguments supporting the existence of many small local governments is that this could lead consumers to reveal their preferences for local public services and hence yield an efficient solution. Efficiency here involves both an efficient allocation of households among communities and efficient levels and mixes of public goods and services in each community. This Tiebout argument is only valid if i) public service provision differs among municipalities, and ii) people move according to taste differences. What do we know about these two conditions in Sweden? We will look at these two issues in turn, first using expenditure data to investigate differences in service levels, and, second, discussing whether people move according to taste differences. For the latter, we will look at both the preferences expressed by citizens in survey data, and discuss what is known from recent research about migration in Sweden. In short, if people have sorted according to preferences for local public services, we should observe inhabitants being satisfied with the current local service level. Also, given that people differ in their preferences, we should observe different levels of output of local public goods and services in different local governments. Is this the case in Sweden today and if so, for which type of goods and services?

Service Levels: Evidence from Expenditure Data

Is there currently any evidence of different level of services in different municipalities and regions, after one has taken structural differences into account? In order to answer this question one can look at empirical data on expenditure levels. In Table 2, summary statistics for the different expenditures are given.

Table 2: Summary Statistics for the Spending, 1995-2000[12]

Variable	Mean	Std. Dev.	Coef of variation	Min	Max
Total/pop	32 568	4 371	0.134	22 484	49 582
Politics/pop	614	302	0.492	85	2 707
Infra/pop	2 712	895	0.330	675	7 451
Culture/pop	760	224	0.295	260	2 015
Leisure/pop	986	323	0.328	139	2 313
Daycare/pop	4277	807	0.189	2277	7272
Schooling/pop	10333	1668	0.161	5036	16934
Care for elderly/pop	10101	2765	0.274	2679	21291
Care/pop	1 817	744	0.409	527	5 658
Targeted/pop	968	462	0.477	25	4 537

Note: The coefficient of variation is calculated by dividing the standard deviation with the mean. The lower the value, the less variation in the variable.

Looking at Table 2, we see that the municipalities are most alike in providing daycare and schooling, and to some extent care for the elderly. These are also the largest spending categories for the municipalities. When it comes to more typically local public services, such as infrastructure, culture and leisure, the variation is larger. We can also note (the figures are available upon request) that for most of the categories, it is the variation across municipalities rather than across time that accounts for the largest share of the variation. This means that municipalities differ more from each other than what a given municipality does over time. This observation is expected, since we have 289 municipalities and only five years.

Hence, there is in fact variation in the spending pattern over municipalities. Without analyzing the figures more, it is hard to say whether this difference is really due to different service levels and differing quality. A high spending level might for example depend on high structural costs in the municipality or its demographic composition, or it simply be a indication of misbehavior.

In order to control for different structural cost we can study an index published by the Swedish Association of Local Authorities that describes the difference between actual municipal costs, and those costs implied by the municipalities' structural conditions. Table 3 presents summary statistics on the difference between municipal actual cost and the cost implied by structural factors. These resulting differences may be a consequence of both a high ambition level and inefficiency. In any case, from the minimum and maximum values we can see that the municipalities differ a

[12] The same pattern emerges if we divide Daycare with the population younger that 7, Schooling with the population between 7 and 19, and Care for the elderly with population older than 79.

great deal in their cost even after accounting for different structural costs. Hence, inhabitants do have some possibility to sort according to their tastes for local public services.

Table 3: Differences between Actual Cost and the Cost Level Implied by Structural Factors, 2000

	Mean	Std. Dev.	Min	Max
Daycare	0.82	12.77	-34.27	29.68
Primary School	-1.42	7.63	-18.80	24.42
Secondary School	2.51	10.76	-28.46	50.01
Care for elderly	4.23	11.48	-25.51	49.53
Individual and family care	5.47	25.54	-60.87	98.17

Degree of Satisfaction: Evidence from Survey Data

If the Tiebout-type mechanism worked perfectly and different levels of local public spending together with local taxes were the only reasons for people to move, everyone would be satisfied with the spending/tax mix in the municipality. Is this the case? In order to answer this question, one can use survey data. In the 1998 HUS-survey, people are asked about their preferences for local public services. More precise, they are asked the following question: "Assume that your municipality has to choose one of the three stated alternatives. What do you think that the municipality ought to choose: 1) Reduce local taxes and spend less on total municipal spending; 2) Keep the current level of local taxes and spend as much as today; 3) Increase local taxes and increase total municipal spending."[13] The same question is asked for a number of specific municipal services.

In Table 4 we present the respondents' answers to this question.

Table 4: Satisfaction with the Current Spending at Local Public Services, Percent

	Total services	Social care	Daycare	Care for the elderly	Education	Culture and leisure
Reduce taxes and spending	10.77	5.33	4.85	1.60	2.90	13.76
Keep the current level of taxes and spending	67.15	59.74	63.09	43.61	59.68	72.62
Raise taxes and spending	22.07	34.93	32.06	54.79	37.42	13.62

From Table 4, we see that approximately 67 percent of the respondents were satisfied with the level of total services. Most satisfaction was found with respect to

[13] To be completely true, there is a fourth alternative, stating "No opinion" but we have excluded the respondents giving this answer.

culture and leisure, followed by daycare. Most dissatisfied were the citizens with the care for the elderly, in which case as many as 55 percent wanted increased spending even if this was accompanied by higher local taxes. One thing worth mentioning is that people seem to be most satisfied with culture and leisure, services that, according to Table 2, differ the most.

From the discussion above we can conclude that the Tiebout mechanism does not work perfectly, which is perhaps not that surprising given the many hard assumptions behind this model. For example, in order to work perfectly as a community-sorting device, the Tiebout model demands that there is an indefinitely large number of municipalities. So even if people have actually sorted according to preferences for local public services, we should still expect some to be dissatisfied: there are simply not enough municipalities to match all citizens' preferences exactly. As argued by Howard Chernick in chapter four, the Swedish equalization grants might also increase the incentives to allow income mixing in the municipalities and hence deteriorate the working of the Tiebout model.

Next, we turn to empirical evidence from Sweden that people move according to differences in local public spending? This is another way of testing for the Tiebout hypothesis.

Migration Behavior in Sweden: Empirical Evidence

Most studies examining migration patterns in Sweden study migration across local labor markets and focus on the impact of labor market characteristics and labor market policy on migration. Westerlund (2001) gives a survey of these studies. He concludes that migration is especially influenced by changes in regional employment (in-migration to regions with low unemployment and out-migration from regions with high unemployment). In addition, active labor market programs seem to have some effects on migration.

The interesting thing to study for our purpose is rather the effect of local public services on migration. Ahlin & Johansson (2000) use survey data from 28 municipalities allocated across the country to examine individual preferences for locally provided schooling. Doing this, they also control for potential Tiebout sorting, of which they find no evidence. Boije & Dahlberg (1997) combine the Tiebout model with the housing market. They use a random utility model to investigate the residential choice of movers in the Stockholm area in 1990. They find that people prefer to live in municipalities where public spending is high. The most thorough analysis of Tiebout-related migration in Sweden is the paper by Dahlberg & Fredriksson (2001). They study movers to the local labor market of Stockholm in 1990 and 1991. In addition, they separate short-distance movers, who move within the Stockholm area, and long-distance movers, who come from outside the Stockholm area. They find that local public services and taxes matter, with the expected signs, for short-distance movers (movers within the Stockholm area) but not for long distance movers. Among the local public services, it is spending on education and spending on other services (including, e.g., recreation and transfer programs) that seem to matter. Spending on daycare and care for the elderly is not that important. Aronsson, Lundberg & Wikström (2001) and Lundberg (2001b) study the effect of regional and local taxes and expenditures on net migration at the county level and the municipal level, respectively. Their results however are ambiguous.

Overall, this evidence suggests that the mechanism suggested by the Tiebout model for determining the provision of local public services is of limited relevance for the Swedish case. This is not surprising given the nature of many of the services that Swedish local governments provide. Some of the most important of them are major public services that serve redistributional objectives, are of some national interest, and are heavily influenced by financing obtained from the state government. The Tiebout model, by focusing mainly on purely local public goods, does not capture the fact that local governments are responsible for providing key public services in the areas of health, education and welfare. Any recommendations for constitutional reform should take account of this feature of the Swedish system of government. It is a feature that is also common among other similar nations, including those elsewhere in the Nordic countries.

Conclusions from the Swedish Evidence

What conclusions can we draw from Swedish empirical evidence?

We first note that the extent to which the central government has let the municipalities handle their own matters has changed over time. The grant reform in 1993 meant that municipal freedom was enhanced considerably. Leaving the municipalities to handle their own business led to different service levels and different level of fees, as the discussion about social assistance and fees for care for the elderly above indicates. Lately, however, we have seen cases where the central government regulates the actions of local governments more, the maximum fees in daycare and care for the elderly being examples of this. This phenomena highlights one of the tradeoffs present in the division of power: To what extent can the central state allow municipal service levels to differ, and to what extent might national objectives call for equal treatment of equals? It is unfortunate if the rules change too often since this might lead to accountability problems. Moreover, the mere ability of the central government to change the intensity of oversight of local government operations will detract from the benefits of decentralized decision-making. These can only be attained if the local governments have real discretionary responsibility. It might therefore be suitable to state some clear principles governing the division of responsibilities in a constitution.

Accountability problems arising from blurred lines of authority ought to be avoided. We saw above, that the School Act is a potential source of accountability problems, and might therefore be worth reconsidering.

In addition, the division of responsibilities for care for elderly might be more carefully arranged and prescribed, in order to avoid accountability problems between municipalities and counties. The same is true for hospital and primary care.

The Tiebout argument itself might not be enough to motivate and discipline local governments with a large self-governing powers, since mobility in accordance to preferences for public goods are only present in the larger cities. However, there is evidence both that people's preferences for public goods differ and that the service levels in local governments differ. These two facts speak in favor of having many self-governing local governments. In addition, almost 70 percent of the population in the HUS-survey states that they are satisfied with the municipal level of total spending.

IMPLICATIONS FOR CONSTITUTIONAL DESIGN

To return to the basic purpose of our paper, what conclusions can we draw from the discussion above concerning the appropriate division of powers between different levels of government? What ought to be the relationship between the central government and the local governments with respect to each area of local responsibility? And, how ought these assignments and relationships be implemented? These are all difficult and politically charged questions, and their resolution must take into consideration much more than economic factors. Nonetheless, it is worth identifying some elements that might be considered as useful components of a constitution designed for the important role that local governments play in delivering public goods and services, some of them serving national objectives.

As we have emphasized, any constitutionally defined principles of the division of responsibilities between the state and local governments must take into consideration the types of public services that local governments are asked to provide. In Sweden, as in most other OECD countries, these are of three broad types. They include a) relatively uncontroversial public goods and services that are of local interest, b) public goods and services that are of mainly local interest but that may involves spillovers to other communities, and c) public services of national interest that are decentralized to local governments to exploit the efficiency advantages of local provision. The latter include services that serve important redistributive roles. (This view might be contrasted with that proposed by Mueller and Uddhammar in chapter eight, where it is advocated that redistribution be solely the responsibility of the state government, and local governments follow the benefit principle. This would involve a major realignment of responsibilities from the current ones.) The constitution ought to reflect not only the efficiency advantages of local provision that are presumed to exist,[14] and the fact that these can only be attained if local governments have some minimal amount of discretion over program design and delivery, but also the means by which the national interest can be served. More generally, the division of responsibilities must accommodate the need for the state government to set general standards for important public services with the desire for accountability. The latter requires some clarity of the lines of

[14] In fact, we say presumed because there is no clear empirical evidence to support the view that decentralization of service provision necessarily increases efficiency. Nonetheless, the efficiency case for decentralization is usually taken as given by most commentators.

responsibility, as well as a relatively high degree of autonomy of local decision-making.

We proceed by setting out the main features of the constitutional provisions that would be consistent with this desire to balance the benefits of decentralized decision-making with the maintenance of national economic and social objectives.

A Statement of Principles

It might be useful to spell out in general terms what ultimate principles guide the roles of the respective governments in serving the public interest. These could include:

- The efficient functioning of the internal common market, that is, the free and non-distorted flow of goods, services, labor and capital across internal borders;
- The principle of equalization, which states that all localities should be able to provide comparable levels of public services at comparable rates of taxation, if they so choose;
- The principles of the social union, which might include the notions of equality of opportunity, social insurance, and the right to a minimum standard of living;
- A statement of individual rights, which might include equality before the law, non-discrimination, mobility, and the various freedoms.

A Statement of the National Interest

Related to the above, it might be useful to specify in general terms what the national economic interest is in order to provide some constitutional basis for state government guidance or intervention in local decision-making. This could include:

- Efficiency in the national economy;
- Nationwide redistributive equity and social justice;
- Equality of opportunity;
- Regional development;
- Relations with other nations.

Local Government Responsibilities

The constitution could include a section outlining the responsibilities of local governments. This could include items over which they have exclusive legislative responsibility, as well as items whose jurisdiction is shared with the state government. The former could be specified in detail, or in general terms. In the latter case, local governments might have exclusive legislative jurisdiction over matters of a mainly local nature. This would be a flexible way to proceed, but it would also require some mechanism for ongoing interpretation. For areas of jurisdiction that involve services to local residents, but serve partly national objectives (that have been spelled out), jurisdiction could be joint, with either the national or the state level of government having paramountcy depending on whether one subscribes to a top-down or bottom-up approach to the nation. State paramountcy would have the advantage that the state government could ensure that local programs were designed to serve the national interest. On the other hand, state paramountcy would lead to more accountability, and would not necessarily preclude the state government from influencing local governments using other means (e.g., conditional grants). Another method to strengthen accountability issues might be to give municipalities the right to pass local laws.

The Residual Power and the Power of Delegation

Having specified the powers of the localities, and presumably also of the state, it is important to assign the residual power. Again, one's choice depends on whether one takes a top-down or bottom-up approach. One might be tempted to suggest that in the case of Sweden, especially given the large number of local governments as well as the presumed high degree of national solidarity, it makes sense to assign the residual power to the state.

At the same time, a useful complement to the residual power is the power of delegation. This would allow either level of government to delegate certain responsibilities to the other level. Presumably some safeguards would be important in defining the power of delegation. For one, one might want the use of the power to be mutually agreed so that one level cannot oblige the other to take on certain responsibilities. For another, there might be some limits to its use to ensure that its use does not give rise to instability or purely short-run changes in jurisdiction.

State Influence over Local Decisions

As we have seen, combining the efficiency benefits of decentralized decision-making with the national interest sometimes means it is useful for the state government to exercise influence over the states, while at the same time leaving states the discretion to operate their own programs. There are many possible instruments for state oversight that are used in federations around the world. Two blunt instruments include the power of disallowance and the power of mandate. These represent the extreme cases of negative and positive control.

The power of disallowance enables the state government to rule out local legislation that is deemed to violate the national interest. This power could be restricted to items that are deemed to be against the constitution (in which case, perhaps some judicial authority would be required to verify its use). Alternatively, it could be more widely available as a means of ruling out local decisions that the state deems not to be in the national interest. In either case, it is fairly blunt instrument, and one that runs the significant risk of overriding local autonomy and muddying accountability.

Mandates are even more intrusive on local authority. They involve requiring the local governments to take certain actions, and thereby usurp the democratic decision-making authority of the local governments. This can be even more damaging to accountability.

The main alternative to these rather strong instruments is the use of the spending power, that is, use of conditional grants to influence local behavior. This represents the use of the carrot rather than the stick. Virtually every federation in the world uses the spending power, though with varying degrees of intensity. (See the survey by Watts (1999).) Its benefit is that if used without too much intrusion, it can induce local governments to take account of state or national objectives, while at the same time preserving their autonomy and accountability. The dangers are that it will be used with too much vigor by the state government, and that it will engender a state of dependency among local governments. In the extreme, it can lead to a soft budget constraint and its associated problems, whichare dealt with in another paper. Nonetheless, there seems little choice but for the state to use the spending power. The challenge is to device a set of rules that safeguards against its misuse.

Inter-governmental Institutions

One such safeguard might be the existence of intergovernmental advisory bodies that can be used to provide long-term advice and proposals for dealing with intergovernmental disputes. Such bodies have been found to be effective in federal settings as means of preventing state decisions from being driven by short-term budgetary considerations, as a way of seconding local governments into the policy-making process, and as a useful body for resolving disputes and for looking for alternative solutions to state-local disputes.

Some Final Words

Given that accountability problems are the main current concern, strict rules of who is responsible might be more important than how power is divided between the different governmental levels. In order to give any strict advice on the appropriate assignment of power, we need more research that investigates whether local provision is really more efficient. The number of reforms that have been undertaken in Sweden makes it possible to investigate this. In addition, we need to know whether the different spending levels in the municipalities are really a consequence of different preferences and if there is any evidence of a race to the bottom.

REFERENCES

Ahlin, Å. & E. Johansson (2000) "Demand for Local Public Schooling: Another Brick in the Wall", Working Paper 2000:12, Department of Economics, Uppsala University.

Ahlin, Å. & E. Johansson (2001) "Individual Demand for Local Public Schooling: Evidence from Swedish Survey Data", *International Tax and Public Finance*, 8(4) 331-351.

Andersson, B.-E (1989) "Effects of Public Day-Care: A Longitudinal Study", *Child Development* 60, 857-866.

Andersson, B.-E (1992) "Effects of Day-Care on Cognitive and Socioemotional Competence of 13-Year-Old Swedish Schoolchildren", *Child Development* 63, 20-36.

Aronsson, T., J. Lundberg & M. Wikström (2001) "The Impact of Regional Public Expenditures on the Local Decision to Spend", in J. Lundberg *Local Government Expenditures and Regional Growth in Sweden*, Umeå Economic Studies No. 554, Umeå University.

Bergstrom, T. & S. Blomquist (1996) "The Political Economy of Subsidized Day Care", *European Journal of Political Economy* 12, 443-458.

Bergström, P., M. Dahlberg & E. Johansson, (1999) "Municipal Labor Demand: Sweden 1988-1995", in E. Johansson *Essays on Local Public Finance and Intergovernmental Grants*, Economic Studies 45, Department of Economics, Uppsala University.

Blomquist, S. & V. Christiansen (1995) "Public Provision of Private Goods as a Redistributive Device in an Optimum Income Tax Model", *Scandinavian Journal of Economics* 97, 547-567.

Blomquist, S. & V. Christiansen (1998) "Price Subsidies versus Public Provision", *International Tax and Public Finance* 5, 283-306.

Boadway, R. (2001) "Inter-Governmental Fiscal Relations, the Facilitator of Fiscal Decentralization", *Constitutional Political Economy* 12, 93-121.

Boadway, R. & M. Marchand (1995) "The Use of Public Expenditures for Redistributive Purposes", *Oxford Economic Papers* 47, 45-59.

Boadway, R., M. Marchand & M. Sato (1998) "Subsidies versus Public Provision of Private Goods as Instruments for Redistribution", *Scandinavian Journal of Economics* 100, 545-564.

Boije, R. & M. Dahlberg (1997) "Discrete Choice and the Demand for Local Public Services", in R. Boije *Capitalisation, Efficiency and the Demand for Local Public Services*, Economic Studies 33, Department of Economics, Uppsala University

Brueckner, J. K. (2000) "Welfare Reform and the Race to the Bottom: Theory and Evidence", *Southern Economic Journal*, 66(3), 505-525.

Dahlberg, M. & P. Fredriksson (2001) "Migration and Local Public Services", Working Paper 2001:12, Department of Economics, Uppsala University.

Jonsson, J.O. (1994) "Förskola – en strategi för jämlikhet?" in R. Erikssson & J.O. Jonsson (eds) *Sortering i skolan*, Carlssons bokförlag, Stockholm.

Lundberg, J. (2001a) "A Spatial Interaction Model of Benefit Spillovers from Locally Provided Public Services", in J. Lundberg *Local Government Expenditures and Regional Growth in Sweden*, Umeå Economic Studies No. 554, Umeå University.

Lundberg, J. (2001b) "On the Determinants of Average Income Growth and Net Migration at the Municipal Level in Sweden", in J. Lundberg *Local Government Expenditures and Regional Growth in Sweden*, Umeå Economic Studies No. 554, Umeå University.

Lundin, M. & P. Skedinger (2000) "Decentralisation of Active Labour Market Policy: The Case of Swedish Local Employment Service Committees", Working Paper 2000:6, Institute for Labor Market Policy Evaluation, Uppsala.

Lundmark, C. (1995) "Pensionärernas flyttningar över kommungräns i Sverige under perioden 1972-1992", Gerum Nr 29, Kulturgeografiska institutionen, Umeå University.

McLure, C.E., Jr. (2001). "The Tax Assignment Problem: Ruminations on How Theory and Practice Depend on History", *National Tax Journal* LIV, 339-363.

Murray R. (1985) "Central Control of the Local Government Sector in Sweden", In E. Gramlich and B.-C. Ysander (eds) *Control of Local Governments*, IUI Conference Reports series 1985:1.

Musgrave, R.A. (1959) *The Iheory of Public Finance*, New York: McGraw-Hill.

Oates, W.E. (1972) *Fiscal Federalism*, New York: Harcourt Brace Jovanovich.

Peterson, Olof (2001) Kommunalpolitik, fjärde upplagan, Nordstedts juridik, Stockholm.

Socialstyrelsen (2000) Taxor och avgifter för vård och omsorg, Äldreuppdraget 2000:1.

Söderström, Lars, Anders Björklund, Per Gunnar Edelback & Agneta Kruse (1999) *Från dagis till servicehus, välfärdspolitik i livets olika skeden.* (Stockholm: SNS förlag).

Tiebout, C.M. (1956) "A Pure Theory of Local Expenditures", *Journal of Political Economy* 64, 416-24.

Uddhammar, E. (1997) *Arbete, välfärd, bidrag: En dynamisk analys av folkets välstånd och välfärdsforskningens missförstånd*, Stockholm: City University Press.

Watts, R.L. (1999) *The Spending Power in Federal Systems: A Comparative Study*, Kingston, Canada: Institute of Intergovernmental Relations.

Westerlund, O. (2001) "Arbetslöshet, arbetsmarknadspolitik och geografisk rörlighet" *Ekonomisk Debatt*, 29(4), 263-272.

Wildasin, D.E. (1986) *Urban Public Finance*, Harwood Academic Publishers, Chur, Switzerland.

APPENDIX

The municipalities are by law responsible for:

social services including care for elderly, social assistance and daycare

public schooling

local planning

health and environmental protection

cleaning and waste disposal

rescue services

water and drainage

order and security

On a voluntary basis, the municipalities can engage in, e.g.,:

leisure activities

culture

dwellings

energy

trade and industry

Counties are responsible for

health care (80%)

national dental health service

secondary health schools/ folk high-school

public transportation

culture (e.g. county museums, county libraries etc.)

3

SWEDISH LOCAL GOVERNMENT: IS THERE A BAILOUT PROBLEM?

Jürgen von Hagen* and Matz Dahlberg

ZEI, University of Bonn, Indiana University, and CEPR

Uppsala University

INTRODUCTION

The vertical structure of government in all OECD countries is characterized by a hierarchy of two or three layers of governments, with the national government at the top and local government at the bottom. Typically, unitary states like Sweden have two layers, while federal states like Germany have three layers of more. This structure serves as a basis for assigning specific tasks to local governments, which, due to their closer proximity to the citizen and their better knowledge of local economic conditions, they can fulfil better than the central government.[1] Decentralization of the public sector also serves to create competition for taxpayers among local governments. Such competition is regarded as a check on rent-seeking behavior of selfish politicians and on excessive growth of government.[2]

The dark side of decentralization of the public sector is the risk that local governments engage in strategic behavior to attract financial resources from the central government and that, as a result, decentralization leads to soft budget constraints at the local level. The local budget constraint defines the total amount of resources, collected from local sources and received as transfers from other governments, expected to be available to finance local public policies during a fiscal year. Following Maskin (1996), the budget constraint is soft, if local governments perceive that the central government lacks the ability or will to keep them to fixed budget constraints. That is, the local government anticipate that they can extract subsidies from the central government during the fiscal year that exceed the levels determined ex ante. Bailouts are an important type of soft budget constraints in practice (Pisauro, 2001). We define bailouts as incidents in which the central government provides more financial resources to local governments than determined ex ante when the latter declare themselves unable to fulfil their obligations otherwise (Rodden, 2001). This may involve local governments unable to service financial debts out of their own revenues, and local governments unable to pay for critical

---

* Correspondence: Jürgen von Hagen, ZEI, Walter Flex Strasse 3, D-53113 Bonn, Germany, Tel +49-228-739199, Email vonhagen@uni-bonn.de

[1] Proximity to the citizen is the basic reason for justifying local government in the context of the economic theory of federalism; see Oates (1999), Olson (1969).

[2] This is an outflow of the "Leviathan" view of government (Brennan and Buchanan, 1977).

public services such as health or education, because they spent their regular revenues on other items.

The bailout problem has received considerable attention in recent years, as international organizations have conducted empirical research into the causes and determinants of bailout problems. Rodden et al (2001) report the results of a study commissioned by the World Bank that looks at the explanation and the resolution of bailouts and at strategies to prevent bailouts in various countries around the world. Fernandez-Arias et al. (2002) present the results of a study on bailouts focusing on Latin American countries. There is also a recent theoretical literature dealing with bailouts, see Careaga and Weingast (2000), Inman (2002), Wildasin (1998), and Goodspeed (2001).

In this paper, we discuss the potential bailout problem of local government in Sweden, a country with a long history of strong and relatively autonomous local government. In the early 1990s, numerous Swedish municipalities found themselves in financial crises and turned to the Swedish government for help. Some of them obtained financial aid to resolve the crisis, although a much larger number of municipalities applied for similar assistance. This experience could be an indication of a severe weakness of local public finances, but it might also just reflect the efforts of communities, which were fundamentally financially healthy, to obtain extra funding. Reforms of public finances during the 1990s have addressed local financial conditions. An important question is whether they solve any potential bailout problem.

In section II, we discuss the bailout problem more generally, reviewing the theoretical literature and the empirical evidence. In section III, we review the state of local public finances in Sweden. In section IV, we consider the bailout problem of Swedish local governments. Section V concludes.

BAILOUTS IN THEORY AND PRACTICE

Theory

In a bailout, a central government assumes obligations of a local government, which the latter declares itself unable to serve. It is useful to distinguish bailouts from insurance, where the central government provides financial assistance to local governments under a set of rules and contingences defined ex ante. In contrast, a characteristic feature of bailouts is that there are no contingent rules obliging the central government to come forth with any assistance. Bailouts involve a local government financial crisis, i.e., a demand for a bailout, and a central government decision to supply additional funds. An important question is, to what extent the former is the result of strategic behavior on the part of the local government, including fiscal negligence or excessive risk taking. For example, the inability of a local government to service its debt may be due to extremely harsh and unexpected macro economic developments that are outside its control, even if the government observed reasonable standards of financial responsibility. If the debts incurred were used to finance projects that local governments can undertake and manage more efficiently than the central government, a bailout may be efficient under such circumstances, as risk averse local authorities might not engage in such projects sufficiently otherwise.

In contrast, local financial crises may be the result of excessive risk-taking by local authorities or of deliberate overspending local financial means anticipating that the central government will pick up the bill. This is the essence of a soft local budget constraint. The principal reason why bailouts are economically undesirable is that they give rise to a common-pool problem.[3] With a hard budget constraint, a local government can increase local spending only by raising additional taxes in its jurisdiction and it will choose its optimal level of spending by equating the marginal cost of raising an extra tax euro from local taxpayers with the marginal benefit of spending that euro on all local government activities. When local governments can borrow, this condition includes an intertemporal dimension in the sense that the marginal cost of borrowing an extra euro and financing it by future tax revenues must equal the current and expected future, discounted marginal benefit of spending it. With a soft budget constraint, in contrast, part of the cost of financing additional local government spending falls on the central government, i.e., on all tax payers in the country. Since local government is likely to disregard the cost of taxation in other jurisdictions, the soft budget constraint faces the local government with a reduced marginal cost of spending on local projects and, therefore, induces spending beyond efficient levels.

A corollary of this is that soft budget constraints affect not only the size but also the composition of local government spending. Careaga and Weingast (2000) consider a local government choosing between local investment projects that increase future economic activity and, thus, revenues from local taxes, and projects that merely increase the local government's popularity or perks. Note that the former might well include investments that are economically not viable. With a hard budget constraint, any borrowing by the local government goes to financing investment. With a soft budget constraint, however, the local government also borrows to finance more perks and non-viable projects and less sound investment, anticipating that the central government will eventually pay for the former. In their terminology, the soft budget constraint results in a 'fiscal pact with the devil' of local fiscal profligacy and neglected local development policies.

An important implication is that any financial assistance granted to local governments in financial crisis should be structured such that the distortion of marginal costs and benefits at the local level is minimized. One way to do this is to impose strict repayment requirements including interest or political penalties on the local administration. Alternatively, Goodspeed (2001) shows that the spending distortion can be rectified, and the demand for bailouts reduced, by increasing central government grants to all local governments every time an individual local government receives a bailout. Since central government grants are paid out of taxes raised in all local jurisdictions, this rule implies that a local government asking for

[3] For a discussion of common pool problems in public finance, see von Hagen and Harden (1995), von Hagen and Hallerberg (1999), and Velasco (1999).

a bailout anticipates an increase in central government taxes as a result of its own excessive spending.

Bailouts are best understood as sequential games between a central and a local government. In the first move of this game, the central government specifies the vertical grants it wants to pay to local governments and any conditional rules for financial assistance in the case of local financial crises. In the second move, the local government considers its optimal spending, taxing, and borrowing policy. The local government can choose prudent policies that do not lead to financial crises, or imprudent policies that can lead to situations where it is unable to serve its obligations. Importantly, its actions are based on the expected central government response to a financial crisis. In the third move, the central government observes whether a local financial crisis has occurred or not. If no crisis has emerged, the central government simply pays out the vertical grants determined at the first stage. If a crisis has occurred, the central government pays additional grants to the local government concerned, if the benefits exceed the costs of providing crisis relief. The costs of doing so may include reputational costs of encouraging imprudent behavior leading to more local financial crises in the future.

In his analysis of the bailout game, Inman (2001) focuses on the central government's ability to commit to a no-bailout rule announced at the first stage. If the central government's announcement is fully credible, the local government does not borrow and there is never a crisis. Credibility depends critically on the central government's ex-post cost of denying a bailout compared to the cost of granting it. The cost of denying a bailout has a financial and a distributional element. The former relates to spill-overs of a local default through the financial system, such as the ripple effects of bank failures or reputational costs resulting in an increased risk premium on international loans. It is larger in less developed financial systems and when a large part of local borrowing is in the international capital market. Distributional costs arise when the central government favors local taxpayers or those owning the local government debt over the general taxpayer. Regarding bond holders, this might be the case when the local government has borrowed in the international market and the central government fears losing market access altogether. Favoring local taxpayers may have to do with the political importance of the locality concerned, as in the case of the bailout of the City of Medellin, Colombia, in the 1980s (Renteria et al, 2000).

Wildasin (1998) focuses on externalities caused by refusing bailouts. In his model, a local government provides a local public service with positive spill-overs to other jurisdictions. These spill-overs imply that citizens of other jurisdictions have an interest in a (minimum) provision of this activity in the jurisdiction under consideration. Examples could be local health services or education. The local government receives a Pigovian grant from the central government to correct for the externality. Given this grant, it may choose to finance too little of the externality-generating service out of local taxes or spend too much of its local taxes on purely local public goods. If that occurs, the central government can provide a bailout, i.e., an additional grant to the local government to achieve a higher level of the externality-generating service. The central government finances this grant by reducing the level of a national pure public good benefiting all citizens. Importantly,

Wildasin assumes that the central government makes this decision by maximizing the welfare of citizens in all other local jurisdictions. One key point of his analysis is, therefore, that bailouts can be compatible with democratic government.

In this setting, bailouts are never granted for small deviations from the optimal level of local provision of the externality-generating service. Bailouts are, therefore, never of small size. Furthermore, the likelihood of bailouts increases with the intensity of the externality. One should, therefore, observe more bailouts connected to the failure of local governments to provide services, which are considered critical from the point of view of other jurisdictions. Furthermore, large local jurisdictions are more likely to obtain bailouts that small ones, because they cause larger externalities. This is a version of the popular 'too-big-to-fail' hypothesis that large cities or regions are too important to be left alone and are, therefore, more likely to attract bailouts.

Finally, Wildasin shows that inducing a bailout is not necessarily in the interest of the local government, even if the central government is willing to grant it. The reason is that a bailout can only be obtained, if the local government chooses a large deviation from the optimal level of public services. As a result, obtaining a bailout may require a combination of local public services and private consumption that is strongly inferior to the optimal one from the point of view of the local citizen. Thus, bailouts have an opportunity cost in terms of a less desirable composition of local public and private consumption. Local governments are less likely to demand bailouts, if small deviations from the optimal consumption bundle generate large losses in utility, or if the substitutability between the externality-generating public service and private consumption is small.

Goodspeed (2001) considers a bailout scenario in which a central government pays grants to local governments that borrowed excessively in the past, and does so in order to boost its reelection chances. These grants are financed out of general taxes – the common pool property of the bailout. As bailouts reduce the cost of borrowing for the local governments, local borrowing increases. But unless the central government reimburses the local government for all borrowing beyond the efficient level, there is again an opportunity cost in the sense that the local government must engage in excessive borrowing to obtain a bailout, and it must raise taxes to finance its part of the resulting borrowing cost. Goodspeed shows, first, that the central government uses bailouts to equalize its marginal reelection chances in all regions. This suggests that large bailouts are unlikely to occur in regions where the central government enjoys strong support for ideological or non-economic reasons, as the marginal benefit from bailouts is small in such regions. Contrary to popular wisdom, one should not expect bailouts to go to local jurisdictions whose governments have strong allegiances to the central government.[4]

Once again, the size of the bailout depends on the central government's and the local government's behavior. If a local jurisdiction's share in the central government tax pool is large, it will anticipate that a bailout will lead to higher central government

[4] This reasoning is consistent with related political economy research in Lindbeck and Weibull (1993) and Dixit and Londregan (1996, 1998).

taxes. Thus, large jurisdictions internalize part of the common pool effect and, therefore, reduce the demand for bailouts. Since externalities emanating from the public services provided by local governments play no role in this analysis, this means that bailouts are more likely to go to small communities, i.e., the 'too-big-to-fail' hypothesis does not hold.

Empirical Evidence

Bailout episodes have attracted considerable attention of academics and international economic institutions such as the World Bank and the Interamerican Development Bank. This is partly at least a reflection of the movement towards greater decentralization of the government in many developing and post-socialist countries. Two collections of case studies currently in preparation (Rodden and Eskeland, 2002, and Fernandez-Arias, Stein and von Hagen, 2002) present rich empirical material relating to bailouts. A first point to note is that bailouts are in no way special to developing or transition economies. Von Hagen et al. (2000) review he experience with bailouts in four OECD countries; Australia, Germany, Italy, and Sweden. The case studies also show that the factors leading to local financial crises and, sometimes, to bailouts, are quite similar in OECD and other countries.

The empirical evidence confirms the critical role of the central government's ability to commit to a hard budget constraint at the local level. Several constitutional and administrative characteristics can be identified that potentially weaken the central government's commitment power. One is the "ambition" (Rodden and Eskeland, 2002) of the central government to equalize living standards or the provision of public service throughout the country. Germany provides a good example. Germany's constitutional court mandated the federal government in the early 1990s to bailout two of the German states (Saarland and Bremen) that had accumulated large debts during the 1980s. The court's reasoning was based on the argument that the German federation owes its member states financial solidarity: Given that the constitution charges the states with certain responsibilities, the federation must assure that the states have the means to fulfil these tasks not only in a minimal way but sufficiently to guarantee their citizens equal living standards. As the two states declared themselves unable to do so due to their high debt burdens, the court concluded that the federal government had to provide financial assistance. According to one reading of Argentina's constitution, there is a similar mandate for the central government to provide the provinces with sufficient financial means in times of crises in that country. In the past, this has repeatedly encouraged the provinces to demand extra grants from the central government, which the latter could not deny. Among the OECD countries, Italy is another example where the ambition to provide equal public services throughout the country was the root of fiscal problems and bailouts at the local level (Bordignon, 2000). In contrast, the US is a case of a federation with an "unambitious" federal government in this regard and one that has proven its ability to deny bailouts in the past (Rodden and Eskeland, 2002).

A related, though not exactly the same factor is the lack of clarity in the assignment of responsibilities to local and central governments. In the Italian case (Bordignon, 2000), many local and regional public services were administered simultaneously by local and central authorities. Its direct involvement made the central government responsible for a continued provision of such services, even if the local governments diverted funds from their proper use. As a result, the central government had little choice but to provide extra grants when the local governments threatened to discontinue health and education services due to local financial stress. Similar problems seem to have played a role in bailouts in the Ukraine and India. In Brazil, the same issue appears in the form of overlapping tax bases and uncoordinated tax administration between the central government and the states (Rodden and Eskeland, 2002).

Another aspect of this is the transfer of responsibilities from the center to local governments when the latter do not wish to assume these responsibilities and the center does not provide the means necessary to fulfil them to the local governments. This factor looms large behind the bailout episodes in Colombia, where local governments were charged with new responsibilities in education and had to pay teachers whose wages were negotiated with the central government (Renteria et al., 2000).

The empirical cases presented in Fernandez-Arias et al. (2002) and von Hagen (2000) point to another aspect. Bailouts often occur in the context of macroeconomic stabilization efforts including significant fiscal tightening at the level of the national government. On the one hand, this may be because the central bank previously financed local government deficits that simply became more visible with a more disciplined monetary and fiscal regime. On the other hand, this could be a result of an effort by the central government to shift financial responsibilities to other levels of government in an attempt to solve its own deficit problems. In either case, large swings in macroeconomic conditions seem to make it harder to refuse bailouts.

The organization of federal fiscal relations is a second, important factor in the commitment power of the central government. The more local governments participate in the determination of vertical grants, the greater the risk that they will exploit the center through bailouts. Brazil is a prime example. Here, the Senat, which is the representation of the states, can require the central government to provide bailouts to state governments. Indeed, the large bailouts of 1989, 1993, and 1997 were the result of coalitions of states in the Senat (Bevilaqua, 2000). Local governments' access to the money printing-press, as it effectively existed in Argentina and Brazil during the 1970s and 1980s, is a similar mechanism increasing the likelihood of bailouts (Aizenman, 1998). Similarly, the absence of fixed and transparent rules determining the size and distribution of vertical grants tends to undermine the commitment power of the central government. As Rodden and Eskeland (2002) point out, the combination of discretionary transfers and ad-hoc political bargaining contributed to the bailout problems in Brazil, China, the Ukraine, and India.

A third, important factor determining the central government's commitment power is the dependence of local governments on vertical grants. The weaker the local government's own tax base, the more difficult it is for the central government to deny a bailout, as doing so would force the local government to shut down services such as school education, hospital care, or local police. Strong vertical dependence coupled with the authority over public policies that generate strong externalities or political pressures in case of unsatisfactory provision, such as health or schooling, gives local governments the opportunity for strategic behavior. In such scenarios, local governments may spend their vertical grants early and on different items and then take the central government hostage with the threat of closing down critical services. Strategic behavior of this kind was a major factor in the repeated bailouts of local and regional governments in Italy. The Italian case also shows that constraining local government borrowing in the capital markets or from financial institutions does not solve the problem of bailouts. Italian local governments and regions simply generated debts in the form of payment arrears, which were later covered by the central government. In fact, that local governments could borrow probably made things worse, as the central government could not force them to borrow enough to pay their obligations and use future central government transfers to repay their debts. A significant increase in local tax and borrowing autonomy was an essential element of the reforms solving the bailout problem in the 1980s and 1990s (Bordignon, 2000).

An interesting observation emerging from the case studies presented in Fernandez-Arias, Stein and von Hagen (2002) is that there is very little evidence supporting the "too-big-to-fail" hypothesis. The case of the metro of Medellin, Columbia, is the only clear-cut example of a "too-big-to-fail" bailout, and even there, the principal reason for granting the bailout was Medellin's political importance for the incumbent president rather than large spillover effects to other regions. Several case studies suggest that it is often the small states or cities that are most likely to obtain bailouts. This suggests that externalities positively related to the size of the local jurisdiction are relatively unimportant for bailouts in practice, and that the inability of central governments to stick to a no-bailout commitment in the face of what at first seems a small cost is a more important factor.

Similarly, there is little evidence in the Latin American bailout episodes that money flows systematically in the direction of political alliances. On the contrary, one Argentine bailout incident suggests that a large political ally of the central government was denied a bailout in the 1990s, while smaller provincial governments adhering to the opposition party did receive bailouts (Nicolini et al., 2000). Similarly, the famous bailout of New South Wales in the 1930s came to rescue a state ruled by the party opposing the central government (von Hagen, 2000). In Germany, the two states receiving bailouts in the early 1990s did not belong to the central government's party, either. This evidence supports the idea developed in Goodspeed (2001), i.e., that central governments use bailouts to maximize the political pay-off, which implies that money does not typically flow to jurisdictions firmly tied to the ruling party by the same ideology.

LOCAL PUBLIC FINANCE IN SWEDEN[5]

There are two layers of local government in Sweden, municipalities and counties. There are 289 municipalities, with an average size of 30,827 inhabitants and ranging from 2,639 to 754,948 inhabitants. The median municipality has 15,264 inhabitants. The 21 counties have an average size of 424,244 inhabitants, ranging from 57,412 to approximately 1.84 million inhabitants. Note that the two layers of local government are not related to each other in a hierarchical way; instead, they are charged with different functions.

Local self-government is protected by the Swedish constitution. Taken together, the local public sector is fairly large in Sweden compared to other countries: It stands for about a third of total public expenditure and two thirds of public sector consumption and more than 80 percent of total public employment. Figure 1 indicates that the local government sector is particularly important for public investment in Sweden. Its share in total public investment stood at 70 percent in the early 1980s and is now around 60 percent. In real terms, local public investment has roughly remained at the same level in the past 20 years. In 1999, investment spending was 7.5 percent of total spending at the local level. Thus, Sweden's government is characterized by a relatively large degree of decentralization. As the total public sector is large relative to the Swedish economy, this implies that the local government sector is economically important; it accounts for approximately 21 percent of GDP and 25 percent of Swedish employment.

Figure 1: Local Government Investment Spending

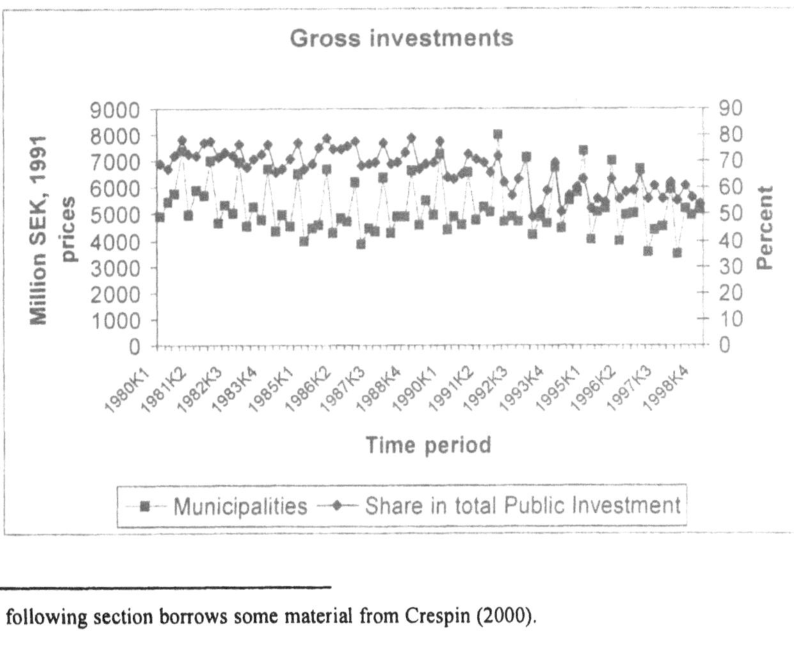

[5] The following section borrows some material from Crespin (2000).

Municipalities fulfil a range of tasks assigned to them by law. Social care and assistance is the most important among them. This comprizes special care programs for families, children, and the elderly. Together, these take up 48 percent of all municipal spending. Education services, which include primary and secondary schooling take up the largest individual item in total municipal spending, accounting for 28 percent. Municipalities also have some tasks regarding public health, safety, street maintenance, water and sewage services, the environment, parks, and recreational services. Even where municipalities are required to offer certain types of services by law, they still retain the freedom to choose their level and quality of these services above a certain minimum level or quality set by the central government. Murray (1985) estimates that about 40 percent of local expenditures are obligatory, implying that the local governments could decide on approximately 60 percent of their own expenditures.[6] To put this statement in perspective we can look at the cross-sectional variation in expenditures. During the period from 1974 to 1994, average expenditures were about 28,000 SEK per capita in real terms, with a standard deviation of roughly 5,600 SEK. Thus, there is substantial cross-sectional variation.

Municipalities also undertake the planning of land use for residential and commercial purposes. Many municipalities own local housing companies that build and rent apartment buildings. County councils are much more limited in their activities. 89 percent of their total spending is for health care, dental care and education in the health field. Municipalities account for about 70 percent of all local government spending, while county councils account for about 30 percent.

The financing of local government consists mainly of own tax revenues (obtained from a proportional local income tax), general (including tax equalizing grants) and specific central government grants, and fees. Property taxes, which were more important in the past, have completely lost importance. Local governments also have the authority to borrow in their own responsibility. An important rule regarding the relationship between local and central government is the *financing principle*. Under this principle, the Swedish Parliament has entered a commitment not to pass legislation affecting local government expenditures without providing the local level with the required resources. In principle, therefore, there should be no unfunded central government mandates imposed on Swedish local governments.

Local Government Revenues

Table 1 reports the composition of local government revenues from 1981 to 1999. It shows that tax revenues constitute the main source of revenues for local governments. The share of own tax revenues increased from 41 percent in 1981 to 53 percent in 1999. Over the past two decades, intergovernmental grants had a stable share of 20 to 25 percent. In contrast, the share of fee income has decreased from slightly less than 20 percent in the early 1980s to less than 10 percent in the late 1990s. Local income taxes are proportional with the tax base defined by national

---

[6] Spending on the partly mandatory services constitutes about 80 percent of all expenditures (Petersson, 2001).

law and tax rates set by the municipalities, although the central government can interfere in this decision as it did when it imposed a tax rate freeze between 1991 and 1994 and again between 1997 and 1999. These interventions came with the purpose of reducing the overall tax burden in the country and, in the second episode, they were framed in an agreement that allowed municipalities to increase rates at the cost of paying part of the extra revenue to the central government. In 1998, tax rates varied between 26 percent and 34 percent. Although municipalities do not have the right to create new taxes, they thus have a considerable degree of autonomy in taxation.

Fees are generated in the context of municipal services such as child care. They vary between municipalities and different types of service; thus, fee income covers over 90 percent of local current expenditures for energy, water sand sewage, and waste management, but less than 3 percent for current spending on education. Taking local tax income and fee income as own resources, Swedish local government today has a share of 61 percent own resources. In international standards this indicates a rather low degree of vertical imbalance. Tax collection is administered by the central government on behalf of the municipalities.

Table 1 also indicates that the composition of central government grants changed dramatically due to two grant reforms in 1993 and 1996. Before 1993, specific grants were the dominant type of grant. They accounted for about 20 percent of local government revenues. After 1993, their share dropped to three percent, while general, or unconditional grants now account for about 20 percent of all revenues. Since specific grants have a stronger impact on local government choices of certain activities, this indicates a decrease in the intensity of central government control over local government behavior, at least in this regard.

In Figure 2, we plot the evolution of the three main revenue sources (expressed in per capita terms and in 1999 prices) during the last two decades. Until the early 1990s, the three series followed fairly similar patterns; local government revenues were, in fact, almost flat after correcting for inflation and population growth. After 1991, the picture began to change. Total revenues grew driven first exclusively by an increase in tax revenues. Grant revenues, which declined between 1992 and 1995, started to increase, too, after 1995. Fee income seems to settle at a lower level during the 1990s than during the 1980s.

Table 1: Local Government Revenue Sources (Percent of Total Revenues)

Year	Taxes	Fees	General Grants	Specific Grants	Other
1981	0,41	0,17	0,04	0.21	0,16
1982	0,42	0,18	0,04	0.21	0,15
1983	0,42	0,19	0,04	0.22	0,14
1984	0,42	0,19	0,04	0.22	0,13
1985	0,41	0,20	0,04	0.22	0,14
1986	0,41	0,19	0,04	0.21	0,16
1987	0,43	0,19	0,04	0.21	0,14
1988	0,46	0,19	0,04	0.21	0,10
1989	0,46	0,18	0,04	0.21	0,11
1990	0,48	0,16	0,04	0.22	0,10
1991	0,49	0,17	0,04	0.22	0,08
1992	0,52	0,14	0,05	0.21	0,07
1993	0,55	0,09	0,14	0.08	0,14
1994	0,56	0,09	0,13	0.07	0,15
1995	0,57	0,10	0,13	0.05	0,16
1996	0,55	0,09	0,18	0.04	0,14
1997	0,54	0,08	0,19	0.03	0,16
1998	0,54	0,08	0,20	0.04	0,14
1999	0,53	0,08	0,19	0.03	0,17

Source: Statistical Yearbook

Figure 2: The Evolution of Municipal Revenues, 1981-1999

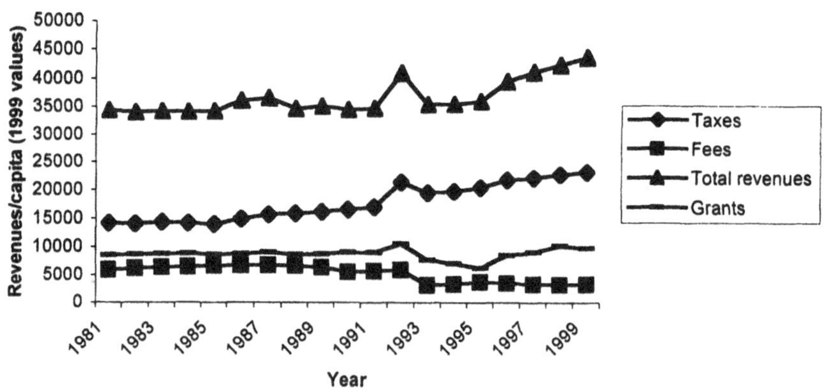

Source: Statistical Yearbook

Equalization

In 1998, the average taxable per-capita income in Sweden stood at SEK 109,852, with a range from SEK 80,373 (Borgholm) to SEK 199,237 (Danderyd). There is thus considerable variation in the local income tax base and, therefore, in local income tax revenues between municipalities. This variation is mainly due to differences in employment levels and stands in contrast to the political objective to ensure that all municipalities and county councils should be able to provide similar levels and standards of public services. In the terminology of Rodden et al. (2002), Sweden is a highly "ambitious" country regarding this objective. To achieve it, a system of revenue and expenditure equalization was introduced in 1996.[7]

The purpose of revenue equalization is to bring per capita tax revenues in all municipalities close to the national average. A municipality's contribution C to the equalization system is calculated as follows:

$$C_i = 0.95 n_i t^* (y_i - y),$$

where n_i is the number of inhabitants as of the previous year's November 1, t^* is the average tax rate prevailing in 1995, y_i is the municipality's average taxable income, and y is the country-wide average taxable income. A municipality thus pays into the equalization system depending on its average taxable income compared to the national average. Net income tax revenue then is

$$T_i - C_i = n_i (t_i - 0.95 t^*) y_i + 0.95 n_i t^* y,$$

where $T_i = n_i t_i$ and t_i is the tax rate of the municipality. After equalization, most municipalities had per capita revenues between 98 and 104 percent of the national average in 1998.

Revenue equalization affects the incentives for municipal tax and development policies. The effect of a change in the tax rate on net tax income is

$$\frac{\partial(T_i - C_i)}{\partial t_i} = n_i y_i \left(1 + \frac{t_i \partial n_i}{n_i \partial t_i} + \frac{t_i \partial y_i}{y_i \partial t_i}\right) - 0.95 \frac{t^*}{t_i} n_i y_i \left[\left(1 - \frac{y}{y_i}\right) \frac{t_i \partial n_i}{n_i \partial t_i} + \frac{t_i \partial y_i}{y_i \partial t_i}\right].$$

The first term gives the response of local tax revenues to a change in the tax rate. If the tax-paying population is attracted by declining local tax rates and local per-capita income rises due to declining tax rates, the two elasticites in the parenthesis are negative. Thus, if the combined elasticities are sufficiently large, a rate hike may reduce tax revenues. The second term shows that this disciplining effect of tax-payer mobility is weakened by revenue equalization, as the losses in tax revenues are partially offset by equalization payments. This effect is stronger for low-tax rate municipalities (where t^*/t_i is large) and for relatively rich municipalities (where $y/y_i < 1$.) As a result, equalization creates a tendency for tax rates to converge at the 1995 average level. For similar reasons, relatively low-tax rate municipalities loose

[7] Such a system had existed earlier as well, although less visible.

tax revenues, if they engage in successful local development policies raising employment or average taxable incomes. Equalization thus discourages the use of local development policies to raise additional income. Complaints about the system voiced in the context of a 1998 public review process suggest that such perverse effects do occur in practice (Crespin, 2000).

In practice, the total volume of tax revenues redistributed by the equalization scheme seems rather low. In 1998, it amounted to a mere 3.3 percent of total municipal revenues. But note that this does not imply that equalization and the incentive effects it creates for local economic policies are unimportant. The small amount of redistribution may just be the result of an equilibrium process of convergence.

Expenditure equalization seeks to reduce differences in structural cost conditions of public services across municipalities. This is done for 16 different service blocks separately. Cost conditions for each service block reflect local social and demographic structures and other characteristics of the municipalities. A per-capita standard structural cost is calculated as a reference value, which is equal to the national average cost. Local governments with unfavorable cost conditions receive an equalization grant, while those with favorable conditions pay a fee. The grant or fee compensates for the full per-capita difference between the local and average cost conditions. Since the payments are based on cost conditions rather than actual costs, local governments have an incentive to minimize actual costs and generate windfall profits. Total funds redistributed through the system are small, amounting to about one percent of total revenues of the local public sector in 1998.

Vertical Grants

As indicated above, Swedish local governments receive general (unconditional) and conditional grants. The former are per-capita grants, which are the same for all municipalities, and age-related grants, which depend on the number of inhabitants below the age of 15 and above the age of 65. The per-capita basis introduces a further element of revenue equalization among municipalities. General grants are also used to compensate municipalities for the financial consequences of national legislation under the financial principle explained above. Conditional grants are paid mainly in areas where local governments act as agents executing central government policies, e.g. in the labor market. There are also some investment grants paid to municipalities.

A third, largely discretionary type of grant was paid to local governments under the *Financial Relief Program*, which was operative between 1974 and 1992. Under this program, local governments in financial distress could apply annually to the national government for financial assistance, and the national government decided discretionarily who to grant assistance at the end of each year. On average over this period, the national government spent an annual SEK 282 million (in 1991 prices) on this program. While less than 50 local governments received such funds between 1975 and 1980, between 100 and 150 governments did so during the 1980s and until 1992. Similar programs existed during the 1990s. They are the core of the bailout incidents reviewed below.

Local Borrowing

Swedish municipalities are allowed to borrow in their own responsibility both domestically and abroad. A bit more than 25 percent of total local debt was foreign in 1994, about 15 percent was borrowing from banks and financial institutions. Local government deficits rarely exceeded investment spending at the local level, and typically amounted to less than half of it. There is a fair amount of heterogeneity in the borrowing behavior of local governments. For example, in 1994 the average level of debt was 14,900 SEK[8] per capita and the standard deviation was SEK 6,200. The minimum level of debt was 4,000 and the maximum 49,400 SEK per capita.

Figure 3: Local Government Debt

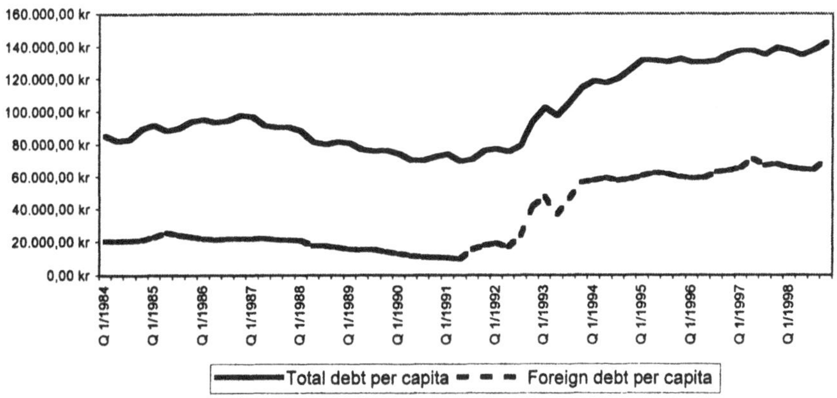

Source: IMF, Public Finance Statistics

Figure 3 shows the development of per-capita local government debt in 1995 prices from 1984 to 1999. Throughout the 1980s, local government debt was stable and even declining. This changed dramatically with the economic crisis in the early 1990s, when per-capita debt almost doubled within a couple of years. We return to this episode in section IV.1.

A peculiarity of the Swedish constitution is that, despite the financial autonomy of local government, municipalities cannot legally default. There is no exact rule on what happens if default is imminent, but the constitutional presumption seems to be that the national government will have to step in under such circumstances. This exposes the national government to the risk of having to accept the financial consequences of fiscal profligacy at the local level.

[8] The figures presented here are in real terms, deflated by the implicit GDP deflator (deflated to 1991 prices).

In order to mitigate this risk, and based on the experiences of the early 1990s – see section IV below – the national government introduced a new Local Government Act in 1997 which requires a balanced budget for local governments from 2000 onwards. Accordingly, local governments have to present and pass balanced budgets or surpluses each year. Should a local government incur a deficit during the fiscal year nevertheless, it is required to balance this deficit with surpluses during the next two years. The financial report of the year in which the deficit occurred must contain an explanation of how and when this will be achieved. The balancing requirement, however, is currently not tied to effective sanctions.

MUNICIPAL BAILOUTS

The past 30 years have seen two episodes that potentially qualify as bailouts in Sweden. One relates to the recurrent payment of central government grants under the *Financial Relief* program. The other has to do with financial assistance granted to municipalities in the 1990s.

The Financial Relief Program

Between 1974 and 1992, the central government had a special program for financial support of financially distressed municipalities. Local governments could apply for funding directly to the central government, which discretionally decided who was to be supported. During this period, a total of SEK 5,361 million (in 1991 prices) was spent under this program, or an SEK 282 million each year, which corresponds to 23.5 percent of average municipal spending in 1991. During 1975 to 1980, less than 50 governments per year received any money, whereas in the period 1981 to 1992, (with some exceptions) roughly 100 to 150 governments were supported each year. The average relief grant amounted to 0.36 percent of annual local government spending, which is quite small. However, the largest grant received was 5.3 percent of annual spending. Thus, the grants could be substantial in individual cases.

Dahlberg and Pettersson-Lidbom (2002) present an empirical analysis of this program. They show that the incidents of relief transfers were highly persistent, i.e., past payments of financial relief transfers are the most important predictors of present transfers. Furthermore, the authors show that the likelihood of receiving a financial relief transfer appears highly significant in a regression explaining debt growth among Swedish municipalities. This says that municipalities that received transfers in the past allowed their debts to grow faster than others. Dahlberg and Pettersson-Lidbom try to discriminate whether local government fiscal misbehavior is consistent with an adverse selection explanation or a moral hazard explanation, where adverse selection refers to fiscal behavior caused by some particular feature (the "type") of a local government and where moral hazard refers to whether a previous experience of a bailout causes a local government to change its fiscal behavior. Their base-line estimate of the combined effect of adverse selection and moral hazard ranges from 3,000-4,700 SEK per capita. This is roughly 30 to 50 percent of the total debt (10,200). Isolating the moral hazard effect, they find that debt is increased with 1,200-1,600 SEK per capita due to moral hazard, which is roughly 25-50 percent of the combined effect. Thus, the behavior of the central government in providing a bailout seems to have had a rather substantial effect on the bailed out municipalities' debt behavior. Taken together, these results imply that relief transfers could be anticipated and rewarded weak fiscal discipline at the local level.[9]

From the data used in Dahlberg and Pettersson-Lidbom, it can also be shown that the majority of municipalities receiving relief transfers had left-wing governments. More interestingly, the share of funds flowing to left-wing local governments increased from 45-48 percent under the Social Democratic Palme government to as much as 64 percent under the Center-Right governments of the late 1970s and early 1980s. Under the Social Democrat governments of the late 1980s, the share of leftist local governments receiving relief funds remained hovered around 70 percent, but the share of center and independent governments increased from 12 percent in 1982 to 19 percent in 1985-86. However, the Center-Right coalition inaugurated in 1991 boosted the share of right-wing local governments from 20 to 41 percent. At a first glance at least, the observation that the central governments tended to increase the share of local governments headed by an opposition party is compatible with the suggestion from Goodspeed's analysis that they used bailouts to promote their local election chances, and that maximizing reelection chances implies channeling bailout funds primarily to localities where the central government's own political support is not secured.

We can use the Dahlberg and Pettersson-Lidbom data to test this hypothesis more rigorously. For this purpose, we run two probit regressions to investigate whether the incumbent government extended bailouts to municipalities where it already had strong support or not. The dependent variable, $bailind_{i,t}$, is a dummy variable which is one if municipal government i received a financial relief transfer in a given year t, and zero otherwise. The explanatory variables are time fixed effects for each year to control for exogenous macro economic shocks affecting all municipalities and two dummy variable, $leftmaj_{i,t}$ and $rightmaj_{i,t}$, which are one if municipality i was ruled by a left-wing (right-wing) majority in year t. In the first probit, we use the years in which Sweden had a socialist central government (1974-1976, 1983-1991). In the second probit, we use the years in which Sweden had a right-wing central government (1977-1982, 1992). Panels 1 and 2 in Table 2 show the results.

[9] Dahlberg and Pettersson-Lidbom also test if there exists a real bailout problem in Sweden in the first place, that is, they test if bailouts have been extended to sub-national government with fiscal (debt) problems related to their own actions. They strongly reject the null hypothesis that the central government has not provided bailouts to the part of debt that is determined by actions taken by the municipality. In fact, they find that the central government has put very little attention to the part of debt that is explained by exogenous factors.

Table 2: Probit Estimates for Bailouts

1. Left-wing Central Governments

Number of observations = 3382

Likelihood Ratio Test for Significance chi-square(12) = 440.5 (p-value = 0.0000)

Log likelihood = -1959.5 Pseudo R-square = 0.10

$$\text{Bailind}_{i,t} = \underset{(4.9)}{-0.39} + \underset{(13.8)}{0.64}\ \text{leftmaj}_{i,t} + \text{time fixed effects.}$$

2. Right-wing Central Governments

Number of observations = 1954

Likelihood Ratio Test for Significance: chi-square(7) = 370.2 (p-value=0.0000)

Log Likelihood = -956.0 Pseudo R-square = 0.16

$$\text{Bailind}_{i,t} = \underset{(4.1)}{-0.77} - \underset{(7.8)}{0.77}\ \text{rightmaj}_{i,t} + \text{time fixed effects.}$$

3. All Central Governments

Number of observations = 4481

Likelihood Ratio Test for Significance: chi-square(19) = 552.5 (p-value=0.0000)

Log Likelihood = -2531.3 Pseudo R-square = 0.10

$$\text{Bailind}_{i,t} = \underset{(1.9)}{-0.16} + \underset{(0.6)}{0.001}\ \text{close}_{i,t} + \text{time fixed effects.}$$

The numbers in parenthesis are z-values. The first part of this table shows that left-wing municipal governments had a greater chance of attracting bailouts from socialist central governments than right-wing governments. The second part shows that right-wing governments had a smaller chance of obtaining bailouts from conservative central governments than left-wing municipal governments. This second result is clearly in line with Goodspeed's hypothesis. At a first glance, the first result seems to contradict the hypothesis. However, the left-wing central governments during this period were minority governments whose support may have been weak even in local jurisdictions governed by left-wing parties. Thus, we find at least some support for strategic behavior as suggested by Goodspeed.[10]

Another way of testing this is to use a measure of how many swing voters there are in a municipality. Here we use the closeness between the two blocs in the preceding municipal elections. It is based on the idea (see, e.g., Dahlberg and Johansson, 2002), that there are more swing voters in very close municipal election races than in very clearly determined ones. Our measure, $close_{i,t}$, is the share of seats in the municipal council that the ruling bloc obtained in the last election (by definition more than 50) minus 50. Under the hypothesis that governments use bailout grants to boost election chances in municipalities where there support is weak, we should expect a negative coefficient on $close_{i,t}$. The results reported in Table 2 show a positive but non-significant coefficient, so that the evidence is inconclusive.

Bailouts in the 1990s

During the early 1990s, several of the Swedish local governments ran into severe economic problems manifested in large recurrent deficits. Many of the financially distressed local governments turned to the central government for financial support.[11] Among the first to apply for financial help from the central government were the municipalities of Haninge and Bjuv, which were very close to bankruptcy at the time. The main event triggering the problems in 1992 was the municipality-owned housing company's (Haningehem) acute payment crisis. Being the main creditor, the municipality faced a payment crisis, too. At the time, the municipality had to regulate approximately SEK 1.3 billion for the housing company. As a result, it was very close to bankruptcy.

After lengthy negotiations, the national government enforced the following solution on Haninge:

- The state assumed responsibility for the housing company. Haninge was allowed to keep one share in it, the rest of the shares had to be handed over to a holding company created by the national government with the only purpose of taking care of Haningehem.
- The holding company was refinanced by a central government loan amounting to 600 million SEK.

---

[10] As mentioned earlier, the hypothesis that one should not expect bailouts to go to local jurisdictions in which the central governments already has strong support is closely related to the hypothesis derived in Lindbeck and Weibull (1993) and Dixit and Londregan (1996, 1998). Using Swedish data from a temporary grant program in 1998 that is rather similar to the bailout grants used in the estimations of Table 2, Dahlberg and Johansson (2002) find strong support for the prediction derived from the Lindbeck-WeibullD ixit-Londregan model saying that the incumbent government purchases votes by investing in those municipalities where there exist a lot of swing voters. They do *not* find support for the hypothesis that the incumbent government purchases votes by investing in their own supporters.

[11] There were mainly municipalities that applied for financial relief, but also some of the county councils did so. Here we focus on the municipalities.

- In 1995, Haninge received an extra, non-refundable central government grant of 850 million SEK largely taken from the fund for all municipality grants. The grant was to be used to pay the remaining debt in Haningehem.
- The municipality had to raise the local tax rate by one percentage point.

In the Bjuv case, the financial crisis also started with problems of the municipality-owned housing company (Bjuvsbyggen). The form of the extended bailout from the central government was, however, different compared to that extended to Haninge. In 1995, the municipality informed the State about its problematic economic situation. In 1996, it considered that it could no longer handle the situation itself, and applied for an extra grant of SEK 200 million from the central government. By March 1998, the municipality's total debt amounted to SEK 627 million. The central government and Bjuv agreed on the following solution:

- Bjuv was allowed to keep its housing company, although the central government has the option to overtake it at any time until May 31, 2003.
- Bjuv received an extra, non-refundable central government grant of SEK 159 million. The main condition for this grant was to repay some of the municipality's loans of SEK 150 million and to put SEK 9 million into the housing company.
- As the sole owner of the housing company, the municipality bound itself to take a larger responsibility of the management of the company.
- As long as the central government has the option to own the housing company, Bjuv must continuously inform it on its financial consolidation program stated in the written agreement between the central government and the municipality.

Following these incidents, a larger number of municipalities turned to the central government for financial relief. To handle their demands, the central government set up two committees, the *Housing Delegation* and the *Local Authority Delegation*. The *Housing Delegation* was established on July 1, 1998. Its work focused primarily on cases where the municipalities' financial problems were connected to a municipal housing company. The Housing Delegation considered only municipalities with severe financial problems. Its decisions were final and taken continuously over the period 1998-2001. The basis for the decisions taken by the Housing Delegation was less clearly laid out by the central government compared to the Local Authority Delegation. The Housing Delegation does not exist anymore.

The *Local Authority Delegation* was established on August 19, 1999, after the central government realized that many municipalities would not meet the balanced budget requirement by the year 2000. TheLocal governments concerned claimed that their inability to balance their budgets was due to external factors. Responding to such claims, the central government decided to establish a transfer program for municipalities where this was found to be true. Municipalities could apply for such funds and the Local Authority Delegation was appointed to prepare the cases and to propose which municipalities that were to be granted a positive response. The central government did, however, have the final decision. The decisions made by the

Local Authority Delegation were all made at the same time in the year 2000. The Local Authority Delegation was dissolved subsequently.

Note that the central government took some transfer decisions itself without handing over the application to any of the two committees. Furthermore, the Housing Delegation and the Local Authority Delegation handled some of the applications jointly. In these cases, the central government made the final decision.

Table 3 shows how the applications were allocated among the different decision-making authorities. The 136 applications summarized in the table were from 107 different municipalities. Of the 28 municipalities that applied twice, seven had one application decided upon directly by the central government and one handled by the Housing Delegation.[12] The other 21 had one application handled by the Housing Delegation and one by the Local Authority Delegation.[13]

Table 3: Relief Applications in the Late 1990s

Decision maker	Granted applications	Rejected applications	Total
Housing Delegation	24	38	62
Central government (after suggestion from Local Authority Delegation)	22	23	45
Central government (after suggestion from both committees)	14	0	14
Central government (without suggestion from any committee)	0	15	15
Total	60	76	136

Since the Local Authority Delegation gave more detailed reasoning for its decisions than the Local Housing Delegation, we provide some more descriptive information for the former. Both delegations were supposed to make their decisions primarily on the basis of the debt performance of the municipalities under consideration.[14]

Figure 4 shows the difference between the average per capita debt of the municipalities applying for financial relief and the non-applicant municipalities from 1974 to 1998, together with 90-percent confidence bands around these averages.[15] In the mid-1970s, the applicant municipalities had significantly lower per-capita debt than the non-applicants. In 1998, however, the difference was significantly positive.

---

[12] While all of the seven municipalities were rejected by the central government, two were granted by the Housing Delegation (Nordanstig and Timrå).

[13] Eleven municipalities were rejected by both of the committees (Boxholm, Finspång, Gullspång, Hallstahammar, Karlskoga, Norberg, Robertsfors, Skinnskatteberg, Sävsjö, Älvkarleby, and Övertorneå). Seven of the municipalities were granted by both committees (Dorotea, Gällivare, Haparanda, Karlsborg, Kristinehamn, Olofström, and Surahammar). Three municipalities were rejected by one of the committees but granted by the other (Grums and Munkedal were granted by the Housing Delegation while Nordmaling was granted by the Local Authority Delegation).

[14] See Finansdepartementet (1999), "Slutrapport från delegationen för stöd till vissa kommuner och landsting med svårigheter att klara balanskravet", Fi 1999:09. The evolution of trend in expenditures is very similar to that in debt.

[15] Figures 4 and 5 are taken from Dahlberg and Pettersson-Lidbom (2002).

This indicates that applicant municipalities were characterized by much faster debt growth than non-applicant ones during this period. Note that the difference was stable in the early 1990s, but the tendency of faster debt growth resumed among the applicants after 1995. Furthermore, as shown in Figure 5, average per-capita spending in the applicant municipalities was lower than in the non-applicant ones in the 1970s and early 1980s, but higher thereafter. The correlation between the difference in debt and the difference in expenditures is 0.93. Thus, the applicant group has had a much higher rate of spending growth relative to the non-applicant group, a possible indication of weak fiscal discipline.

Figure 4: Municipal Debt: Difference Between Applicants and Non-Applicants

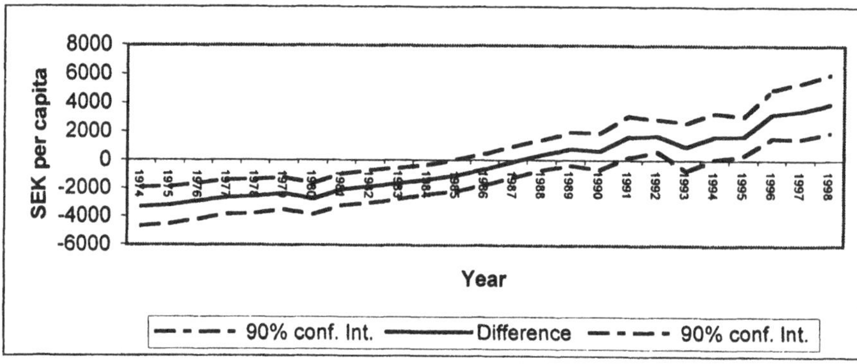

Source: Dahlberg and Pettersson-Lidbom (2002)

Figure 5: Local Spending: Difference Between Applicants and Non-Applicants

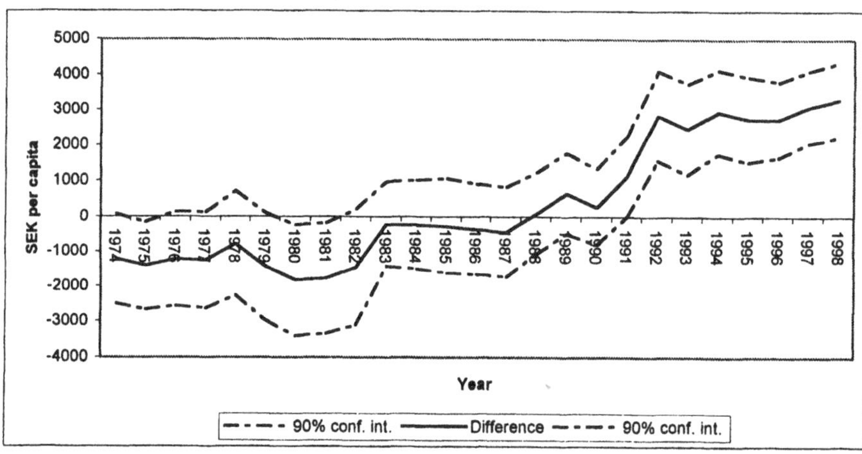

Source: Dahlberg and Pettersson-Lidbom (2002)

Table 4 reports a regression of the change in per-capita debt of all municipalities between 1974 and 1998 on dummies for the two groups of applicants. Municipalities that applied for relief but were not granted (ANG) increased their debts by SEK 7,067 more than the non-applying municipalities, while municipalities that were granted relief (AG) increased their debts by SEK 5,271 more per capita than the non-applying ones. The differences between applicants and non-applicants are statistically significant, while the difference between the groups of applicants is not. Hence, the ANG municipalities increased their debts by an average of SEK 6,453 per capita over this period, compared to SEK 4,658 for the AG group and a decrease of SEK 613 per capita in the non-applying group of municipalities.

Table 4: Debt Changes Between 1974 and 1998

Variable	ANG Dummy	AG Dummy	Constant
Coefficient	7066.7	5271.3	-613.3
(Standard error)	(2135.18)	(1394.42)	(597.14)
t-ratio	3.31	3.78	-1.03
R^2	0.073		
# of observations	277		

Note: ANG = 'Applied, not granted' is a dummy taking on the value 1 if the municipality was applying for grants but was denied money, zero otherwise. AG = 'Applied, granted' is a dummy taking on the value 1 if the municipality was applying for grants and was granted, zero otherwise. OLS estimation with heteroscedasticity consistent standard errors.

Table 5: Empirical Models of Debt Growth

Variable	Coefficient (Standard error)	t-ratio
Applied, not granted	5950.3	2.82
	(2103.87)	
Applied, granted	4716.4	3.23
	(1461.65)	
Δ Population	-8151.5	-2.67
	(3055.19)	
Δ Share of persons aged 0-15	244.4	.73
	(334.83)	
Δ Share of persons aged 65+	-413.9	-1.081
	(382.98)	
Δ Tax base	.091	.92
	(.099)	
Constant	-1575.0	-.43
	(3672.94)	
R^2	0.123	
# of observations	277	

Note: 'Applied, not granted' is a dummy taking on the value 1 if the municipality was applying for grants but was denied money, zero otherwise. 'Applied, granted' is a dummy taking on the value 1 if the municipality was applying for grants and was granted, zero otherwise. OLS estimation with heteroscedasticity consistent standard errors.

Empirical debt performance is typically estimated as a function of population change (Δ Population), changes in shares of persons younger than 16 (Δ Share of persons aged 0 –15) and aged 65 or older (Δ Share of persons aged 65+), and changes in the tax base (Δ Tax base). These variables were also considered as the main causes of "external effects" affecting municipality finances by the central government[16]. To check the influence of these external factors on the increase in municipal debt over the same period, we run the regression reported in Table 5. The results show that the two dummy variables for relief applicants are reduced by 11 percent for the AG group and 16 percent for the ANG group, respectively. The differences to the non-applying group of municipalities remain statistically significant. This suggests that only a small part of the debt increase of the applicants relative to the non-applicants is due to different external factors. A closer look at the data shows that the external factors and past patterns of debt growth were quite similar for those applicants that obtained relief and those that did not. Thus, the decision to grant or refuse relief was not related to either external factors or past debt performance. In sum, the empirical evidence shows that financial relief was granted primarily to municipalities that had incurred much larger debts than others, and that the external factors considered in the relief program did not explain their financial distress. Whether or not these bailouts arose from strategic behavior is more difficult to judge.[17]

An important consideration in this context is that the financial difficulties of local governments in the early 1990s occurred under exceptional circumstances beyond their control and, indeed, caused by central government policies. The year 1992, when the crisis began to emerge, marks the collapse of Sweden's attempt to "shadow the D-mark", i.e., to maintain a fixed exchange rate with the DM. When the Swedish Krona came under massive speculative attacks in 1992, the Riksbank raised interest rates to record highs in an attempt to defend the peg. Figure 7 shows the resulting, huge increase in real interest rates both at the long and the short end of the market. It is reasonable to assume that local housing companies became non-viable as a result of this. To put this crisis in perspective, note that the Swedish government paid capital expenditures to rescue financially distressed banks of about 3.5 percent of GDP in 1992/3. Thus, it can be argued that municipalities with financial obligations that would have been manageable in normal times found themselves in a crisis due to bad macroeconomic management.

This view is further supported by the observation that the high-interest rate policy lead to a severe recession with rapidly rising and persistent unemployment, see Figure 6. Given the large dependence of local governments on income tax revenues, the observation that this had dire budgetary consequences is no surprise.

---

[16] See Finansdepartementet (1999), "Slutrapport fran delegationen för stöd till vissa kommuner och landsting med svarigheter att klare balanskravet", Fi 1999:09.

[17] An interesting thing to note though is that those municipalities that got many bailouts in the 1974-1992 relief program are also to a larger extent bailed out in the bailout program in the late 1990s (Dahlberg and Pettersson-Lidbom, 2002). For example, Dahlberg and Pettersson-Lidbom find that there is a 74 percent chance of finding a municipality applying in the 1998 program that had received seven or more bailouts in the 1974-1992 program, whereas it is only a 32 percent chance of finding a non-applying municipality that had received as many bailouts in the earlier program.

Figure 6: Swedish Real GDP Growth and Unemployment

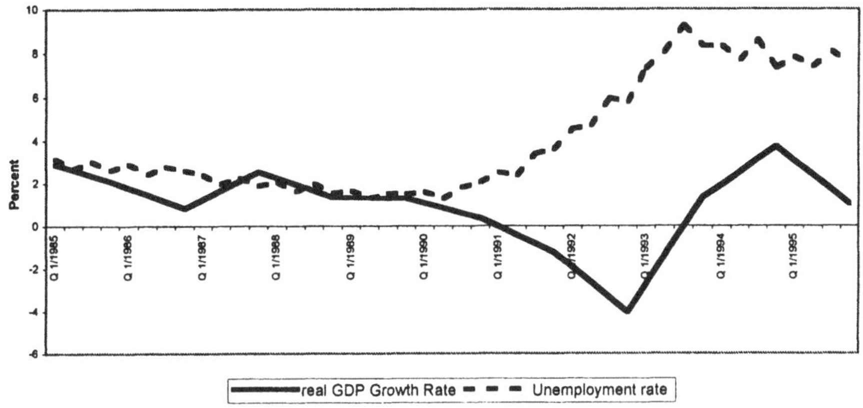

Figure 7: Swedish Real Interest Rates

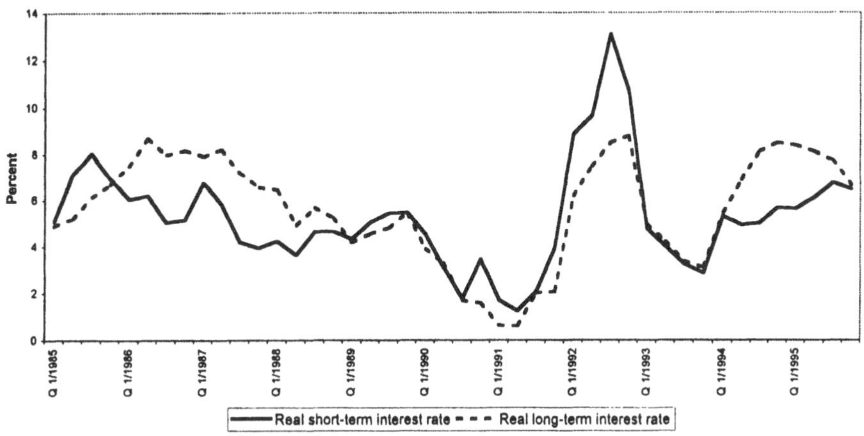

In Figure 8, we illustrate several aspects of local government fiscal performance during this crisis. First, the late 1980s saw a period of rather expansionary wage and personnel spending at the local level, which, however, was reversed already in 1990. Throughout the 1980s, the ratio of local income tax revenues to total spending increased, which suggests that local governments made efforts to increase their own revenues. These two observations indicate, that the crisis did not follow a period of fiscal profligacy at the local level. However, the ratio of income tax revenue to spending fell after 1992, the combined result of the recession and the central government's ban on local tax increases, which was imposed for macro economic reasons. Figure 8 also shows that in 1994, after the imposition of this ban, local government deficits for the first time exceeded local government investments. This gives some credibility to the argument that the central government's interference with local finances made it more difficult for local governments to provide their services at desired levels and quality and to achieve prudent financial management at the same time. In sum, the financial distress of local government seems closely connected to the central government's macro economic (mis)management at the time. Note also that the central government itself was plagued with huge deficits at the time, which were promoted by weak fiscal institutions at the national level.[18] It is not surprising that the demand for bailouts would go up under such circumstances.

Figure 8: Local Public Finance: Performance 1985-99

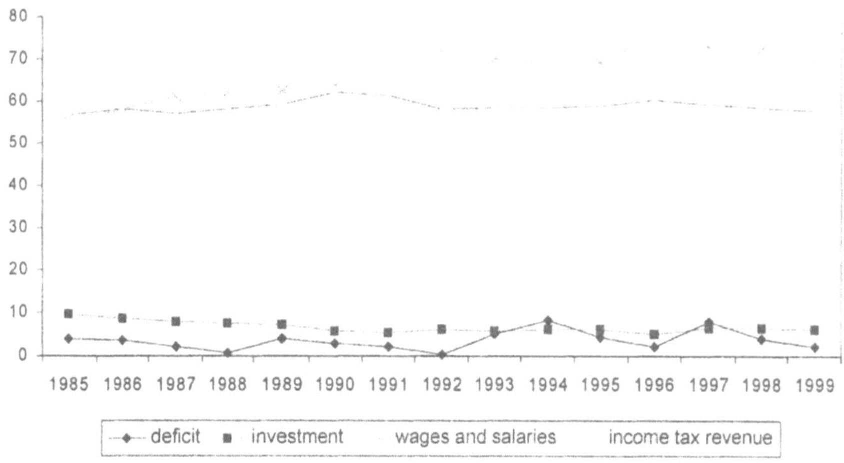

IS THERE A BAILOUT PROBLEM IN SWEDISH LOCAL GOVERNMENT?

Our review of Swedish local public finances during the last three decades gives us a basis for answering the main question of this paper: How large is the bailout problem of local government in Sweden? To answer this question, we refer back to the empirical and theoretical literature discussed in section II.

We begin with the supply side of bailouts. Theory and empirical evidence suggest that the central government's ability to stick to a no-bailout commitment is critical for the existence of a bailout problem. The picture emerging from the Swedish evidence is rather bleak in this regard.

[18] See Molander (1999).

The Swedish central government is "ambitious" in the terminology of Rodden et al. (2002), i.e. it is an officially acknowledged goal of Swedish economic policy to achieve equal living standards, including equal provision of public services, throughout the country. The strong equalization programs, both of revenues and of costs are direct outflows of this ambition. This ambition creates a presumption for central government responsibility when local governments find themselves in financial difficulties. Such a presumption is particularly important in cases where, as in Sweden, local governments provide services that are politically sensitive, such as education and health care. At the same time, constraining local governments' ability to self-finance their expenditures, e.g. through a centrally imposed ban on raising local taxes can only make this presumption of central government responsibility stronger, as local governments have some reason to argue that the central government reduces their ability to provide satisfactory levels and quality of public services.

The constitutional rule that local governments cannot default is an open flank for the central government's no-bailout commitment, and the more so the less specific is the interpretation of this rule. The central government ought to have an interest in clarifying ex ante who has what responsibilities when a default is imminent, and to devise rules that strengthen the accountability of local governments in such situations. Importantly, theory and empirical evidence show that a balancing requirement is not a good protection against bailouts.

Ambiguity and discretion in dealing with local governments in financial distress weaken the ability to commit to a no-bailout policy. The Swedish central government has a rather weak record in this regard, stemming from a tradition of financial relief grants in the 1970s and 1980s. The same tradition reappeared in its dealing with the financial crisis of the 1990s. Comparing the Bjuv case with that of Haninge and the relief program of the 1970s and 1980s, the central government seemed to impose stricter bailout conditions that might discourage future demands for bailouts from local jurisdictions. The subsequent wave of applications, however, suggests that this effort was not enough and was not carried through with sufficient resolve.

Finally, central government interference with local public finance for reasons of macro economic management in the 1990s weakened the local governments' ability to control and, therefore, their accountability for local public finances. This is particularly significant in the context of the Swedish debate on entering European Monetary Union. Losing the autonomy over monetary policy to the European Central Bank will imply that the Swedish economy will be exposed to interest rate policies that are not consistent with its own development. Under conditions of high real interest rates due to ECB monetary policy and little room for manouvre at the local level, the central government will find it difficult to deny demands for financial assistance from local governments arguing that their difficulties arise from a macro economic regime chosen by the central government.

In sum, the Swedish central government's ability to commit to a no-bailout rule is rather weak. A more explicit framework for dealing with local governments in financial distress could help to overcome this weakness.

Turning to local governments, a first point is that the large degree of financial autonomy, including the very low vertical imbalance of Swedish public finances is, perhaps, the best protection of the central government against bailouts. Local governments that spend up to 70 percent out of own taxes and enjoy autonomy to borrow can reasonably be expected to make even strong adjustments to local spending programs if a financial crisis hits. Given this starting point, constraints on local public finances such as the balancing requirement can only weaken fiscal autonomy at the local level and reduce the central government's protection against bailouts.

A second point is the design of the equalization programs, which reduces accountability at the local level and weakens the incentives for successful local development policies and efforts to improve efficiency in public service production.

A third point concerns the sources of revenues at the local level. With its strong dependence on income taxes, Swedish local government is strongly exposed to business cycle risk and interference of macro economic policies with the stability of local finances. Although the episode was exceptional, the early 1990s illustrate that local ownership of capital-intensive businesses such as housing companies increases such exposure. Less vulnerability to macro economic fluctuations and swings in real interest rates would probably strengthen accountability at the local level. One way to achieve that would be to find alternative sources of local government revenue, such as property taxes, which are less variable over time.

On balance, the majority of the bailout risk in Sweden is on the supply side. Strengthening the central government's ability to commit to clear ex ante rules and to deny bailout demands are key to reduce this risk. The macro policy reforms of the Swedish government in the 1990s, of which the reform of the budget process is an important element, is a good basis for further effort in this direction.

REFERENCES

Aizenman, Joshua (1998) "Fiscal Disciplin in a Union" in F. Sturzenegger and M. Tomassi (eds.), *The Political Economy of Reform*. Boston: MIT Press.

Bevilaqua, A. (2000) "State Government Bailouts in Brazil." Working Paper, Catholic University of Rio de Janeiro.

Bordignon M. (2000) "Problems of Soft Budget Constraint in Intergovernmental Relationship: The Case of Italy", *Working Paper*, Catholic University of Milan, Milan.

Brennan G. and J.M. Buchanan (1977) "Towards a Tax Constitution for Leviathan", *Journal of Public Economics*, 8, 255-273.

Careaga, Maite, and Barry R. Weingast (2000) "The Fiscal Pact with the Devil: A Positive Approach to Fiscal Federalism, Revenue Sharing, and Good Governance." Working paper, Stanford University.

Crespin, Herman (2000) "Local Government in Sweden – Tasks and Financing." Mimeo, Swedish Association of Local Authorities, Stockholm.

Dahlberg, Matz, and Eva Johansson (2002) "On the Vote Purchasing Behavior of Incumbent Governments." *American Political Science Review* 96, 27-40.

Dahlberg, Matz, and Per Pettersson-Lidbloom (2002) "The Bailout Problem: An Empirical Approach." Mimeo, Uppsala University.

Dixit, Avinash, and John Londregan (1996) "The Determinants of Success of Special Interests in Redistributive Politics." *Journal of Politics* 58, 1132-1155.

Dixit, Avinash, and John Londregan (1998) "Ideology, Tactics, and Efficiency in Redistributive Politics." *Quarterly Journal of Economics* 113, 497-529.

Fernandez-Arias, Eduardo, Ernesto Stein, and Jürgen von Hagen (2002) *Subnational Government Bailouts*. Washington DC: Interamerican Development Bank. forthcoming.

Goodspeed, Tim (2001) "Bailouts in a Federation." Working Paper, City University of New York.

Inman, Robert P. (2002) "Transfers and Bailouts: Enforcing Local Fiscal Discipline with Lessons from US Federalism." in: Rodden and Eskeland (2002).

Lindbeck, Assar, and Jörgen Weibull (1993) "A Model of Political Equilibrium in a Representative Democracy." *Journal of Public Economics* 51: 195-209.

Murray, Richard (1985) "Central Control of the Local Government Sector in Sweden." in Edward Gramlich and Bengt-Christer Ysander (eds), *Control of Local Governments*, IUI Conference Reports series 1985:1.

Nicolini, J. P., J. Sanguinetti, P. Sanguinetti, and M. Tommasi (2000) "Decentralization, Fiscal Discipline in Subcentral Governments, and the Bailout Problem: The Argentine Case." Working Paper, Interamerican Development Bank.

Molander, P. (1999) "Reforming Budgetary Institutins: Swedish Experiences." In: R. Strauch and J. von Hagen (eds.) *Institutions, Politics, and Fiscal Policy*. ZEI Studies in European Economics and Law II, Boston: Kluwer Academic Publishers.

Oates W. (1999) "An Essay on Fiscal Federalism", *Journal of Economic Literature*, vol. XXXVII, pages 1120-1149.

Olson M. Jr. (1969) "The Principle of 'Fiscal Equivalence': The Division of Responsibilities Among Different Levels of Government." *American Economic Review Papers and Proceedings* 59, 479-87.

Peterson, Olof (2001) *Kommunalpolitik*, fjärde upplagan, Nordstedts juridik, Stockholm.

Pisauro, Giuseppe (2001) "Intergovernmental Relations and Fiscal Discipline: Between Commons and Soft Budget Constraints." IMF Working Paper 01/65.

Renteria, Carolina, Roberto Steiner, and Juan J. Echevarria (2000) "Bailouts of Territorial Entities by the Central Government of Colombia." Working Paper, FEDESARROLLO.

Rodden, Jonathan (2001) "The Dilemma of Fiscal Federalism: Grants and Fiscal Performance around the World." Mimeo: Department of Political Science, MIT.

Rodden, Jonathan, and Gunnar S. Eskeland (2002) "Decentralization and Bailouts." Mimeo, MIT.

Rodden, Jonanthan, and Gunnar S. Eskeland (2002) "Summary and Conclusions", in Rodden and Eskeland (2002).

Rodden, Jonathan, Gunnar S. Eskeland, and Jennie Litvack (2002) "Introduction and Overview." in Rodden and Eskeland (2002).

Velasco A. (1999) "A Model of Endogenous Fiscal Deficits and Delayed Fiscal Reforms." in Poterba and Von Hagen (eds.) *Fiscal Institutions and Fiscal Performance*. Chicago: University of Chicago Press.

Von Hagen, Jürgen (2000) "Subnational Government Bailouts in OECD Countries: Four Case Studies." ZEI Working Paper, University of Bonn.

Von Hagen J. and M. Hallerberg (1999) "Electoral Institutions, Cabinet Negotiations, and Budget Deficits in the EU." in Poterba and von Hagen (eds.) *Fiscal Institutions and Fiscal Performance*. University of Chicago Press 1999.

Von Hagen J. and I. Harden (1995) "Budget Processes and Commitment to Fiscal Discipline." *European Economic Review* 39, 771-79.

Wildasin, David (1998) "Externalities and Bailouts: Hard and Soft Budget Constraints in Intergovernmental Fiscal Relations." Mimeo: Vanderbilt University.

4

FISCAL EQUALISATION BETWEEN SWEDISH MUNICIPALITIES

Howard Chernick[*]

Hunter College, City University of New York

INTRODUCTION

In its 1993 reform of the intergovernmental grant system, Sweden adopted an ambitious program of fiscal equalisation, one which is among the most comprehensive in the developed world. This paper examines the structure of equalisation in Sweden. I focus on the overall effectiveness of the program, and the incentives built into its major components; capacity equalisation, cost equalisation, and capitation aid. Incentives for individual and firm location, and the fiscal behavior of municipalities are considered. I argue that some of these incentives are positive, while other effects may be adverse. The variety of possible effects in the Swedish system illustrates the potential tradeoffs between equity and efficiency in a fiscal system. Where possible, I adduce evidence as to the actual responses to these incentives. The paper also considers the mix of equalisation policies, and the extent to which substitution between one or another component is either possible or desirable. At various points, comparisons are made to other fiscal systems around the world.

The plan of the chapter is as follows. Section I presents the rationale for fiscal equalisation, and discusses factors affecting the need for equalisation. The second section considers the relationship between equalisation objectives and the structure of intergovernmental finance. Section III analyses the overall degree of equalisation in the Swedish system. Section IV, which has four subsections, focuses on the capacity equalisation grant. The first presents a general analysis of this form of grant. The second discusses the actual Swedish formula. The third considers the fiscal insurance aspect of the grant, while the fourth analyses the incentives built into the capacity equalisation grant. Section V, divided into three sub-sections, considers the cost equalisation grant. The first sub-section discusses the general structure of such grants. The second sub-section considers in some detail the Swedish cost formula for child day-care services, while the third discusses the incentives built into the cost equalisation formulae. Section VI considers Sweden's mix of equalisation policies. Section VII addresses briefly the tradeoff between

[*] Address for Correspondence. Economics Department, 695 Park Ave., New York, New York 10021. E-mail: Howard.Chernick@hunter.cuny.edu; I would like to thank Per Molander, Jürgen von Hagen, Robin Boadway, Jorn Rattso, and Andrew Reschovsky for helpful comments, and Clas Olsson, and Henrik Berggren both for comments and for their considerable help in providing data and in understanding the Swedish system of grants-in-aid. I would also like to thank Jennifer Tennant for her able research assistance.

equalising transfers to individuals and equalising transfers to governments. Section VIII summarizes and concludes.

WHY FISCAL EQUALISATION?

Fiscal equalisation is a necessary component of a decentralized public economy. All national states that rely on their sub-national sector to provide important public services provide some measure of equalising assistance from higher level governments to help finance lower level governments. The rationale for such assistance is twofold. First, equalization promotes efficiency in the allocation of labor and capital across space. Second, it is a means of promoting equity in the distribution of public services.

If fiscal capacity or fiscal costs differs across jurisdictions, as is usually the case, people and businesses have an incentive to locate in those jurisdictions with the highest fiscal capacity, or the lowest fiscal cost. The social costs of such location decisions may exceed the private benefits, if the marginal productivity of the mobile factor is lower in the destination jurisdiction than in the place of origin.

Even if mobility in response to fiscal differentials is limited, there is a strong case on grounds of horizontal equity for fiscal equalization. Equity has been interpreted in different ways, but at the core is the concept that all members of a federation, regardless of where they live, are entitled to certain minimum standards of public services, at a cost in foregone private income which is "not excessive". While most federations accept this basic principle, there are enormous differences across federations in what constitutes "minimum standards", and "not excessive". These differences reflect many factors, including the manner in which the federation came together, the geographic and population size of the country, and the culture of the country regarding the degree of aversion to income inequality.[1] In Canada, for example, minimum standards are viewed as separate from the goal of avoiding excessive taxation. The former is a question of vertical equity, while the latter is justified in terms of horizontal equity.

A separate issue is the vehicle for stating minimum standards - constitutional or legislative, the degree of specificity in those standards, and the mechanisms for resolving disputes about standards. Compared with many other countries, Sweden has a relatively high minimum standard for local public services. However, the constitutional basis for these standards is general and non-specific. (For a discussion of constitutional design issues, see the chapter by Boadway and Johansson.)

Many U.S. states have a constitutional provision requiring the state to provide elementary and secondary education to all children. The standard is usually stated as providing an "adequate" or "efficient" level. However, the operational definition of adequacy is defined by the state legislature, with numerous interventions by the judicial branch. The new constitution of South Africa includes the requirement that

---

[1] In Canada the equalisation system is treated as being separate from the issue of national standards. The goal of equalisation is to provide "reasonably comparable levels of public services at reasonably comparable rates of taxation."

all citizens are entitled to basic services in health, education, and income security, but recognizes resource constraints by stating that the goal is to be achieved progressively. The constitution assigns responsibility for guaranteeing these services to both the national government and the provinces. The working definition of standards is developed by national government, in consultation with the provinces.

Standards of equity in service levels and tax burdens are likely to evolve over time, as the economy grows and competitive pressures change. Despite the fact that horizontal equity across jurisdictions and locational efficiency may both be enhanced by some degree of fiscal equalization, as the stringency of the standard of equalization is increased there may be increasing costs in terms of public sector efficiency. Sensitivity to this tradeoff can cause a country to cycle between lesser and greater degrees of equalization.[2]

Whatever the standard of equity, the degree of equalization also depends on the "need" for fiscal equalization. Need can be absolute or relative. Absolute need can be thought of as the extent to which any given community would fall short of national standards of public services, assuming that the community taxed itself at a reasonable level. Relative need refers to the dispersion in levels of public services and/or tax burdens that would exist if there were no equalizing grants. Need will depend on the dispersion in the local fiscal base and dispersion in the costs of providing given levels of services. Dispersion in the fiscal base depends on the personal income distribution, and the extent to which individual jurisdictions are stratified by income.[3] Ceteris paribus, the more equal the distribution of family income, the less the degree of inequality at the jurisdictional level. Less jurisdictional inequality implies a lower cost or price of equalization, in the sense that a smaller transfer of fiscal resources would be required to achieve complete equality of fiscal conditions across jurisdictions. However, whether less need leads to less equalization will depend on preferences.

In Sweden, fiscal capacity, as measured by labor income per capita, ranges from 75 percent of the national average in the poorest jurisdiction (Borgholm) to 188 percent in the richest (Danderyd). Some 51 percent of municipalities are within 10 percent of the national average, while 75 percent are within 15 percent of the national average. The range in Sweden is much smaller than in many other developed countries. In American states, many of which are roughly comparable in population size to Sweden, per capita income in many suburban areas is more than twice as high as per capita income in the central city. Similar disparities hold for property values. (Chernick and Reschovsky, 2001) In four U.S. states, the ratio of the 95th

[2] In the United States, an important factor in explaining the overturning of the basic local public finance mechanism in at least two states - Michigan, which moved to mainly state finance of elementary and secondary education in 1994, and Massachusetts, which imposed a severe tax limitation in the 1980's - was wide variations in local fiscal capacity and tax burdens.

[3] Note that income stratification is partly endogenous to equalization policies, because location decisions may be influenced by fiscal differentials.

to the 5th percentile of district income per pupil ranges from 3 to almost 5. (Oates and Schwab, 2002) The comparable figure for Sweden is 1.56.[4]

Despite this relative equality in the distribution of fiscal capacity, Sweden, like other Scandinavian countries, has a rigorous standard for equity in the local public sector. The operating principle is that "all municipalities will be able to operate on equivalent economic terms." Defining minimum standards in this way leads to an ambitious program of fiscal equalization.

EQUALISATION AND THE FORM OF INTERGOVERNMENTAL ASSISTANCE

What type of grant system does the goal of minimum standards point towards? If minimum standards are defined for a narrow range of services, then categorical or relatively narrow block grants, with equalizing conditions, are appropriate. In the United States, the focus has been on categorical equity. There is currently no general untied grant from the national government to the states, and little or no general purpose aid from states to municipalities.

By contrast, the national government provides a categorical matching grant to the states to help pay for medical care for the poor. Fiscal equalization is built into the grant through a federal matching rate which varies inversely with a state's relative income level. Under the impetus of the courts, states have moved to the provision of education grants to local school districts which are typically inverse to fiscal capacity. However, the U.S. Supreme Court has decisively rejected the notion that there is a national constitutional basis for equity in the financing of education (San Antonio, 1973).

If minimum standards are extended to a broad range of local public services, then multiple programs of categorical aid, one for each service, can become intrusive of local autonomy, and destructive of efficiency in local government decision-making. The 1993 reform of local government finance in Sweden, which converted the grant system from a set of categorical grants to an unconditional block grant, was based on the notion that enhanced local autonomy would lead to greater efficiency in decision making.

The problem with broad untied intergovernmental assistance is that by definition it reduces the "categorical leverage" of the national government, making it harder to influence local priorities. An intermediate form of aid is the conditional block grant. This form allows the government to retain some leverage over local programs, while still allowing for considerable local independence.[5] Over time, greater reliance on either conditional or block aid tends to highlight the disadvantages of each type, leading to a pattern of cycling between the two types of assistance. Aid which is originally untied may be recategorized by attaching

[4] The relative equality of municipal income per capita in Sweden is related to the high level of equality of the personal income distribution. Of 23 countries in western and eastern Europe, and Canada, Israel, and Japan, Sweden's income distribution in the 1990's, as measured by the Gini coefficient, was more equal than any of the other countries except Hungary. (Suhrcke, 2001)

[5] Canada relies on such a grant for provision of health services.

conditions, or else new categorical programs will be introduced which supplement, and may eventually supplant the block grants.

One way to achieve equalisation is to centralise both financing and service delivery. This approach allows the nation (or province) to achieve uniformity in service levels, and a uniform national standard of equity in financial sacrifice for all individuals, regardless of where they live. The greater the extent to which particular functions or services are centralised, the less the need for equalisation between municipalities. Recent changes in education finance in the state of Michigan in the United States, and Ontario province in Canada have followed this course, by moving financing from the municipal to the state level. Centralisation sacrifices the advantages of decentralised public finance in meeting diverse preferences for local public goods, and stimulating beneficial fiscal competition.

An alternative way to achieve the desired degree of equalisation between municipalities is to use intergovernmental transfers and regulatory mechanisms. The preferred type of grant depends on the particular dimensions of equalisation on which the country puts the most weight. Equalisation of fiscal capacity is best achieved by broad lump-sum block grants, distributed inversely to a broad measure of the ability to raise revenue.[6] Cost equalisation requires grants which vary according to interjurisdictional differences in the minimum cost of providing services to the eligible population. Equalisation of service provision typically requires a combination of mandates for minimum levels of provision, together with cost and/or capacity equalisation. Horizontal equity for similar individuals living in jurisdictions with differing fiscal capacities or costs will be enhanced by any form of intergovernmental grant, so long as the distribution of the grant is more equal than the distribution of the taxes used to finance the grant.

THE SWEDISH FISCAL EQUALISATION SYSTEM

In 1993, a major reform of the Swedish grant system took place. Substantial modifications were made in 1996. A number of categorical grants were replaced by a single block grant, and an equalisation system was introduced. The block grant is distributed on a capitation basis (an equal amount per capita in all municipalities). The equalisation component consists of two sub-systems: a fiscal capacity equalizing component, and a cost equalizing component. The equalisation system is technically not a grant from the central government, but rather a set of fiscal flows between municipalities. Positive flows just offset negative flows, so the system is self-financing.

Revenue in each municipality is the sum of own tax revenue, fees, grants, and equalisation aid. While the major grant is a capitation block grant, there are also some conditional grants. To investigate overall equalisation in the Swedish system, I start with a set of regression equations that explain variation in per capita assistance as a function of population, income, and density. Population is the best

---

[6] In its equalisation grant, Canada uses the "representative tax system" approach, which defines fiscal capacity as the weighted average of all the taxes used by provinces.

general measure of workload. Relative Income is a measure of fiscal capacity, and density is a proxy for the cost per unit of service delivery.

Table 1: Regression Analysis of the Distribution of Grants in Sweden in 2000

Grant Type	Log Population	Fiscal Capacity[+]	Density	Adj R^2
1.Capacity Equalisation	169*	-26,321*	1507	.90
2. Cost Equalisation	-1,154*	-8385	17,357*	.30
3. Total Grants	-1,012*	-30,477*	15,738*	.73

* Significant at the 5 percent level.
[+] Fiscal Capacity defined as per capita income relative to the national average.

The results in Table 1 show that overall the Swedish grant system favors jurisdictions that are smaller in population, have lower fiscal capacity, and are more densely populated. The positive coefficient on density results from the fact that density is a cost factor in many of the formulae for the cost equalisation grant. However, since smaller jurisdictions tend to be less dense, it is somewhat surprising that both small and dense municipalities get more aid. The overall degree of fiscal equalisation in the Swedish system is quite strong. Taking the coefficient on fiscal capacity from the total grant equation – **the third row of Table 1 -** a jurisdiction with fiscal capacity at 90 percent of the median would get an additional SEK 3,048 per capita [-30,477 X (-0.1)], or about 35 percent of the average grant amount to all municipalities.

In 1999, grants comprised 22 percent of total municipal revenues. Thus, the additional 35 percent of grants received by the jurisdiction with fiscal capacity 10 percent below the median represents a revenue offset of roughly 35 percent of 22 percent, or about 8 percent of total revenues.[7] The loss in potential revenue due to a 10 percent fiscal capacity gap would be somewhere between 5 and 8 percent. Thus the grant system offsets somewhere between 62.5 (5/8) and 100 (8/8) percent of the potential revenue loss from lower fiscal capacity.

The implied degree of redistribution of revenues under the Swedish grant-in-aid system is high relative to most federalist states. A recent study of fiscal redistribution in Germany finds that about 50 percent of the long-run differences in tax revenue across states are offset by federal revenue sharing. (Von Hagen and Hepp, 2000). In the United States, slightly less than fifty percent of the inequality in education spending within states is eliminated by equalising grants. (Evans, Murray and Schwab, 1997)[8] In France, the reduction in inequality of fiscal capacity among municipalities is about 30 percent. (Gilbert and Guengant, 2001)

---

[7] In 1999 tax revenues comprised 53 percent of municipal revenue in Sweden. Assuming that the tax rate is unchanged, a ten percent reduction in fiscal capacity relative to the median implies a 10 percent reduction in tax revenue. If fees and other revenue sources remain the same, then the implied reduction in total revenue would equal (0.1) X (53%) = 5.3%. Own source revenues comprised 78% of total revenues. If all own source revenues, rather than just taxes, are reduced in a jurisdiction with low fiscal capacity, then the revenue reduction could be as high as 10 percent of 78 %, or 7.8%.

[8] Education spending makes up about 46 percent of total local spending. Since most other types of local spending are effectively unequalised, the overall degree of capacity equalisation in the U.S. is probably

CAPACITY EQUALIZATION GRANTS

General Principles

We first consider some general characteristics of a capacity equalisation grant, and then turn to the Swedish formula. The equalisation grant for jurisdiction i is equal to

$$G^{equal}_i = t^*(Y^* - Y_i)^9 \quad (1)$$

t^* = target tax rate

Y^* = target fiscal capacity.

Formula (1) can be rewritten as

$$G^{equal}_i = \alpha t_{bar} [\beta Y_{bar} - Y_i] \quad (2)$$

t_{bar} = national average tax rate

Y_{bar} = national average fiscal capacity

$\alpha = t^*/t_{bar}$, the ratio of the target tax rate to the national average tax rate.

$\beta = Y^*/Y_{bar}$, the ratio of the target fiscal capacity to the national average fiscal capacity,.

Both α and β are parameters chosen by the government. To achieve full equalisation of fiscal capacity with zero net fiscal cost to the central government, α and β would both be set equal to one. The amount of the grant or payment is equal to the fiscal gap times the national average tax rate. All jurisdictions with below average fiscal capacity (a negative fiscal gap) would get positive equalization grants, while all jurisdictions with above average fiscal capacity (a positive fiscal gap) would pay into the national system, i.e. get negative grants. The average grant to a jurisdiction is zero, with half of the jurisdictions getting a negative grant, and half getting a positive grant.

As β rises above one, the proportion of jurisdictions with positive grants rises, as does the total cost of the equalisation scheme. Hence, there is a tradeoff between the tax rate needed to fund the grant, and the number of municipalities getting positive grants. Because it is politically costly to have jurisdictions get negative grants, it is rare in most federalist countries to have negative grants. Negative grants can be

---

closer to 25 percent. In a study of municipalities in the state of Minnesota, Ladd, Reschovsky and Yinger (1991) find a very low correlation between the level of state grants and a measure of fiscal need.

[9] This formula is similar to the standard foundation grant for education in the United States. The foundation grant is equal to $G_i = E^* - t^*Y_i$, where $E^* = t^*Y^*$. The difference between the U.S. and the Swedish formulation is that in the U.S. E^* represents a spending norm for education, while in Sweden t^*Y^* is a hypothetical national average expenditure level.
An alternative type of equalisation grant is known as the power equalisation grant. Under this scheme, $G^{equal} = t_i (Y^* - Y_i)$. This scheme guarantees that each municipality is guaranteed the same tax base Y^*. Revenue is equal to t_iY^*. This general type of equalisation grant is used for education finance in about a third of U.S. states. (Reschovsky, 1994)

avoided by setting β high enough that the target tax base exceeds that of all or most jurisdictions. This approach achieves net equalisation through a large vertical transfer.[10]

Even if Y* is set equal to Y_{bar}, the total cost of the grant could still be positive or negative, depending on the relation between municipal population and income. If richer municipalities have a higher average population than poorer municipalities, as is the case in Sweden, then for the net amount of aid (positive aid minus negative aid) to be zero, β would have to be set at a level greater than one. In this case, more communities would get positive amounts of aid than would get negative amounts. However, the program would still be self-financing, because the average negative grant would be larger than average positive grant.

As the equalising percentage α falls below one, the proportion of a jurisdiction's fiscal gap which is offset diminishes. Gross fiscal flows from high to low capacity municipalities fall, but the net fiscal cost to the of the equalisation scheme remains the same.

If there is only an equalization grant, the jurisdiction's revenue constraint becomes

$$REVi = t_iY_i + t^*[Y^* - Y_i] = t^*Y^* + [t_i - t^*]Yi \qquad (3)$$

As shown in (3), a municipality's revenue is equal to a common national standard, the national target tax rate times the national average tax base, plus an amount based on its own tax base. Revenue will be higher than the national standard if the community's own tax rate is higher than the standard rate, and lower if its tax rate is set below the national rate. The first term represents the pooling of all local fiscal bases into a national per capita fiscal base. Each jurisdiction receives an equal per capita share of the national base. The second term represents the contribution to revenue from the jurisdiction's choice of its own tax rate.

Equation (3) shows that the municipality can always increases its revenue by raising its tax rate. However, the "fiscal return" from an increase in tax rates depends on community income. If a relatively rich municipality ($Y_i > Y^*$) sets its tax rate below t*, it incurs a greater loss in the form of a tax-back of fiscal resources than would be incurred by a relatively poor community following the same fiscal strategy. Rewriting (3) as

$$REVi = t_iY_i + t^*[Y^* - Y_i] = t^*Y^* + t_iY_i - t^*Y_i \qquad (3')$$

shows that municipal revenue consists of three components: a common national grant t*Y*, a purely local component t_iY_i, and a tax back or negative component which is a function of the municipal fiscal base. The greater the tax back component, the more the municipality must raise its own tax rate as an offset.

A community with a tax base greater than Y* has an incentive to raise its tax rate at least up to the national rate t*, so that its revenues will not fall below the national average. A municipality with a tax base less than Y* can lower its tax rate to the national average, and still get the national average revenues per capita. Thus the

---

[10] Examples are Australia and South Africa.

capacity equalisation grant creates an incentive for local tax rates to converge to the national average. The evidence from Sweden indicates that municipalities have already begun to respond to this incentive, with the gap between the highest and the lowest municipal tax rate falling from 8.2 percentage points in 1996 to 6.3 percentage points in 2002.

The lower the target tax rate t*, relative to the national average tax rate (the smaller is α in equation 2), the smaller the share of a jurisdiction's revenue which comes from the common national pool, and the larger the share from taxation of the jurisdiction's own fiscal base. The higher the target fiscal base (the larger is β in equation 2), the greater the share of revenue from the common national pool, and the greater each community's revenue, for any local tax rate.

Equation (3) also illustrates the potential negative effect of capacity equalisation on the incentive to develop its fiscal base, because the jurisdiction is able to capture only a fraction of the increase in local capacity. It a jurisdiction's tax rate is less than the national target rate ($t_i < t^*$), then the net revenue received by the municipality would actually decline if its fiscal base were to increase.

The Swedish Formula

The local tax base in Sweden is equal to earned income (wages) plus benefits from social insurance systems (e.g. sickness, parental leave, unemployment benefits), minus certain deductions. This base will henceforth be referred to simply as income. The equalisation grant is determined by the level of municipal income relative to the national average. The standard tax rate t* is set at 95 percent of the national average tax rate in 1995. Hence the per capita grant or charge to municipality i is equal to

$$G^{equal}_i = .95\ t_{bar}\,(Y_{bar} - Y_i) \qquad (4)$$

where Y_{bar} is the (weighted) national average fiscal base per capita, and t_{bar} is the national average tax rate, equal to 30.3 percent in 1995. Equation (4) indicates that 95 percent of any difference in local revenue which results from a difference in fiscal capacity is offset by the equalisation grant. For local income ranging from 20 percent above to 20 percent below Y_{bar}, if the municipality taxed were to tax itself at the national average rate, its revenue would range from 101 to 99 percent of the national average. The actual rate of equalisation may be slightly lower than 95 percent, because the current national average rate is slightly higher than the 1995 rate. However, even if the equalisation rate fell to 90 percent, the range in fiscal capacity would still be between 98 and 102 percent.

In the year 2000 eighty percent of municipalities (232 out of 289) received positive equalisation grants, and twenty percent received negative grants. Reflecting the preponderance of positive grants, the average grant by municipality was equal to SEK 1357. However, the population weighted average grant was only a slightly above zero, equaling SEK 31.

The difference between the number of communities that get positive equalisation grants and the percentage of population living in these jurisdictions reflects the fact that larger jurisdictions tend to have higher fiscal capacity. To see this, I regressed the per capita equalisation grant for the year 2000 on the log of population. The estimated equation, with the standard error in parentheses, is

$$\text{EQUALIZATION AID} = 14{,}536 - \underset{(163)}{1342}\,(\text{log population}) \quad R^2 = .19$$

The significant negative coefficient on population indicates that a ten percent increase in population size leads to a reduction in the per capita capacity equalisation grant of SEK134. This result contrasts with the regression presented in Table 1, where population has a positive relation to capacity equalisation grant. The difference in result reflects the fact that the regression in Table 1 shows the marginal effect of population, controlling for fiscal capacity. The negative effect of population is in part a reflection of the fact that most of the jurisdictions in the Stockholm metropolitan area have both above average fiscal capacity and above average populations. The city of Stockholm alone, with 8.4 percent of the total population, has a fiscal capacity 23.4 percent higher than the national target. Thus the capacity equalisation grant redistributes fiscal resources not only between jurisdictions, but also from the richer more populous urban centers to the poorer and smaller rural jurisdictions.

Because each municipality receives a capitation grant that is large relative to the capacity and cost equalisation grants, as well as some conditional aid, almost all municipalities receive positive grant amounts in total. Nonetheless, a striking feature of the Swedish system is that the capacity equalisation grant is negative for some jurisdictions. Even though the net fiscal flow between the central government and particular jurisdictions may be negative, direct and visible recovery of fiscal resources from high capacity jurisdictions through negative grants is rare.

For example, Canada offsets differences in provincial fiscal capacity by an equalizing fiscal transfer from the federal government to the provinces. However, no province is required to make direct payments into the equalisation fund, so unlike Sweden, there are no visibly negative grants.[11] While a number of U.S. states use variants of the capacity equalisation grant to finance education, no state imposes negative grants.[12] (Reschovsky, 1994)

[11] The transfer is based on the constitutional standard that each province be able to provide "reasonably comparable levels of public services at reasonably comparable rates of taxation." In 2000-01, seven provinces received payments totalling $9.8 billion. An important difference between Canada's equalisation scheme and Sweden's is that in Canada not all provinces are used to determine the equalisation standard. Rather, the standard of comparison in determining net fiscal benefit is the average revenue raising capacity of five of the nine provinces, but excluding the richest province and the four poorest. Revenue raising capacity is the weighted average of all the tax bases used in the country. Because Alberta, the richest province, is not in the standard, poor provinces's natural resource acquisitions are fully taxed away, while at the same time they receive no equalisation payments on account of Alberta's large endowment. The favored treatment of Alberta, where mineral wealth is concentrated, creates problems of fiscal competition with the neighboring Canadian provinces of Manitoba, Saskatchewan, and British Columbia.

[12] The typical U.S. formula for school equalisation aid is $G_i^{equal} = \max\{t^*(Y^* - Y_i), G_{min}\}$, where t^*Y^* is the spending norm, and G_{min} is a minimum grant guaranteed to all districts. In Wisconsin negative aid has actually been declared unconstitutional.

Fiscal Insurance

The equalization grant provides both long-term redistribution from richer to poorer municipalities, as well as insurance against short-term risk from differences in regional business cycles.[13] The effectiveness of the grant as fiscal insurance depends on how long it takes for grant amounts to reflect a change in fiscal conditions. In Sweden this adjustment should be relatively rapid. When the local fiscal base is earned income, short run fluctuations in base over the business cycle are likely to be high relative to countries that rely on the local property tax. To minimise instability in the provision of public services, countries that rely more heavily on income taxation at the sub-national level require aid systems that respond more promptly to fluctuation in the overall rate of economic activity than would be the case in property base countries. The fiscal capacity grant, which provides automatic and timely adjustments to fluctuations in a jurisdiction's relative tax base, is likely to be effective at reducing fluctuations in public services levels due to regional business cycles. However, the equalisation mechanism will not offset pressures on public services due to the national business cycle.

The compensation for differences in fiscal capacity, together with the cost equalisation grant, should reduce the role of fiscal considerations in the choice of residential location. Because the benefits of a higher tax base are mostly taxed away by the equalisation grant, an individual has little direct fiscal incentive to prefer a higher to a lower income municipality. The fiscal gain from relatively rapid growth in community income is shared with the nation, rather than benefiting only that community. In general, the reduction in purely fiscal incentives for factor location should encourage factors of production to locate in those municipalities where their marginal private product is highest, thus promoting efficiency in regional development.

Incentives for Municipalities

Regarding the fiscal behavior of the municipality, the fact that capacity equalisation taxes away most of the fiscal gain from economic development reduces the incentive for municipalities to pursue policies that increase their average fiscal base. As compared to a system with little or no direct equalisation (as in the United States), the Swedish system is likely to have both positive and negative effects on economic efficiency. On the positive side, there is less incentive to pursue policies which increase a jurisdiction's own base at the expense of its neighbors. For example, there is less incentive to exclude low-income persons through such strategies as reducing construction of low-income housing, or relying heavily on fees for services. Thus the negative externalities generated by fiscal competition will be reduced.

However, fiscal competition also has the beneficial effect of encouraging efficiency and innovation in service delivery. The problem with the capacity equalisation

[13] The aggregate stabilisation properties of a capacity equalisation system depend on the covariance of t^*, Y^*, and Y_i. In Canada, which uses a scheme similar to Sweden's, equalisation has been found to be somewhat destabilising.

grant is that offsets all variation in the tax base, whether the source is exogenous shocks or endogenous changes in the fiscal behavior of the municipality. Thus fiscal policies which raise the average income of a municipality but do not lessen, or perhaps even enhance, the income of its neighbors, are also less likely to be pursued. Municipalities will face less direct pressure to improve efficiency in service delivery, and keep expenditure levels at the minimum necessary to provide desired services. Whether the advantages of limiting fiscal competition outweigh the disadvantages depends on the strength of other forces which can keep local spending in check.

There is an enormous literature on the effect of fiscal policies on economic development. In the United States literature, there is a reasonably consistent body of evidence that higher taxes do have a negative effect on the fiscal base of communities, while spending, especially education, can increase the fiscal base. (Bartik, 1991) However, the typical economic development subsidy that many states and cities offer to specific firms can be quite costly per new job or job retained (Netzer, 1997)

A number of studies have found that Tiebout type competition between jurisdictions tends to restrain municipal spending (Sjoquist, 1982). Competition is typically measured by the number of jurisdictions in a metropolitan area. Hoxby (2000) finds that metropolitan areas with more school districts tend to have both lower tax rates, and higher test scores. A potential danger from more Tiebout type competition is that it leads to greater municipal segregation, both by income level, as expected, but also by racial composition, and previous studies have found such an effect. (Harrison, 1982) Such segregation might be expected to lower the educational performance of students from low-income and minority families. However, Hoxby's study finds that competition seems to benefit all groups.

In the Tiebout choice model of local public goods, communities must have some way of restricting entrance. (Hamilton, 1975) If they do not, then the poor will have a continuous incentive to chase the rich to get better public services at a lower tax price, and the rich will have a similar incentive to flee the poor. Hence there is no stable equilibrium. For stability, municipalities must be able to impose a minimum tax base requirement - called zoning. The effect of the minimum tax base requirement is to limit fiscal redistribution within a municipality. By contrast, the Swedish equalisation grant reduces fiscal redistribution within communities by instead shifting that redistribution to the nation as a whole. The result is that there should be a greater incentive to allow income mixing within municipalities than in systems that rely more extensively on purely local finance. Greater income mixing could have positive effects on educational output, through peer group effects (Evans, Murray, and Schwab, 1992)

The negative incentive effects of capacity equalisation result from the reduced responsiveness of the fiscal base to the tax and spending decisions of municipalities. In the U.S. version of the Tiebout model, an important factor in inducing efficient levels of public expenditure comes from the capitalisation of local fiscal decisions into the fiscal base, i.e. property values. Bruckner (1979) argues that policies which maximize property values will lead to the efficient level of local public expenditures. Municipalities that overspend relative to the preferences of their residents, or deliver public services inefficiently, will have relatively high taxes, or low levels of public services. Undesirable fiscal characteristics lead to reduced demand for housing and a decline in property values. Such a decline in the fiscal base provides a strong signal to municipal officials to adjust their fiscal behavior towards the optimum.

The incentive problem that results from the capacity equalisation grant is that it helps to insulate local officials from the consequences of "bad" fiscal behavior. Suppose a community overspends, causing a decline in property values. To the extent that the decline in property values translates into a decline in average income, the municipality receives an offsetting transfer through increased equalisation aid. The offset mitigates the increase in tax rates that would be required to maintain the same level of public expenditures. The tax rate is an important signal as to the efficiency of the community. By reducing the responsiveness of the tax price to a municipality's fiscal choices, its signalling value is weakened, and the community is less likely to achieve the optimal (property value maximising) tax rate.[14] [See the appendix for a graphical demonstration.]

Borge and Rattso (2002) finds that in Norway municipalities with a local property tax have lower unit costs. Boije (1997) presents some evidence that even before the introduction of the capacity equalising grant, Swedish municipalities were overspending relative to the property value maximising rate. Such overspending may be amplified under the new Swedish grant structure. However, it is important to stress that the tax price argument could also lead to underspending, since a community is equally protected against the fiscal-base consequences of spending too little. Moreover, because the capacity equalisation grant is a zero sum grant, and depends on relative fiscal capacity, if all communities reduce their fiscal base by increasing expenditures, there would be no net compensation. Only if a subset of municipalities respond to the capacity equalisation incentive by inefficiently raising their spending levels would the offsetting mechanism take effect.

Though capacity equalizing grants reduce the incentive for economic development, the strength of this effect may be mitigated because of Sweden's reliance on local income taxation, as opposed to property taxation. If industrial development occurs in a particular jurisdiction, bringing with it new employment or higher wage levels, some of the additional wage income will benefit jurisdictions other than the jurisdiction where the new development is sited. The extent of this diffusion depends on the extent to which workers tend to live in jurisdictions other than their place of employment. While this diffusion of the fiscal benefits of economic development reduces the incentive to pursue such activities, it also means that the tax-back on economic development will apply to only a fraction of the increase in wage income generated within a jurisdiction.

---

[14] The argument is shown graphically in the Appendix. Without capacity equalisation, the relationship between the change in tax rates and the change in revenue is given by $dRev/dt = Y(1 + \varepsilon_Y)$, where ε_Y is the elasticity of the tax base Y with respect to the tax rate. With capacity equalisation, the relationship becomes $dRev/dt = Y[1 + \varepsilon_Y - (t^*/t)\varepsilon_Y]$. If ε_Y is negative (an increase in tax rates decreases the base), then the revenue responsiveness to an increase in tax rates is greater with capacity equalisation.

COST EQUALISATION AID

General Discussion

Cost equalisation is one aspect of the general issue of fiscal equalisation. In the academic literature on this subject in the United States, costs are used in the economic sense of the minimum expenditure necessary to produce a given quality of public services, given the characteristics of the environment.[15] The basic idea is that the cost of providing a given level of public output is influenced both by the size of the eligible population and certain exogenous characteristics of the environment in which a jurisdiction operates. Conceptually, a sharp distinction is made between expenditure variation due to factors that are outside the control of local officials, versus expenditure variation that reflects the choices of public officials. In principle, only exogenous factors should be reflected in the cost equalisation formula. If factors under the control of the local jurisdiction are used in the cost equalising formula, then jurisdictions will have an incentive to manipulate those factors to increase the level of aid.

To give an example, education costs may vary depending on the characteristics of the students, e.g. the extent of poverty (Downes and Pogue, 1994) Expenditures may also be higher if a jurisdiction has a higher administrative ratio than the typical school, or chooses small class sizes. Cost equalisation should compensate for cost-related differences in student characteristics, but should not reward districts that spend more simply because they have a higher preference for education. While there is widespread agreement that demographic sources of cost differentials should be compensated, other factors are more controversial. For example, it has been argued that density, though it may affect costs, should not be included in the cost formula, because density related cost differentials provide a useful signal in making locational choices.

In the European context, the distinction between "costs" and expenditures is less sharp. Costs are the expenditures required to satisfy the "needs" of a jurisdiction. The calculation of such costs is closely related to current expenditure levels. Implicitly, therefore, the average level of current expenditures is assumed to reflect the cost of providing a nationally defined standard of service. By contrast, in the U.S. model, current expenditures are taken to indicate a combination of preferences and costs. The greater the extent to which variation in expenditures reflects preferences rather than "needs", the weaker the justification for using current expenditures as the basis for cost equalisation.

On an empirical level, the needs approach is proabably easier to implement than the cost approach. The obstacles to reliable cost estimation, in terms of data availability, estimation, and transparency of the results, are formidable. The "needs" approach, if well designed, may be the most practical alternative.

---

15 The rationale that underlies adjusting grants for differences in the cost of service provision is discussed in the papers by Reschovsky, and Ladd and Yinger in "Symposium on Fiscal Equalisation", *National Tax Journal*, March 1994. Oakland (same issue) presents an opposing view, arguing that attempts to offset differences in municipal costs will increase inefficiency.

The prototype cost equalization formula is of the form

$$G^{cost}_{i} = \gamma C_{bar} + (C_i - C_{bar}) \tag{5}$$

G^{cost}_{i} = per capita cost grant for cost equalization in jurisdiction i.

Ci = the standardized cost of providing the mandated services in i.

C_{bar} = the standardized national average cost of providing the mandated activities.

The parameter γ, which ranges from zero to one, represents the proportion of the national average cost which is subsidised by the central government. As γ rises, the net cost of the grant increases. If γ equals zero, the grant compensates only for differences in standardized cost, and the cost to the central government is zero. At γ equal to one, standardised cost is fully subsidised in each community. Treating the capitation grant as a subsidy for required expenditures, γ is on the order of .2 for Sweden.[16]

The cost-based grant formula usually starts with the size of the population to be served. Thus, if the grant is for education, the major determinant of the size of the grant is the number of eligible pupils. The grant amount may then be adjusted to reflect differential costs for students of different ages, and in a few countries for cost differences by type of student.

The Swedish cost equalisation formula for year t is

$$G^{cost}_{i,t} = [C_i (ADJ_t) - C_{bar,t}] \tag{6}$$

ADJ_t is an adjustment factor that guarantees that the estimated average cost in any year is equal to the actual weighted average net cost. The adjustment factor accounts for lags in estimating cost factors, and for inflation. Swedish cost equalisation differs from the general formula in (5) in that the communities receive only the difference between their own structural cost and the national average cost. However, given that population is the basic determinant of costs, the capitation grant may be viewed as supporting C_{bar}. Mandated activities of local government for which costs are equalised include child care, individual and family care, care of the elderly, compulsory school, and upper secondary school, public transport, streets and roads, and water and wastewater .

A standard cost is computed for each of these services by taking a weighted average of the eligible population, where the weights reflect differences in the cost of providing services to different subgroups among the eligible population. This standardized cost may be interpreted as what it would cost any municipality to provide the nationwide average level of the mandated service to its population. As such, the standard cost constitutes a kind of spending norm for each service.

In the year 2000 more than 50 percent of municipalities had standardized costs below the national average, and hence got negative grants. The average per capita grant amount was SEK 540. However, as this average is the sum of both negative and positive grants, it is misleading as to the overall importance of the cost

---

[16] In South Africa, the value of γ is closer to .9. (Reschovsky and Chernick, 2001)

equalisation component of the grant system. A better way to assess its importance is to note that some SEK 10 billion are reallocated through cost equalisation. This is about the same amount as through capacity equalisation, and about one fifth of the general purpose capitation grant.

Child Daycare Services

To analyse some potential issues in the Swedish cost equalisation grant, we consider in detail the cost formula for child day-care services. Demographic cost is calculated as the sum of the number of children nine years or less, with higher cost weights on very young children than for older children. The weights on the differerent age groups are based on observed expenditure differences across communities with different age distributions of children.

Next the demographic cost of child care is multiplied by a "volume" index, which is designed to account for sources of difference in expenditure other than the proportion of children in the population. The volume index is computed by a regression equation that includes a factor for potential eligibility or need (number of full-time working mothers), number of part-time working mothers, and a measure of density. The particular variables in the volume index seem to be those that "work well", in the statistical sense. However, the rationale for their inclusion is unclear.

For example, the potential need factor (number of working mothers or single fathers) in the child care volume index is multiplied by a measure of the relative fiscal capacity of the jurisdiction. Thus the formula adjusts standard cost upward for richer communities. The inclusion of fiscal capacity in the volume index reflects the fact that the demand for publicly provided child care in Sweden is a normal good, with higher income families using the service more intensively than lower income families.[17] In the U.S. model of cost differentials, community income serves primarily as a measure of demand for public services. By contrast, in Sweden child care seems to be viewed as a basic need to which all are entitled, to be provided mainly free of direct charges by local governments. Systematic variations in the use of the service, for example by municipal income or density, reflect differences in need, and are compensated through the cost equalisation grant.

By including fiscal capacity in the determination of standard cost, the cost formula is conflating preferences for child care with the costs of providing the service. In explaining differences in expenditures, it is appropriate for the regression equation to contain both cost and preference factors. However, in constructing the cost index, one should attempt to distinguish costs from preferences.[18] That said, one should recognize that it is difficult, both conceptually and empirically, to construct a true

[17] One might argue that costs of day care are higher in richer municipalities, because more parents are working, or because salaries for day-care workers are higher. However, the volume index already takes account of differences in the proportion of mothers working full-time.

[18] Duncombe and Yinger (1997) estimate costs for school districts in New York State by regressing expenditures on community characteristics, such as the percent of children in poverty, and wage levels for teachers. The equation includes several measures of educational outputs. With this specification, the coefficient on, say poverty, is interpreted as the extra expenditures required by an increase in poverty, in order to achieve a given level of educational performance.

frontier of minimum cost, and that minimum cost must always be a weighted average of actual municipal expenditures.

Regarding cost equalisation for education, it is notable that the Swedish formula does not include a factor for children from low-income families. Undoubtedly, this means that income level is not an important factor in explaining differences in education expenditures across Swedish municipalities. It is possible that poverty or relative income deprivation has no effect on the cost of providing education services in Sweden. However, the U.S. literature stresses that it is more costly to achieve a given level of educational output for poor children than for higher income children. If this result holds for Sweden, then it would suggest that Swedish municipalities are responding to the higher "price" of educating poor children by cutting back on expenditures. If this is the case, poverty would not be seen to cause higher costs, but it would still leave municipalities with high proportions of poor uncompensated for the higher costs of providing educational services. I would encourage attempts to investigate this issue further, following the methodology presented in Duncombe and Yinger (1997).

Demographic cost and the volume index are multiplied together to give a "standard cost" for each municipality. This standard cost is then adjusted by an index which guarantees that the (weighted) average standard cost is equal to the actual average cost of child care in Sweden in a given year. This adjusted standard cost is then further adjusted to take account of inflation. The same adjustment up to the national average is made in the cost calculation for each of the mandated areas of spending.

Incentives for Cost Control

As discussed above, the rationale for cost adjustments is to compensate communities for costs over which they have no control, while avoiding the perverse incentive of rewarding communities simply for spending more. Because the Swedish cost equalisation grant is not a function of the municipality's actual expenditures, it goes some way toward accomplishing this basic purpose. If a municipality spends more than its standardized (predicted) cost, whether because it is inefficient, or chooses a higher level of public services, the extra expenditures must be funded from own sources. If a municipality spends less than its expected amount its cost equalisation grant would also be unaffected. Because expenditure reductions in a particular service free up resources for other purposes, the cost equalisation grant may on balance encourage spending reductions in specific functional areas. The extent of such reductions, and whether they might derive from greater efficiencies or reductions in service levels, is basically an empirical question.[19] (The ability of municipalities to choose the quality of public services such as care for the elderly is discussed in the chapter by Boadway and Johanson.)

---

[19] To the extent that cost factors are unable to fully capture differences in needs, the equalisation grant may enhance the incentive for "cream-skimming". For example, the elder-care component is weighted by the age distribution of the elderly in a community, but not by their health condition. Therefore, a

At the aggregate level, the cost equalisation grant is likely to be neutral in terms of expenditure incentives. Basically, what the formula does is to take national average spending per capita, adjust each community upward or downward from that national average, and provide a grant equal to that difference. Hence, the structure of the cost equalisation grant neither constrains nor encourages the overall growth of local government expenditures over time.[20] If exogenous factors (e.g. public sector wage inflation, or increased mandation) push up aggregate costs, then all municipalities will face a fiscal squeeze. In such an event, the mechanism for relief would have to be an increase in capitation or conditional aid.

THE MIX OF EQUALISATION POLICIES

Fiscal equalisation in Sweden is accomplished through capacity equalisation, cost equalisation, and the capitation grant. The capitation grant establishes a base of intergovernmental funding for mandated activities, while the two equalisation grants move fiscal resources between jurisdictions as a function of fiscal capacity and cost. The above discussion has analysed the incentives, both positive and negative, that are built into the various grant types. To a certain extent the three grants schemes are substitutes in achieving fiscal equalisation. Is the mix of the three optimal?

The capitation grant, whose amount is decided annually by Parliament, is the biggest grant in Sweden. In magnitude it is more than five times the size of the cost or capacity equalisation reallocations. The grant subsidises the cost to each locality of providing the mandated minimum set of public services. It may also be viewed as a component of Sweden's fiscal equalisation policy. Whereas the capacity and cost equalisation components represent a set of interjurisdictional taxes and subsidies, the capitation grant transfers fiscal resources from high income individuals to low income communities. It does this by imposing a uniform national tax rate on income, and refunding the money to municipalities on a per capita basis. The equalisation effect results from the fact that high income individuals, and by extension high income jurisdictions, contribute more in taxes than they receive in grant funds.

The opportunity cost of the capitation grant stems from the tax which must be imposed to fund the grant. Because the grant provides an equal per capita amount, any increase in revenue to the poorest jurisdictions is quite costly, because it must be accompanied by an equal increase in all other jurisdictions. For example, to increase potential revenue in the poorest jurisdiction (with 80 percent of the national average fiscal capacity) by 10 percent, would require an increase in the national tax rate of approximately 2.4 percentage points. With even modest assumptions about the marginal excess burden of national taxation in a high tax country such as Sweden, the efficiency costs of this additional taxation are likely to rather high. Thus the extreme lack of target efficiency in capitation grant makes it a costly way

---

municipality, perhaps through its housing policies, might attempt to recruit relatively healthy elderly, while discouraging those who are relatively sick.

[20] Potential efficiency incentives can be built into a scheme of vertical transfers, by using costed norms to determine each jurisdiction's grant amount. This approach, as applied to South Africa, is described in Reschovsky and Chernick (2001).

to achieve fiscal equalisation. To the tax cost one should also add any reduction in local government efficiency that stems from relying on grants rather than locally raised funds.

The offsetting benefit of the capitation grant can be seen from equation (4) above. For convenience we rewrite (4) here.

$$G^{equal}_i = .95\ t_{bar}\,(Y_{bar} - Y_i) \qquad (4)$$

Because the capitation grant allows municipalities to substitute intergovernmental aid for local taxation, the lower the level of capitation aid, the higher will be t_{bar}, the average local tax rate.

As shown in (4), a higher t_{bar} means that the loss in equalisation aid as a municipality raises its fiscal base is greater, thus further reducing the incentive for economic development. In general, all of the negative incentives associated with capacity equalisation are stronger the higher the level of t_{bar}. The higher is t_{bar}, the greater the gross flow of equalisation aid for any given fiscal capacity gap. For high income communities, this increase in the fiscal penalty is likely to increase resistance to the equalisation scheme.

The optimal mix of capitation aid and equalisation aid depends on the local fiscal response to any change in capitation aid, and the magnitudes of the various potential inefficiencies induced by the grant structure. The greater the magnitude of the inefficiency induced by a particular grant type, the less should be the reliance on that type. In principal, the mix of grants should be set so as to equalize the marginal excess burden per kroner of equalisation from each of grant.

The greater the extent to which each kroner of capitation aid substitutes for a kroner of local spending, the greater the strain on equalisation that would result from a reduction in capitation grants. For the capacity grant, the greater the extent to which it induces overspending, the smaller should be the role of that grant. We cannot determine whether Sweden is currently using the optimal grant mix without more knowledge of the relevant behavioural reactions. However, we can predict that if the capitation grant were reduced, the overall degree of fiscal equalisation would probably be reduced, as would be the size of the local public sector in Sweden. This reduction would be accompanied by an increase in interjurisdictional fiscal competition.

The tradeoff between capitation aid and capacity equalisation can be minimised if the national government were to assume greater fiscal responsibility for redistributional services. In this case, t_{bar} would fall, as would the level of interjurisdictional transfers for fiscal equalisation. By reassigning redistributional functions to the national level, the adverse fiscal incentives from differences in fiscal capacity would be weaker, and therefore the need for equalisation would also be diminished. (See the chapter by Mueller and Uddhammar in this volume.)

TRANSFERS TO INDIVIDUALS

Fiscal Incentives and Grant Type

Under the mandated category known as "individual and family care", municipalities provide cash assistance to eligible recipients. Standard cost depends on the number of refugees, the number of unemployed persons, the number of single women with children, population density, and the number of low-income men. The municipality is relied upon to determine eligibility. Eligibility rules are determined nationally. In 2000 the standard cost for this service was SEK 2546. It is notable that this amount is only about a third of the cost of providing care services for the elderly.

The financing of public assistance from a general block grant is an approach that has been adopted in a growing number of federalist countries. The United States, Canada, and France have in the past few years converted the financing of cash assistance from a conditional matching grant program to a broad block grant. The motivation for this change has been to reduce budgetary pressure on the central level, and to give localities more freedom in designing effective programs to aid low-income persons.

The concern with the block-grant approach to financing public assistance is that by forcing communities to bear the full cost for each additional dollar of welfare expenditures, the block grant will exacerbate each jurisdiction's incentive to reduce the level of public assistance. This incentive is commonly referred to as the 'race to the bottom'. Evidence from the U.S. suggests that a very dramatic race to the bottom is not likely to occur, but that over time block grants will lead to some reduction in local willingness to spend on the needy (Chernick, 1998).

In Sweden, the race-to-the-bottom incentive is likely to be muted, in part because, since 1998, the ability of municipalities to deviate from a national norm has been substantially restricted (see Boadway and Johansson, this volume). Hence, the main dimension in which communities can compete is in access - making it more difficult for individuals to qualify for public assistance by raising administrative hurdles. The willingness to do so is probably limited by general social acceptance of the legitimate role of the local public sector in providing fair access to public assistance. The standardized cost for public assistance provides a "notional" norm of what each community could be expected to spend, and there is considerable pressure on municipalities not to deviate substantially from that standard. In addition, the capacity equalisation grant limits the fiscal harm that municipalities face if they accept more public assistance recipients.

Transfers to Individuals versus Transfers to Government

There is a tradeoff between fiscal equalization through the intergovernmental grant system and equalization of individual incomes through the tax and transfer system. The two approaches may be viewed as partial substitutes in promoting horizontal equity for individuals living in different municipalities and assuring minimum levels of public services for all. The greater the extent to which transfers go directly from the federal government to needy individuals, the less is the need for sub-national governments to provide such transfers. To assure that the equalisation system takes appropriate account of direct national transfer programs, income from federal insurance programs is included in the measure of fiscal capacity.

There is an important relation between the extent of decentralisation and the need for equalisation. By reducing local responsibility for redistributional functions, the need for equalisation finance is commensurately reduced. In principle, if one could remove all local responsibility for redistribution, or if all local tax financing was benefit based, then there would be no need at all for equalisation (see the chapter by Boadway and Johansson on the need for equalisation, and the chapter by Mueller and Udhammar for a discussion of local benefits-received taxation).

The component of cost equalisation for low-income assistance includes a factor for the number of unemployed without unemployment benefits. Thus, there is a direct trade-off between the stringency of the rules for getting unemployment benefits and cost compensation for welfare costs. If unemployment insurance coverage is reduced, this should increase the number of persons eligible for public assistance, thus increasing national average welfare costs.

However, because the Swedish cost equalisation grant only compensates (positively or negatively) for cost differences, the total amount of the cost equalisation component for cash assistance grant would be unaffected by changes in unemployment benefits. A change in the national rate of coverage for unemployment would change the average cost of public assistance for the nation. Each community's standard cost would be increased by a higher adjustment factor, but in principal there should be no change in the total grant amount. There would also be an adjustment to fiscal capacity if unemployment benefits were reduced. Again, however, the aggregate grant amount would remain unchanged. Unless there is an implicit compensation to municipalities through an increase in the capitation grant, the national obligation would remain the same. Thus in principal the state could shift costs to municipalities by changing the rules on the duration of coverage for unemployment insurance. Canada has experienced significant intergovernmental conflict in precisely this area.

The appropriate mix between transfers to individuals and equalising grants to governments depends on the importance of the potential disincentives built into each policy. While transfers to individuals may induce reductions in labor supply, transfers to government may promote overspending or inefficiency. The United States has gradually moved towards greater reliance on transfers to individuals, versus transfers to governments. Whether such a direction is warranted in Sweden depends ultimately on fundamental views about the role of governments in redistribution. However, the debate should be informed by information from empirical studies of the importance of the relevant incentives and disincentives.

CONCLUSION

In this review of fiscal equalisation in Sweden, the main findings are the following:

1) Despite the fact that inequalities in fiscal capacity across municipalities are relatively small, the Swedish standard for equity in the local public sector is quite stringent, as is the actual degree of fiscal equalisation. Based on a regression analysis of the overall distribution of grants, I find that the grant system offsets between 62 and 100 percent of potential revenue variation from variations in fiscal capacity.

2) Capacity equalisation grants provide an incentive for the narrowing of tax rate differentials between municipalities. Some narrowing has occurred.

3) Because larger municipalities tend to have higher incomes, more municipalities get positive capacity equalisation grants than get negative grants. However, the net fiscal cost is close to zero.

4) The capacity equalisation grant provides both fiscal insurance against shocks to regional economic activity, and fiscal redistribution in response to long-term shifts in economic activity.

5) The capacity equalisation grant reduces the incentive to pursue economic development. This has both potentially positive and negative effects. The positive effect is that it encourages income mixing within communities, and reduces the incentive for beggar-thy-neighbor policies. The negative effect is that it discourages cost-reducing fiscal competition between municipalities. There is not enough empirical evidence to determine which of these effects is dominant.

6) Cost equalisation adjusts for expenditure differences from national averages, not for underlying cost differentials. As such, the grant is neutral in terms of aggregate incentives for cost reduction.

7) There is a tradeoff between vertical transfers through capitation aid and the need for interjurisdictional fiscal equalisation. A reduction in capitation aid would permit lower rates of national taxation, but would increase the interjurisdictional flows for capacity and cost equalisation, and the potential disincentives which go along with these flows. By contrast, centralisation of redistributional functions would reduce the need for fiscal equalisation.

8) Further research investigating the empirical importance of the various incentives built into the system of fiscal equalisation would be useful in evaluating the Swedish system of intergovernmental finance.

REFERENCES

Boije, Robert (1997) "Capitalisation, Efficiency and the Demand for Local Public Services," *Economic Studies*, 33, Department of Economics, Uppsala University.

Borge, L-E. and J. Rattso (2001) "Property Taxation as Incentive for Cost Control: Empirical Evidence for Utility Services in Norway." unpublished draft.

Chernick, Howard (1998) "Fiscal Effects of Block Grants for the Needy: An Interpretation of the Evidence," *International Tax and Public Finance*, 5, 205-233.

Chernick, Howard and Andrew Reschovsky (2001) "Lost in the Balance: How State Policies Affect the Fiscal Health of Cities," Discussion Paper, The Brookings Institution Center on Urban and Metropolitan Policy. http://www.brook.edu/urban/chernick/chernickexsum.htm.

Downes, Thomas and Thomas Pogue (1994) "Adjusting School Aid Formulas for the Higher Costs of Educating Disadvantaged Students," *National Tax Journal*, 47, 89-110.

Duncombe, William and John Yinger (1997) "Why is it so Hard to Help Central City Schools?" *Journal of Policy Analysis and Management*, Vol 16, Number 1.

Evans, William, Wallace Oates, and Robert Schwab (1992) "Measuring Peer Group Effects: A Study of Teenage Behavior", *Journal of Political Economy*, Vol. 100, Number 5, 966-991.

Evans, William, Sheila Murray, and Robert Schwab (1997) "Schoolhouses, Courthouses, and Statehouses After Serrano," *Journal of Policy Analysis and Management*, Vol 16, Number 1.

Gilbert, Guy and Alain Guengant (2001) "Éffects Redistributifs des Dotations de l'État aux Communes," Commissariat Generale du Plan, Groupement de Recherche sous l'Administration Local en Europe, GIS-CNRS.

Hamilton, Bruce W. (1975) "Zoning and Property Taxation in a System of Local Governments," *Urban Studies* 12, 205-11.

Harrison, Russell S. (1982) "The Effects of Exclusionary Zoning and Residential Segregation on Urban-Service Distributions." in Richard C. Rich (ed.) *The Politics of Urban Public Services*. Lexington Books, D.C. Heath and Company. Lexington, MA., 83-100.

Hoxby, Caroline (2000) "Does Competition Among Public Schools Benefit Students and Taxpayers?" *American Economic Review*, 90, 1209-1238.

Ladd, Helen, Andrew Reschovsky, and John Yinger (1992), "City Fiscal Conditions and State Equalisation Aid: The Case of Minnesota." in *Proceeding of the 84th Annual Conference: 1991, National Tax Association*, 42-49.

Netzer, Dick (1997) "Comments on Tax and Spending Incentives and Enterprise Zones," in The Effects of State and Local Public Policies on Economic Development, *New England Economic Review*.

Oates, Wallace E. and Robert M. Schwab (forthcoming) "What Should Local Governments Tax: Income or Property?", in Amy Ellen Schwartz (ed.) *Urban Issues and Public Finance: Essays in Honor of Dick Netzer*, Northampton, MA: Edward Elgar Publishing.

Reschovsky, Andrew (1994) "Fiscal Equalization and School Finance" in Symposium on Fiscal Equalisation, *National Tax Journal*.

Reschovsky, Andrew and Howard Chernick (2001) "Financing Health, Education, and Welfare in the New South Africa," La Follette Policy Report, Robert M. La Follette School of Public Affairs, Volume 12, Number 1.

San Antonio Independent School District versus Rodriguez, 1973.

Sjoquist, David L. (1982) "The Effect of the Number of Local Governments on Central City Expenditures," *National Tax Journal* 35 (1), 79-88.

Suhrcke, Marc (2001) "Preferences for Inequality: East vs. West" Innocenti Working Paper No. 89, United Nations Children's Fund, Innocenti Research Centre, Florence Italy.

Von Hagen, Jürgen, and Ralf Hepp (2000) "Regional Risks Haring and Redistribution in the German Federation", Center for European Integration Studies, Working Paper B15, http://www.zei.de/zei_deutsch/f_publ.html.

APPENDIX

ON THE RELATIONSHIP BETWEEN LOCAL TAX RATES AND LOCAL PROPERTY VALUES

The figure shows the potential effect of fiscal equalisation on municipal spending. The municipality's fiscal base is assumed to first increase as the tax rate is raised, then decrease. The base maximizing rate is at t*. Following the argument in the text, Curve I, without fiscal equalisation, is assumed to be more elastic with respect to the municipal tax rate than curve II. Assume that the community chooses a tax rate t_2 that exceeds the base maximizing rate. In the absence of fiscal equalisation, the resultant decline in the average fiscal base is equal to B_{max} minus B_2. The amount of overspending is equal to the difference between t_2B_2 and t^*B_{max}. With capacity equalisation, the revenue t_2B_2 can be realized at a lower tax rate t_1, where by construction t_1B_1 equals t_2B_2. Because the negative effect on the tax base from overspending is reduced under capacity equalisation, the tax price fluctuates less, thus reducing the incentive to achieve the optimal tax rate t*.

The decrease in the tax base from B_{max} to B_2 is a measure of the deadweight loss from overspending, in the absence of capacity equalisation. However, because of capacity equalisation, the tax base declines only to B_1. Hence the difference between B_1 and B_2 may be interpreted as a measure of the excess burden from capacity equalisation, i.e. the difference between the value of the additional services financed by the equalisation grant and the capitalised value of the additional local taxes that would be required to finance those expenditures.

Figure 1: The Relationship between the Tax Rate and the Tax Base

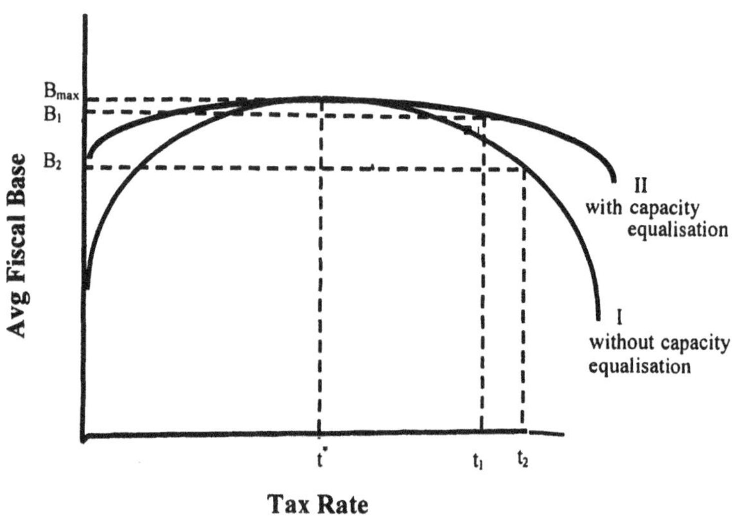

5

CONSTRAINING MISUSE OF FUNDS FROM INTERGOVERNMENTAL GRANTS: A LEGAL ANALYSIS

Clayton P. Gillette*

New York University School of Law

INTRODUCTION

Sources of Diversions of Grant Funds

Intergovernmental grants allow centralized governments to ensure that decentralized units have sufficient funds to make available a minimal level of a particular good to all constituents, or to induce decentralized governments (which I refer to as "localities") to produce a greater level of public goods than they would produce if they employed only internally generated funds. King (1984) distinguishes four reasons for making grants: (1) to encourage localities to take account of the external effects of their services; (2) to enforce grantor preferences; (3) to correct for fiscal imbalance between the various tiers of government (revenue sharing); and (4) for equalization. I refer to grants that satisfy any of these conditions as an "ideal" grant and to the requirements that the central government imposes for use of the grant and the ways in which the locality expends grant funds as the "terms" of the grant. Although grants are not costless, in that they require additional bureaucracies at both the central and decentralized levels, ideal grants promote either efficiency or distributional goals within a multi-tiered political system.

Grants can roughly be divided into two categories. Central governments utilize conditional matching grants to minimize the fiscal externalities that are inherent in a decentralized system. They make sense where the local government is, relative to the central government, a superior provider of the public good being funded. This may occur because, for instance, the details of administration vary from locality to locality. Central governments utilize block grants to reduce the horizontal inequities that are also inherent in decentralization or to permit greater satisfaction of local preferences for goods beyond those that the locality can generate from its own tax base. Thus, ideal grants allow a nation to obtain the benefits of decentralization — geographic sorting of constituents by preference for specific local public goods, easier monitoring of public officials, efficiencies driven by interlocal competition — while simultaneously negating some of its potential costs — horizontal inequities among localities in the nation, vertical externalities (shifting costs from the local

* Max E. Greenberg Professor of Contract Law, New York University School of Law, 40 Washington Square South, New York, NY 10012, USA

level to the central level), and horizontal externalities (shifting costs from one locality to the other, such as where different localities have different preferences for the same public good and the choice of one affects the other).

Grant terms, however, may deviate significantly from the ideal. Either the grantor, the central government, or the local recipient can use grants in ways that serve none of the desired objectives. Instead, central or local officials may use funds to maximize the scope of their authority, to maximize budgets, or to increase the probability of re-election.[1] To understand how this deviation may occur, consider how grants permit officials to pursue motivations that do not align with national interest. Central officials may employ grants to expand the authority of the central government into areas best left to decentralized decision making. Funds to localities, for instance, may be conditioned on requirements that localities cede authority to the central government, such as by agreeing to regulations that confer few national benefits. Alternatively, the central government may direct grant funds to purposes that are appropriate for local decision making, but that distort local decisions in order to increase the political base of central incumbents. For instance, Dahlberg and Johansson posit that a grant may be used by the incumbent government to fund projects favored by swing voters. While they are agnostic on whether such uses necessarily generate inefficiencies, Dahlberg and Johansson recognize the possibility that such directives may serve central officials' objectives rather than national ones.

Local officials, in turn, may divert grants from their ideal purposes for either of two reasons. The first is a function of the fact that the prices of grants and the identities of the payers are opaque. Local officials may take advantage of the fiscal illusion that grants from the central government may be viewed by local residents as "free" money, which cannot be translated into tax savings. Thus, residents will not subject the expenditure of grant funds to the same level of scrutiny that those same residents would apply to expenditures from locally raised taxes. Officials who are aware of this reduced scrutiny may utilize grant funds for projects that constituents would not consider worth their tax price. Block grants intended to increase local autonomy over expenditure decisions and equalization grants that are intended to redistribute wealth from richer to poorer localities may be particularly susceptible to these diversions, since the funds come with relatively few restrictions on their use. The absence of a centrally designated benchmark for appropriating the funds makes the task of evaluating their expenditure more difficult. For instance, local officials may siphon block grant funds to provide themselves with perquisites or may

---

[1] Gramlich, for instance, notes that "central governments have increasingly become more ambitious is trying to establish minimum service or spending levels for different government-provided goods and services." Gramlich at 222. There is no reason to believe, however, that only central officials will attempt to expand their jurisdiction. Local officials can do the same by using grants in a manner that advances local, rather than the intended national, objectives. This is not to say that officials necessarily act this way. Public officials may attempt to realize the ideal objectives of grants in order to serve general welfare. But even publicly interested officials may define the public welfare in a manner that enhances their authority, so that central officials may believe that the jurisdiction of the central government should be defined more broadly than local officials. Moreover, as Hume suggested, the assumption of self-interested officials allows us to consider constraints on those individuals who act in this manner without limiting the authority of officials who, in fact, act in a publicly interested manner.

otherwise use funds to make expenditures that do not increase private personal incomes.

Alternatively, local officials may prefer to expend grants in pursuit of "the public interest," but their definition of that term may deviate from central government expectations. Local officials may pursue the interests of the local "public" even where doing so conflicts with the interests of the broader public. For instance, local expenditures may impose externalities on neighboring localities or utilize funds that could be appropriated more efficiently by other governmental entities. The common pool nature of grants may exacerbate these tendencies. Local officials who might otherwise eschew funds that could better be utilized elsewhere will be less likely to act on those altruistic motivations if they believe that similarly situated localities are utilizing grants, so that their decision to forgo funds does little to guarantee their efficient use by others. Indeed, given interlocal competition for residents and businesses, localities have incentives to avoid altruistic renunciation of available grant funds.[2]

These tendencies on the part of both central and local officials to deviate from ideal grant terms may be countered by making misuse more salient to potential monitors of official and bureaucratic behavior, that is, by making public officials more accountable to constituents and to national officials who control budgets and the electoral process. In this paper, therefore, I speculate about the legal and structural constraints that a constitutional and statutory system might incorporate to increase the accountability of officials. Many of the constraints that I envision, especially in the context of conditional grants, arise from a bargaining relationship between central and local officials in which the need of each to cooperate with the other over the long term constrains the capacity of either to defect from a cooperative relationship in the short term. This approach does not deny that government officials at any level may act in a self-interested manner. Rather it attempts to create a structure in which the countervailing interests of central and decentralized governments can generate socially optimal intergovernmental arrangements.

ACCOUNTABILITY THROUGH BARGAINS

Accountability for public officials may arise from multiple sources. Most commonly, accountability arises from institutional structures that permit third parties to detect, penalize, or deter deviations from publicly interested behavior. For instance, courts may enjoin or penalize opportunistic behavior by officials, or the electorate can refuse to return to office those officials whose conduct is inconsistent with the perceived objectives of governmental activity. Third party intervention, however, suffers from multiple limitations. Courts in many nations cannot initiate actions, but can only pursue claims that are brought by aggrieved citizens. Since monitoring and prosecuting government misconduct is costly, and the benefits constitute a public good, we would expect such prosecutions to be undersupplied.

---

[2] See, e.g., Hills: 876-77 (asserting that governors of states in the United States are reluctant to turn down federal money in order to avoid grant conditions, because voters will retaliate against politicians who fail to apply for "free" federal money).

In addition, as I discuss more fully below, deviations from ideal grant terms will often be opaque; third parties will have difficulty deriving or applying a consensus definition of governmental misuse of funds. As a result, misuse will be difficult for third parties to observe, and even more difficult to verify to potential enforcers.

An alternative source of accountability, therefore, may be appropriate. In a bilateral relationship like a grant, the most effective constraint on misuse may arise from the competing interests of the parties to the grant. Efforts by central officials to expand their jurisdiction should, in theory, be resisted by local officials, who would suffer a reduction in their own authority. Efforts by local officials to misuse grant funds should, again in theory, be resisted by central officials who prefer that those same funds be directed towards achieving national goals. If divergence between ideal grant terms and actual terms are observable to the other party, then that divergence can be addressed in any bargain between the central and local governments or can be penalized in subsequent interactions between the parties. Fear of retaliation in subsequent interactions and refusal to cooperate even in mutually agreeable objectives can provide the incentives for each actor to limit its opportunistic behavior in a current interaction. Central officials who seek to intrude too far into local affairs will have to raise the price (increase grant amounts) to willing localities; local officials who fail to expend grant funds in a manner that coincides with national interests will find themselves deprived of subsequent funding.

These optimistic predictions of mutual accountability depend, however, on the structure of the underlying grant. For instance, one premise of mutual accountability is that localities will spend grant funds in a manner consistent with central preferences in order to avoid a termination of funding. A locality that spends funds profligately or for nonproductive uses (for instance, purchasing expensive office furniture rather than subsidizing public goods), could be expected to suffer a reduction of subsequent grants. But that assumes that the central government has devised a standard for appropriate use of grant funds and monitors local expenditures to ensure compliance with that standard. Monitoring costs alone suggest that this condition will not be fully satisfied. More importantly, some ideal grants will be made without any central preference about their expenditure. Central governments that make general or block grants are primarily concerned with increasing local autonomy in expenditure decisions or equalization of resources among localities. In those cases, central officials will be less willing to impose accountability on local officials for their substantive decisions. The implicit "bargain" over expenditure will occur between local officials and their constituents, who will remain the primary monitors of expenditure decisions.

Accountability is made more difficult by the fact that deviations between ideal and actual grant terms are highly opaque. There are few sharp jurisdictional boundaries that separate the responsibilities of central and local officials. Consequently, there are few guidelines to distinguish between appropriate and inappropriate uses of grant funds. As a result, misuse often will not readily be observable even to the immediate parties, and, as noted above, will be difficult to verify to third parties.

Finally, central officials may be able to buy out the resistance of local officials simply by raising the personal value of grants to those officials. Central officials, after all, are not spending their own money, but the taxes of their constituents. Unless they are taxing at the limit, they are not facing a serious budget constraint. Hence, they may be able to bribe local officials into accepting nonideal grant terms that expand central functions. Local officials, on the other hand, may perceive grant funds as "free goods" that do not require the imposition of tax increases on their constituents and that are less likely to monitored than expenditures from taxes. The result is that even the bargain relationship can generate overuse of grant funds.

Notwithstanding these limitations, it may be possible to design mechanisms that counter the incentives of central and local officials to chisel at the inherently ambiguous boundaries of their appropriate jurisdiction. Once we perceive grants as bargains between central and local officials, or between local officials and their constituents, grant terms look less like conditions that central and local governments "impose" on each other than like solutions to a bargaining game defined by the environment in which the parties interact. On this view, grant terms are constantly available for negotiation between sophisticated entities that have significant authority to bargain. As a result, the ideal legal rules for administration of grants reflect legal rules that apply generally to incomplete contracts. That is, the legal and structural environment should seek to reduce transactions costs between parties so that the bargain that evolves is one that would have reflected the terms agreed to by informed transactors operating at arm's length. This objective has different consequences for common forms of grants, conditional grants and block grants. For the former, the reduction of transactions costs requires placing the entitlement to impose or resist terms on the appropriate party. For block grants, where accountability is likely to emerge from constituent monitoring, legal rules should promote fiscal transparency in order to reduce the risks associated with unobservability and nonverifiability. In each case, after developing these concepts, I attempt to apply the general principles that I derive to the Swedish experience.

RECENT FORMS OF GRANTS IN SWEDEN

The ability of either central or local governments to engage in opportunistic behavior with respect to grants depends at least in part on the type of grant involved. I discuss the two prevalent forms of grant, specific grants, or conditional grants, for particular projects, and general grants, or block grants that are not limited to particular projects but that can be used for purposes designated within the discretion of recipient localities. In Sweden, municipalities receive approximately 20 percent of their revenue from grants. There is, however, significant variation in these figures depending on the form of locality and the form of grant. The 18 county councils receive less than 10 percent of their income from grants, while 289 municipalities receive closer to 25 percent of their income from grants. This can be contrasted with the United States, where, in 1998-99, states received approximately 21 percent of their revenue from federal grants, and localities received approximately

3 percent of their revenue from federal grants and 31 percent of their revenues from state grants.[3]

In the last decade, the structure of grants in Sweden has changed radically from a system that relied heavily on conditional grants to a system of block grants. This reform was instituted in 1993 for the express purpose of giving local governments greater autonomy and more freedom over their expenditures, and to improve the efficiency with which local public goods were provided. The underlying assumption appears to be that local officials will be better able to adapt to local needs if expenditures for municipal functions are made from local budgets (regardless of the source of funds in those budgets) rather than from centrally dictated directives. As a result, while the percentage of municipal revenues attributable to grants has remained somewhat stable over the past 20 years, the vast majority of grant funds currently takes the form of general grants. From 1990 to 1993, municipal revenue attributable to special grants decreased from 22 percent to 8 percent, while the percentage attributable to block grants rose from 4 percent to 14 percent.

The apparent discretion that Swedish municipalities and county councils have to expend grant funds under the revised system, however, may be somewhat misleading. The Local Government Act and the Social Services Act impose on municipalities obligations to provide and to pay for a wide variety of services. The realistic expectation that municipalities will use general grants for these purposes reduces the latitude with which they can employ grant funds. Municipalities are required to provide child care, care for the elderly, education (up to secondary education), water and sewage treatment, streets and roads, social programs for the poor, planning, emergency services, and environmental and health protection. County councils are responsible for health care. Municipalities and county councils are jointly responsible for regional public transportation. Thus, while as a formal matter, most grants in Sweden are general, as a practical matter, they may share many of the difficulties involved with more traditional categorical grants. At least, this is true insofar as municipalities do not have access to alternative revenues to cover the costs of mandatory requirements.

These constraints are exacerbated by the legal requirement that municipalities operate on a balanced budget and correct deficits within two years. The technical inability to engage in deficit spending or to borrow for operating expenses reduces the likelihood that municipalities will be able to fund significant discretionary expenditures after paying for centrally mandated programs. There is some evidence that the balanced budget requirement is not enforced, so that deficit budgets are, in practice, possible. This, of course, does not solve the problem of inefficient government expenditures, since deficit spending for current expenses simply imposes on future residents the obligation to pay for goods from which prior residents benefited. Thus, the balanced budget requirement may be an appropriate constraint, assuming that localities have sufficient funds to make necessary and mandated public expenditures. While the central government has made equalizing

---

[3] See U.S. Census Bureau, Table 1. These comparisons may be distorted by different definitions of "revenues" and "grants" in different jurisdictions.

funds available for municipalities that do not have the resources necessary to balance their budgets, it is unclear whether those funds would be available to municipalities that had sufficient funds to satisfy mandatory obligations but wanted additional funds to satisfy discretionary functions.[4] Arguably, if the functions mandated by the central government reflect public goods with a national scope, they should be provided at a central level,[5] and equalization funds should be available to local governments to pursue local public goods of the localities choosing. This procedure would permit localities more readily to adjust to the demands of different populations and to compete for residents in a manner often affiliated with the efficient provision of local public services.

CONDITIONAL GRANTS AND LEGAL ENTITLEMENTS

Constitutional Limits on Central Imposition of Local Obligations

Central officials who seek to expand their jurisdiction would presumably prefer to impose obligations on localities and require the latter to pay for implementing them. In this way, central officials can claim responsibility for addressing social issues, while defraying to others the blame for increasing taxes necessary to pay for the programs. Unfunded mandates have frequently been criticized for having this effect. Depending on the constitutional structure of the particular country, and the form of intergovernmental relations it adopts, central officials may face either legal or political constraints in imposing unfunded obligations on localities. For instance, the structure of federalism in the United States guarantees a certain degree of sovereignty for states and, derivatively, for their political subdivisions. These federalism protections make sense at least insofar as they preclude the central government from imposing obligations on localities that can be implemented more efficiently through local regulations.

The structural protections of federalism, however, are not self-enforcing; they must be defined through judicial or political understandings of the appropriate jurisdiction of national and subnational governments. In the United States, for instance, the central government faces constitutional restrictions on its ability to "commandeer" state agencies into using their resources to implement a federally enacted program. While the scope of "commandeering" is vague, judicial interpretations of the central governments efforts to enlist the aid of states and localities to pursue national goals has provided more concrete definition to the concept. Most recently, in *Printz v. United States*,[6] the Supreme Court of the United States invalidated federal legislation that required state and local law enforcement officials to assist in the implementation of a federal law involving registration of handguns. The federal law

[4] Dahlberg (2001) indicates that in 1999, 57 municipalities applied for funds from a transfer program for municipalities unable to meet the balanced budget requirements, and 36 received central relief. See the paper by Chernick in this volume, which indicates that equalization adjusts only for expenditure differences from national averages.
[5] See Mueller and Uddhammar in this volume.
[6] 521 U.S. 898 (1997).

provided no additional funding to defray state and local costs in complying with the federal legislation.

Even within United States federalism, however, it is plausible that the central government would be entitled to impose an obligation on a locality, as long as the central government was willing to bear the full costs of the program. We might think of such a program as one involving a "mandatory grant," that is, one in which the central government required localities to undertake a program, but agreed to pay its full costs. To date, United States courts have used the "commandeering" doctrine only to invalidate programs in which the federal government required state and local officials to bear the costs of complying with a federally enacted program. Given the desire to maintain constitutional autonomy for state governments separate from the federal government, moreover, it is unlikely that the federal government could claim that it was implicitly funding "commandeered" activities through general grants that the locality could use for the mandated activity.

It is unclear, however, whether the Swedish system contains similar protections against the imposition of central obligations. Certainly, the Swedish constitution does not purport to establish a federal system in which subnational governments are granted sovereignty over significant issues not explicitly delegated to the central government. If, therefore, Swedish municipalities are simply functionaries of the central government, created to provide more efficient delivery of local public goods, then there is less of a constitutional basis for local resistance to the imposition of mandates, at least where those mandates are accompanied by full funding.

The absence of a federal system, however, does not entail that subnational governments are without legal rights against incursions by the central government into areas better administered at a decentralized level. Indeed, the structure of Sweden's constitution does provide some degree of constitutional protection for municipalities. Article 1, subsection 2 of Chapter 1 in the Instrument of Government, provides that Swedish democracy is to be provided, in part, through "local self-government." Article 7 of Chapter 1 recites that there are "primary and regional [municipal and county council] local government units in Sweden." It is plausible that these provisions could be interpreted to limit the central government's capacity to impose obligations on localities. In practice, nevertheless, Swedish experience confers on the central government significant authority to dictate obligations to localities, regardless of the source of payment. As noted above, the Local Government Act and the Social Service Act impose broad requirements on localities for the provision of multiple public goods and redistribution. It is not clear whether central grants fully compensate the localities for the costs of these goods and services. Even if they do not, however, the Swedish constitution does not obviously protect localities against the imposition of such unfunded obligations. Municipalities have begun to challenge the capacity of the central government to impose obligations without providing sufficient funding as provided by Acts relating to municipalities. For instance, the Municipality of Vellinge challenged the amount of taxes that the central government owed to the Municipality. When the Supreme Court dismissed the suit, the Municipality brought the claim to the European Court of Justice under Article 11 of the European Convention on the Autonomy of Municipalities.[7] Although the decision of the Supreme Court was based on procedural grounds, concerning the proper forum for a claim against the central government, rather than substantive grounds, and was based on statutory rights of municipalities rather than the constitutional structure of the central government/local government relationship, the case demonstrates the fact that even outside of formal federalist structures, there may be limits on the capacity of central governments to dictate terms to localities.

Even in the absence of constitutional guarantees of local autonomy, political constraints may limit the capacity of the central government to expand its jurisdiction. Typically, central representatives responsible for imposing obligations on localities are elected on a geographic basis, that is, from areas that tend to coincide with the boundaries of localities. Central representatives therefore have some incentive not to overreach the appropriate jurisdiction of the central government, as doing so will increase costs of providing local public goods to their constituents. Local officials who might have to raise taxes to their constituents to pay for centrally mandated programs and potential challengers to incumbent central representatives have incentives to inform constituents about costly overreaching by the central government. The effect is that representatives who serve at the national level will be unable fully to escape accountability for the measures they enact that impose costs on localities.

These political checks on keeping central and local officials within their appropriate realms, however, are highly imperfect. Central officials may seek to demonstrate their familiarity with and attention to problems that are salient in the minds of the electorate by creating federal legislation, notwithstanding that the issues are best dealt with at through local discretion. For instance, commentators in the United States have traced the dramatic increase in crimes punishable under federal law to the electorate's concern about crime, even though most crimes generate minimal externalities beyond the jurisdiction where they are committed. Again, the opacity of the line between central and decentralized activities may make it difficult for local officials to claim convincingly that they are being improperly enlisted to serve national objectives best addressed at a more decentralized level of government.

Limits on Inducing Local Action

Conditional grants, however, do not trigger the constitutional difficulties of either unfunded mandates or mandatory grants because localities are not obligated to accept the funds or to perform the functions on which the funds are contingent. Instead, conditional grants are used to induce the locality to participate in the reduction of negative externalities or the generation of positive externalities that localities would typically ignore (Peterson at 23). Conditional grants can achieve this objective by compensating localities for performing specific functions that have external benefits. Making the grants conditional rather than matching avoids adverse incentives for localities to overinvest in an unnecessary program in order to obtain more central

---

[7] Supreme Court case No. Ö 4777-97.

funding. Alternatively, the central government may use conditional grants to solve a collective action problem that arises when localities seek to avoid attracting the relatively poor by reducing redistributive expenditures. If the central government can use grants to induce all localities to provide such expenditures, no one locality will fear that voluntarily making such expenditures will cause it to become a "welfare magnet."

As in the case of mandatory grants, however, the central government could employ conditional grants to expand its jurisdiction by inducing localities to produce a socially inefficient amount of a local public good. This would occur, for instance, if the grant allows the central government to set conditions that are inappropriate for local implementation, or that are insufficiently responsive to local conditions and that would be better set at the local level, or that otherwise impinge on local autonomy in a manner that is more costly to localities than beneficial to the central government. Nevertheless, central officials who are attempting to expand their authority have incentives to require localities to fulfill central objectives.

Initially, this possibility seems more remote in the case of conditional grants because the localities' capacity to reject the conditions prevents central governments from imposing inefficient terms. Instead, the central government must devise terms that would be acceptable to localities. Hence, conditional grants essentially become hypothetical bargains between the central government and the recipient localities. Ideal conditional grants make sense in this context because they permit the central government to "purchase" the "expertise" of localities in providing a good or service that confers national benefits by inducing a greater or lesser level of production than the locality would otherwise provide. By offering a conditional grant on similar terms to all localities, the central government may make this purchase without incurring the costs of negotiating with every locality that is necessary to implement it. Assuming that central officials were publicly interested and that transactions costs were zero, conditional grants would lead to the same allocation of governmental responsibility as a unitary government that was attempting to optimize the interests of all constituents. Localities would receive an amount necessary to produce the desirable level of external benefit, and central officials would make payments equivalent to the value of those benefits. Bargains would generate efficient outcomes because the central government would be unwilling to pay localities amounts necessary to expand central jurisdiction into areas better addressed through local regulation, since those costs would exceed the benefits to central officials. Central officials, however, would properly compensate localities to engage in activities or activity levels that only generated spillover benefits or avoided spillover costs. Under these Coasean conditions, conditional grants would not create either autonomy or accountability problems. Conditional grants would serve as an ideal constraint on central governments, as they would be required to purchase the cooperation of localities, and presumably would not spend funds in excess of national benefits. (This analysis assumes that there are no agency costs. In the presence of agency costs, central officials, who are, after all, spending the public's money rather than their own, would theoretically be willing to pay localities an inefficiently high amount to surrender some of their autonomy if that expenditure made the central officials better off. But that same reasoning suggests that local officials might also impose agency costs, either by rejecting (for self-interested reasons) a properly priced and nationally desirable central program or by surrendering local autonomy for less than the costs necessary to implement the desired program. There is no *a priori* reason to believe that agency costs at the national or local level will dominate. Thus, I omit agency costs generally from the current discussion.)

Bargaining between central and local governments, however, is not costless. Either the central government or the localities may misestimate the external effects of local action and thus set conditions for the grant too high or too low. Either the central government or the localities may hold out for more of the bargaining surplus than the other is willing to grant. Or the central government may seek to impose conditions that are unwarranted by national welfare, but that the states are willing to accept because they gain more value with the conditional grant than they do without it, notwithstanding that they would have gained still more with a different condition. Since every condition imposes a constraint on local autonomy, ideal grant terms could impose only those conditions that create a benefit for centralization that is more highly valued than the necessary incursion into local autonomy. Given the opacity of the appropriate dividing line between appropriate central and local activities, each party may have difficulty observing efforts of the other to expand or to resist efforts to alter its jurisdiction. Even if it is clear to localities that conditions impose undue constraints or to the central government that it is serving a national interest, the opacity of the proper dividing line between central and local functions frustrates efforts to verify to third parties that a particular condition within the "gray area" is either appropriate or inappropriate. Misuse of grant terms, therefore, can occur at either the central or the local level. As a result, in practice, the extent to which localities will be able to resist undesired (and arguably undesirable) conditions may depend less on the capacity to reach an efficient bargain or to demonstrate misuse to a third party than on the constitutional relationship between the central and local governments.

The constitutional structure of a multi-tiered government implicitly or explicitly assigns initial entitlements to each party in the intergovernmental relationship. For instance, with respect to grants, the constitutional structure will either confer on the central government an entitlement to impose conditions in gray areas or will confer on decentralized governments an entitlement to resist such conditions. The United States reveals both of these presumptions in different contexts. The basic principles of most state constitutions in the United States confer on states the entitlement to impose obligations on localities within their jurisdiction, except where the state constitution provides a specific protection for localities. The Constitution of the United States, however, limits the federal government's capacity to impose obligations on states or their political subdivisions. While this limitation has been interpreted with different degrees of strictness at different points in the nation's history, it creates a presumption that the federal government must make an affirmative demonstration of national purpose before imposing obligations on the states.

In a world of positive transactions costs that might interfere with intergovernmental bargains, it makes sense to allow the central government to impose obligations whenever the failure of localities to purchase the entitlement to be free from such obligations will still tend to promote net savings in administration or the production of national public goods. Conversely, where centrally imposed obligations are less likely to generate net national benefits, legal invalidation of the obligations should more readily be available, thus replicating the optimal result that would obtain if localities were able to bargain costlessly. For instance, even if states within a federation arguably should have a right to set their own tariffs, it may make sense to place the initial entitlement to impose tariffs on the central government, since that allocation avoids holdout problems and races to the bottom that would otherwise interfere with effective tariffs. Should states desire to set tariffs in particular cases, they may be able to purchase that right from the federal government. But it is less likely that transactions costs will interfere with an efficient purchase of that right by the states than that initial assignment of the right to impose tariffs to the states will preclude its efficient purchase by the federal government.

The conditional nature of specific grants implies that the entitlement initially rests with localities, that is, they have a right to reject the grant. This allocation is sensible insofar as grants concern issues that are plausibly, but not necessarily, national in scope. The greater the case for local provision of the service, the stronger the case for any national involvement to take a conditional form, and then only where national involvement arguably reduces costs of interlocal bargains. For instance, nonpolluting localities might bargain with polluting localities to induce the latter not to pollute the former. But if several polluting and nonpolluting jurisdictions are involved, so that costs of negotiating a global settlement are high, central grants arguably perform the same function at lower transactions costs. At the same time, allocation of the entitlement to localities permits them to resist inappropriate central expansion beyond the opaque area in which central participation may be legitimate, though inessential.

Even if localities possess the initial entitlement to resist conditions, a locality facing positive transactions costs may accept a condition that does not reflect a Coasean bargain and that inappropriately allows expansion of federal authority. Assume, for instance, that a central government offers highway funds that would confer on the locality a $10,000,000 gain, but the grant contains a condition that the locality increase its minimum drinking age from 18 to 21. Assume further that the cost of that change to the locality is $1,000,000. Assume, finally, that the increase in the drinking age will benefit the central government by only $900,000. The condition that requires the locality to increase its drinking age is socially inefficient. Nevertheless, it may be retained in the grant. If Coasean bargaining were available, the locality should be able to pay the federal government (by taking a lower grant) something between $900,000 and $1,000,000 to eliminate the condition. It is conceivable, however, that no such bargain could be struck. The parties may have difficulty achieving agreement because they will confront difficulty verifying each other=s expressed preferences over bargaining outcomes, they may face significant enforcement costs, and they may have difficulty agreeing on a division of the bargaining surplus (Inman and Rubinfeld: 1997). Bargaining costs may also increase because the central government wants to impose a uniform drinking age throughout the country, and the locality must coordinate with other states that do not share its preferences (some states will already have minimum drinking ages of 21, so that they will require additional payments to bring them within the coalition against the grant). As a result, bargaining costs for the locality may exceed $100,000. In that case it will accept the inefficient condition that costs it $1,000,000 rather than pay those bargaining costs plus the (minimum) $900,000 compensation to the central government.

Legal Alternatives to Bargains to Constrain Expansive Grants

Given this possibility, are there other legal or structural constraints that could deter efforts by the central government to impose inefficient conditions in order to expand the scope of the central jurisdiction? As noted above with respect to compulsory grants, some structural constraint exists in the political process by which representatives are selected for the central legislature. Again, if legislators are selected geographically, then local constituents who would face higher service costs required by inefficient central conditions would theoretically obtain electoral redress against their representatives. Nevertheless, there is reason to be skeptical that this check would sufficiently limit inappropriate conditional grants. Central representatives would only be subject to electoral check if their behavior is sufficiently monitored, if their favoritism of the conditional grant were salient to a significant number of voters, and if there were no competing interest group that provided representatives with benefits for imposing the condition on localities. Each of these requirements is highly unlikely, as demonstrated in the example above. Given the large number of votes cast by central representatives, the salience of any one vote to a significant number of voters will be low. Hence monitoring all votes will have a low expected value; individual voters will instead tend to focus on issues of particular importance to them and to free ride on monitoring by others in other cases. In the example above, the costs of bargaining and of changing drinking ages will be difficult to calculate, so that only intensely interested voters (those who otherwise would have been able to drink at ages 18-20) are likely to incur those costs. That same group is also likely to include the primary parties with a sufficiently intense interest in the outcome that representatives' votes will be salient. And that group is likely to be outweighed in numbers and influence by competing groups who have organized to express concerns about drunk driving and underage drinking. The result is that political actors may respond to dominant interest groups even if that means expanding federal inducements of local processes beyond an ideal separation of local and central functions. Localities will not necessarily resist, because it may be worthwhile for central officials to satisfy dominant interests by distributing grant funds sufficient to "bribe" the localities notwithstanding the social inefficiency of the program. It is possible, however, to place some constraint on such behavior. If, for instance, the central government is subject to spending limits, it will be less able to act inefficiently with respect to one area (e.g., grants) while simultaneously acting in other areas of its interest.

Other checks may arise from divisions of powers within the central government. While it may be in the interest of the legislative branch to expand its reach in order to maximize electoral support, the executive branch which has to implement grant programs may not share the same incentives. Additionally, judicial review of conditional grants could constrain central officials from inducing localities to participate in areas that lack a need for central involvement. In theory, courts, armed with a way of gauging the proper reach of central authority, could invalidate grant conditions that exceeded that authority. The opacity of the dividing line between appropriate and inappropriate central intervention suggests, however, that judicial review will be of limited utility. Thus, at most, judicial review could address only the most egregious instances of federal incursions. Even those cases, however, may be inappropriate subjects for judicial review, since localities retain the entitlement simply to refuse the grant. In order to suggest that judicial intervention in the process is appropriate, one would essentially have to argue that localities are "coerced" by the benefits of the grant to accept the condition that they prefer to reject or that courts are better arbiters than the localities of determining whether the central "bribe" was offset by local benefits.

Nevertheless, there is some basis for inviting judicial review of conditional grants in some instances in order to protect the dividing line between central and local functions. In United States jurisprudence, the Congress possesses a constitutional power to spend "for the general welfare." Although Congress's ability to legislate outside of its constitutionally enumerated powers is restricted, (that is, the states retain residual governmental authority), the Supreme Court has authorized Congress to use its spending power and the conditional grant of federal funds even for purposes not included in the constitutional enumeration of federal functions. Congress has exercised this power to attach numerous conditions to expenditures that initially appear have some (relatively remote) relationship to the purpose of the federal program. For instance, the Court has upheld a condition that certain recipients of federal money refrain from engaging in political activities.[8]

Numerous commentators have suggested that Congress is prohibited from imposing "unconstitutional conditions" to require localities to alter their behavior in order to qualify for grant funds. The "unconstitutional conditions" doctrine presupposes that some centrally designed grant terms exceed the competence of the central government. As a doctrinal matter, this occurs where the central government conditions receipt of a benefit on the recipient's (1) forgoing an activity in which the recipient has a right to engage, or (2) engaging in an activity on terms that the recipient can typically refuse. This definition, however, seems overly broad. Read literally, it would foreclose many grants that properly fit within the objectives for grants. As long as the prior behavior of the locality was permissible, the grant, if successful, necessarily induces the locality to forgo an activity that it would otherwise have undertaken or to undertake an activity that it would otherwise have forgone.

Consider, for instance, the most prominent American case dealing with the scope of permissible federal conditions. In *South Dakota v. Dole*,[9] Congress enacted a law that, as in the example above, withheld federal highway funds from any state that

[8] State of Oklahoma v. United States Civil Service Commission, 330 U.S. 127 (1947).
[9] 483 U.S. 203 (1987).

did not establish a statutory minimum age of 21 for the purchase or possession of alcoholic beverages. The state of South Dakota, which allowed persons over 19 to possess and purchase certain alcoholic beverages, claimed that the legislation exceeded Congress' constitutional authority. The Supreme Court concluded that Congress could, as it had in this case, use its spending power to achieve indirectly purposes on which it might not be able to legislate directly. That is, even if Congress would have been precluded from enacting a nationwide minimum drinking law, it was not precluded from achieving the same objective through the use of its spending power and the conditional grant of federal funds. The Court, however, did not conclude that the spending power was absolute or that Congress could attach any conditions that it deemed desirable. But the restrictions on Congressional use of its spending power were quite narrow. As long as spending was in pursuit of the "general welfare," contained unambiguous conditions that clearly indicated to the recipients the obligations undertaken by receipt of the funds, and imposed only conditions related to the federal interest in particular projects, conditional grants were permissible. The Court further reiterated that nothing in its federalism jurisprudence that might preclude Congress from regulating affairs of individual states restricted Congress from offering benefits to a state dependent on cooperation by the state with federal objectives. In so concluding, the Court rejected allegations that the conditions placed on grants of federal funds could effectively coerce the states into submission, thus compromising their autonomy. Only if the condition itself required the states to commit unconstitutional acts would the required activity constitute an improper exercise of Congressional spending power.

Notwithstanding what appeared to be a broad grant of authority to Congressional conditions for grants, the Court conceded that "in some circumstances the financial inducement offered by Congress might be so coercive as to pass the point at which 'pressure turns into compulsion.'"[10] In that event, the Court intimated, the unconstitutional conditions doctrine might be used to invalidate the conditions to the grant. The Court, however, was silent on the types of cases that might fall within that category or on any tests by which it might be applied. Subsequent efforts by commentators to fashion such a test have proven remarkably unsuccessful. The mere existence of a condition that alters the behavior of localities, of course, cannot be the measure of inappropriate coercion, since the very objective of categorical grants is to induce behavioral change. Nevertheless, some degree of "germaneness" is perhaps appropriate to draw a limit to the conditions that the central government must attach to the grant. As Justice O'Connor indicated in a dissent in the South Dakota case, there must be some relationship between the condition stated and the federal purpose to be achieved. (Justice O'Conner concluded that regulation of the minimum drinking age was insufficiently related to interstate highway construction to justify the condition imposed on funds appropriated for that purpose.)

While the degree of "germaneness" that is present in any particular case and that is necessary in order to render a condition permissible will always be contestable, the notion that there is some appropriate limitation on conditions is consistent with the

[10] 483 U.S. at 211.

view that grants ideally reflect bargains between central and local governments. The existence of an unrelated condition in a grant may be a signal that the central government is attempting to alter local behavior for some purpose other than generating spillover benefits or solving collective action problems linked to the grant at issue. Instead, the attachment of the unrelated condition may indicate a central government's use of monopoly power over funding to impose costs on localities in excess of national benefits and purchase at a lower than "market" rate an entitlement that is initially awarded to the localities.

LOCAL MISUSE OF BLOCK GRANTS

As noted above, the Swedish system of grants has moved primarily to a system of block grants to municipalities. I have suggested above that these grants do not necessarily satisfy the ideal functions of general grants. In theory, block grants permit localities more flexibility in providing services. Hence, they can increase interlocal competition for residents and tax base, and can allow greater preference satisfaction for mobile residents. In practice, however, the Swedish system does not necessarily achieve those objectives. Because localities face constraints on expenditures, both from the requirements that they provide certain services and from the obligation to enact a balanced budget, block grants may offer limited additional discretion to local officials to satisfy local preferences. In addition, the central government may adjust the size of block grants to limit the discretion of local officials. For instance, the central government apparently responded to municipal efforts to sell housing companies by reducing block grants in an amount approximately equivalent to what was received in those sales, thus negating any additional fiscal flexibility that the municipalities might have obtained through the block grant system.

Nevertheless, local officials will inevitably retain some discretion in deciding how to expend grant funds. Block grants carry fewer specific requirements than conditional grants, even if the funds of each are dedicated to the same general municipal function. The relatively open-ended nature of block grants allows localities greater discretion to advance local autonomy. Simultaneously, however, the system permits localities greater capacity to use grants contrary to the interests of the central government that grants them and to local constituents.

In theory, block grants increase expenditures on public goods by shifting the grantee's budget line so that it intersects with a higher indifference curve of the grantee. Grants from the central government, therefore, can theoretically compensate for any "undertaxation" that might occur at the local level as a result of tax competition among localities. Block grants also permit localities to control unit costs and to make decisions about final output. To this extent, localities also may compete with each other about the specific use of funds for the same specific purpose, such as child care in the Swedish system. This competition should allow individuals in a relatively mobile population to gravitate to the jurisdiction that offers their favored allocation of goods and services. Consequently, there will be a better match between constituent preferences and local services.

To the extent that block grants are intended to increase local autonomy, there are few accountability issues that arise between the central and local governments. The central government's interest is satisfied by the increase in local autonomy, not the target of the expenditure. Local officials who autonomously decide to use grant funds for other than public purposes may be subject to local electoral redress, but do not necessarily violate any central government sanction.

The possibility of electoral redress, however, indicates that block grants do raise accountability issues between the locality and it constituents. Local constituents are likely to believe that all public funds, regardless of their source, should be used to provide goods and services that constituents prefer. Nevertheless, block grants may be more susceptible to misuse, simply because those constituents have less incentive to monitor the use of externally generated funds than of funds derived from taxes and fees that those constituents pay. Local constituents may believe that grants consist of "other people's" money and thus be less concerned with its expenditure. That is, constituents may not see funds from block grants as equivalent to foregone tax increases.

The reduced local monitoring of block grants may become manifest in a variety of ways. First, a block grant may induce expenditures that the locality would not make with locally generated funds. Thus, groups that can influence expenditure decisions at the local level will be able to distort spending decisions, just as groups that can organize at the central level will be able to distort expenditure decisions under a system of conditional grants. It is unclear where the level of distortion is greater. For instance, Gustafsson, Kjulin and Schwarz conclude that the shift in Sweden from specific to matching grants led to a decrease in construction of child-care facilities (because matching grants for that purpose disappeared) and to an increase in the number of children per care center. But that conclusion does not mean that the prior level of child-care facility construction was optimal, only that it was greater than it was subsequently.

As with the case of the central government's expansive use of conditional grants, therefore, evaluation of a locality's use of block grant funds requires some metric for determining "misuse." One might think that misuse is inherent in idiosyncratic uses. That is, if localities ultimately have access to roughly equal fiscal resources, but one provides vastly different levels of mandated services, one might conclude that the outlier locality is diverting grant funds to inappropriate purposes. But the very notion of local autonomy suggests that different localities will have different preferences for public goods. Thus, a locality that provides a level of water and sewage service below the average may simply be signaling that its constituents prefer that a larger percentage of the local budget be devoted to other local public goods rather than that it is siphoning funds to inappropriate uses.

Second, there is the possibility that block grant funds will not be used in a manner consistent with median-voter preferences, which presumably would favor public expenditures that create commensurate private wealth effects. Instead, imperfectly constrained public officials arguably spend grant funds for their own purposes. The existence and extent of this "flypaper effect" remains controversial. According to Oates (1994), criticisms include (1) claims that perceptions of the flypaper effect reflect improperly understood grant terms (Chernick: 1979); (2) claims that any perceived effect is actually consistent with responsive government (Hamilton: 1986); and (3) claims that the flypaper effect accurately reveals the presence of budget-maximizing bureaucrats and the use of fiscal illusion.

It is difficult to design efficient devices that would deter misuses of grant funds by local officials. Judicial review provides a poor mechanism for checking expenditures from municipal budgets. Budgetary decisions are polycentric, requiring attention to multiple variables simultaneously and accommodating trade-offs among municipal services. The local budgetary process, therefore, is far more amenable to the legislative forum of fact-finding and compromise than to the winner-take-all, bilateral system of adjudication. Courts, therefore, largely refuse to review budgetary decisions. The rare exceptions involve only those expenditures that fall so far outside the norms of municipal functions that they fail to satisfy any plausible public purpose.

The potential for local officials to divert grant funds is often attributed to aspects of fiscal illusion. Perhaps the most effective legal mechanism that can be employed to counter these tendencies is to require a certain level of fiscal transparency or other form of disclosure about the use of grants. Fiscal transparency, for instance, has been used in some jurisdictions in the United States to counter the incentives of central governments to impose unfunded mandates on decentralized jurisdictions. Some states have required any unfunded mandate to be accompanied by a "fiscal note" that provides details concerning the costs of the mandate to the affected jurisdictions. Disclosure of this financial impact does not preclude the central government from imposing it, but does make the costs of the program salient and more accessible to potential opponents. Hence, the transparency of information facilitates the organization of groups that might oppose proposed expenditures or review programs to determine whether their costs are worth incurring. Similar "sunshine" requirements for grant expenditures may include itemization requirements for appropriations, limitations on the capacity of a locality to transfer funds itemized as intended for one purpose to another purpose, and "single-subject" requirements that deter logrolling among legislators within an appropriation item. Like fiscal notes, these requirements are expected to provide more visible information to potential monitors of the municipal budget, including ombudsman, political opponents of current local officials, and the press. Appropriation ordinances, however, cannot be required to particularize expenditures with minute precision. In addition, before third parties could determine whether an expenditure was a "misuse," there would have to be some mechanism for evaluating local preferences to determine the fit between the expenditure and those preferences. As a result, these constraints provide, at best, rough disincentives against misuse of grant funds.

A final corrective against misuse may simply lie in the interjurisdictional competition that is implicit in a nationwide block grant program. Sweden's grant program, for instance, purports to confer significantly equal financial resources on all municipalities. The announced objective of the equalization program inaugurated in 1996 was to enable all municipalities to offer their inhabitants "the same standard at the same price." As noted above, if resources are equal, then differences in the level of municipal services should reflect differences in constituent preferences. In a relatively small country like Sweden, differences among municipal services should themselves be transparent. The fact that all municipalities must offer the same services facilitates interjurisdictional comparisons, and thus provides an accessible, if imprecise, metric for determining whether the officials of any particular municipality are making appropriate use of public funds, regardless of their source. Assuming mobility among residents, municipalities that did not provide services consistent in quality or price with constituent preferences would lose residents to municipalities that did.

If interjurisdictional competition is a valuable check on the capacity of local officials to misuse public funds, additional forms of competition conceivably would confer additional benefits. For instance, local services may frequently compete not only with similar services offered by other localities, but also with similar services offered by the private sector. Gustafsson, Kjulin, and Schwarz, for instance, suggest that child care has few of the characteristics of a pure public good. As a result, one would anticipate that private day-care centers could compete with municipally funded centers. Competition between public and private providers of the same service might provide a more significant incentive towards efficient provision than interjurisdictional competition. The latter implies that localities compete with respect to *packages* of public goods and depends on significant constituent mobility. Residents who favored municipality A over municipality B with respect to one service might remain in B because the entire package of services that B offers provides a superior combination to the one offered by A. If that is the case, however, officials of B receive no indication that they may be providing a suboptimal level of that one service.

Competition between a public provider of a service and a private provider of the same service within that municipality allows competitive forces to work with respect to that one service in isolation. In addition, constituents can "vote with their feet" between public and private services in the same jurisdiction without uprooting themselves physically from investments in homes, friends, and jobs. These features suggest that privatization and voucher systems that compete with, but that do not necessarily displace, municipal provision may help to minimize misuse of municipal resources, especially those that are less susceptible to monitoring than tax resources. Nevertheless, it remains to be seen whether such systems confer net benefits in light of possible effects that competition would have on distribution of municipal services, the difficulty of introducing competition for municipal services that have characteristics of natural monopolies, the need to provide information to constituents in order to allow informed choice among alternative service providers, or the consequences for constituents who select a service that fails to perform adequately in the competitive environment.

CONCLUSION

Ideal grants can increase both efficiency and distributional objectives in a multijurisdictional nation. Each level of government, however, has incentives to use grants in a manner that deviates from those objectives and that instead increases its own authority. Implicit bargains and political markets can provide some constraints on those incentives. Legal and institutional structures can similarly be employed to assign entitlements and create legal obligations that counter misuse of grant terms. Given the difficulty of defining and monitoring misuse, these incentives will necessarily be imperfect. But any efforts to design relations between central governments and localities should consider the extent to which such mechanisms may help to achieve the objectives for which grants are made.

Based on the analysis of this paper, possible recommendations for the situation of Swedish include the following:

Constitutional provisions that delineate the roles of central and decentralized government should provide a more detailed allocation of authority than is currently the case. In this way, the background entitlements against which the bargaining over grant terms must exist will be clearer.

Constitutional allocations of local autonomy should be enforceable through judicial review. This would include judicial development of doctrines that limit the extent to which the central government could impose conditions on the receipt of grant funds, similar to the "unconstitutional conditions" doctrine in United States law. While any doctrine is necessarily vague, it creates a disincentive against the inappropriate expansion of central power into matters of purely local concern.

Bargains should be facilitated by the recognition of legal limits on the ability of the central government to impose conditions on localities. While these legal limits may be vague, they implicitly recognize the capacity of localities to resist the expansion of central jurisdiction that does not have offsetting benefits.

In order to increase local autonomy, block grants to localities should exceed the amounts necessary for localities to fund centrally mandated expenditures.

In order to increase the transparency, and hence the accountability, of local expenditures block grants should be accompanied by specific reporting and publication requirements that facilitate the distribution of information to residents of the recipient concerning grant fund expenditures.

In order to increase competition and efficiency in the delivery of local public goods, grant funds should be available to private entities within the locality as well as to the locality itself.

REFERENCES

Baker, L.A. (1995) "Conditional Federal Spending After Lopez", *Columbia Law Review* 95, 1911.

Boadway, R. (2001) "Inter-Governmental Fiscal Relations: The Facilitator of Decentralization", *Constitutional Political Economy* 12, 91.

Chernick, H.A. (1979) "An Economic Model of the Distribution of Project Grants," in Peter Mieszkowski and William H. Oakland (eds.) *Fiscal Federalism and Grants-In-Aid*, Washington D.C.: The Urban Institute, 81-103.

Chernick, H.A., Fiscal Equalisation Between Swedish Municipalities. [chapter 4 of this volume].

Cooter, Robert C. (2000) *The Strategic Constitution*. Princeton, N.J.

Cullis, J. and Philip Jones (1998) *Public Finance and Public Choice*. Oxford. 2nd ed.

Dahlberg, M. (2001) *A Brief Inspection of the Revenue Side for Swedish Municipalities*. [paper prepared for the meeting of our group in Bonn in October 2001].

Dahlberg, M. and Eva Johansson (2002) "On the Vote Purchasing Behavior of Incumbent Governments," *American Political Science Review* 96(1), 27-40.

Gramlich, E. M. (1977) "Intergovernmental Grants: A Review of the Empirical Literature", in Wallace E. Oates (ed.) *The Political Economy of Fiscal Federalism*: Lexington MA: D.C. Heath and Co.

Gustafsson, B., Urban Kjulin, and Brita Schwarz (2002) "Central-Local Government Relations in Transition: The Case of Swedish Child Care", *Public Choice* 110, 305-325.

Hamilton, J.H. (1986) "The Flypaper Effect and the Deadweight Loss from Taxation" *Journal of Urban Economics* 19, 148-155.

Hills, R. M. Jr. (1998) "The Political Economy of Cooperative Federalism: Why State Autonomy Makes Sense and 'Dual Sovereignty' Doesn't." *Michigan Law Review* 96, 813.

Hume, D. (1963) "On the Independency of Parliament", in David Hume, *Essays: Moral, Political and Literary*. Oxford University Press. London.

Inman, R. P. and Daniel L. Rubinfeld (1997) "Making Sense of the Antitrust State-Action Doctrine: Balancing Political Participation and Economic Efficiency in Regulatory Federalism", *Texas Law Review* 75, 1203.

David N. King (1984) *Fiscal Tiers: The Economics of Multi-Level Government*. George Allen & Unwin. London.

Oates, W.E. (1994) "Federalism and Government Finance," in John M. Quigley and Eugene Smolensky (eds.) *Modern Public Finance*, Cambridge, MA: Harvard University Press, 126-151.

Peterson, P. E. (1995) *The Price of Federalism*, Brookings Institution. Washington, D.C.

Rubinfeld, D. (2001) "Structuring Intergovernmental Grants to Local Governments: Lessons from South Africa." *Constitutional Political Economy* 12, 173.

Swedish Institute (2001) *Fact Sheets on Sweden*.

United States Census Bureau (2001) *Government Finances 1998-99*.

6

DEMOCRATIC GOVERNANCE AND LOCAL AUTONOMY

Olof Petersson*

SNS, The Center for Business and Policy Studies, Stockholm

INTRODUCTION

Multilevel democracy means that the citizens belong to several democratic associations at one and the same time: at the local, regional, national and European levels. The fact that this concept has now become established marks a turning-point in the history of political ideas. For centuries philosophers have attempted to discover the most appropriate size for a working community. The village was long deemed to be the ideal; democracy was considered to work best in small communities in which everyone knew everyone else. After the American and French revolutions, the nation state came to be seen as the natural foundation of democratic institutions.

The quest for that perfect size has now been discontinued. It is no longer an either/or question. Multilevel democracy means that democratic units can exist in parallel. The question rather is how the broad notion of multilevel democracy is to be implemented through working institutions.

There are, in fact, two major problems that must be dealt with if multilevel democracy is to be made to work. Both democratic governance and local autonomy have to be realised simultaneously. From the point of view of democratic governance, the problem concerns how to establish working forms of government *within* the level in question. Viewed from the perspective of local autonomy, the problem involves how to structure the reciprocal power relations *between* the different levels.

A CURRENT DEMOCRATIC PROBLEM

As far as Sweden is concerned, the problem of multilevel democracy is of considerable immediate relevance. The contributions in this book make clear that opinion is also divided among researchers as to how power should be shared between the state, the regions and the municipalities. However, all are agreed that the current system does not function satisfactorily. From the point of view of the individual citizen, the problems have actually tended to get worse. Only a few years ago the inhabitants of Gothenburg were faced with just two ballot forms, one for the Riksdag (the national parliament) and one for the municipality. Today the people of

---

* www.sns.se/olof; translation by Frank G. Perry

Gothenburg are represented by politicians at six levels: the European Parliament, Västra Götaland (the county council), the Gothenburg region (indirectly elected), Gothenburg the municipality) and the neighbourhood council (also indirectly elected). How is the popular will to be realised in what is a far from transparent system?

In the Swedish domestic debate, discussion has focussed mainly on the intervention of central government in the work of the municipalities and the county councils. There are many examples of conflicts between the state and local self-government bodies. At the beginning of the 1990s, the government introduced a cap on taxation at the local level with the consent of parliament, despite the provisions of the constitution regarding local self-government and the freedom it accords the municipalities to levy taxation. The design of the rate-equalisation system has also resulted in controversy; the Law Council, for example, set aside a government bill on the matter as unconstitutional. The municipalities and the county councils have repeatedly complained that the courts and the civil service departments establish norms which impose limits on freedom of action at the local level. The conflicts surrounding the provisions of the Social Services Act and social assistance (income support) have attracted most attention in this regard. The municipalities have complained that the legislative provisions governing the right of the functionally impaired to support and service permit no local freedom of manoeuvre and have gone so far as to propose that this being the case the state should take over the entire responsibility. The selling-off by non-Socialist ruled municipalities of council housing and the privatisation of hospitals have led the Social Democratic government to intervene in local government affairs by various means that include legislation setting limits on local autonomy.

The government has appointed a commission of inquiry. "The debate on the regional issue makes clear that a concerted and long-term appraisal of the distribution of tasks and responsibilities among the different political levels of our society is required", the government announced as part of its bill on the organisation of the regions (prop. 2001/02:7).

The actions of central government also serve to illustrate the problems of multilevel democracy in other ways. When the government put forward proposals as part of its bill on democracy aimed at strengthening democratic governance, the focus of interest was on the municipalities (prop. 2001/02:80). One example is the right that has now been accorded the inhabitants of a municipality to put proposals before the municipal council. The state is intervening in the internal workings of local government bodies in order to increase the influence of the individual citizen. Democratic governance is being strengthened at the expense of local autonomy.

The problems of multilevel democracy also rank high on the political agenda as a consequence of Sweden's membership of the EU and the focus on the European Convention. One of the four issues given special priority in the Declaration of Nice in 2000 was this very relationship between the levels of political organisation in a democratic society: "The issue of how to establish and monitor a more precise delimitation of powers between the European Union and the Member States, reflecting the principle of subsidiarity."

The Declaration of Laeken in 2001 provides a description of the disappointment felt by the citizens. The institutions of the EU must be "brought closer to its citizens". Citizens "do not always see a connection between those goals and the Union's everyday action. They want the European institutions to be less unwieldy and rigid and, above all, more efficient and open." It was also felt that the Union should devote itself to its particular concerns, instead of intervening in every detail. The heads of state and government declared: "the citizens feel that deals are all too often cut out of their sight and they want better democratic scrutiny". One of the key areas highlighted was the problem of the vertical separation of powers: "A better division and definition of competence in the European Union."

The issue of the distribution of responsibilities between the EU and the member states is also dealt with in the Commission's white paper on European forms of government published in the summer of 2001. One of the primary tasks of the Convention on the Future of Europe is to put forward proposals on this matter to the Intergovernmental Conference.

DEMOCRATIC GOVERNANCE

Democracy, government by the people, popular sovereignty – such a broad ideal needs to be defined in greater detail if the discussion is to be made more applicable. In what follows democracy is defined as a political system that satisfies three requirements: popular, constitutional and effective government.

Popular government is the requirement derived from the principle of the sovereignty of the people. In a democracy, political decisions must embody the wishes of the citizens. Although individuals may have different interests, tastes, talents and incomes, democracy means that everyone enjoys the same right to participate in making decisions about the common affairs of a society. Democratic governance is based on the free formation of opinion. This means that a public sphere must exist for the exchange of information and for debate and criticism to take place. The citizens must also have the opportunity to participate actively in the shaping of their own future and that of society. Citizenship is based on a combination of rights and obligations; as a result, democracy imposes requirements of tolerance and respect for differences of opinion.

Constitutional government embodies the notion that power is bound by law and clearly defined. The citizen is guaranteed a number of fundamental rights and freedoms in relation to the state. An individual who considers that a right has been infringed is entitled to have the matter heard in an independent court of law. Constitutional government also imposes requirements in terms of due process. Public power is exercised under the law. The principle of the separation of powers is also an integral part of the rule of law. It follows from this principle that the public sector should be divided into various bodies with clearly defined mandates. A number of public authorities are charged with supervising and investigating other public bodies.

A working democracy also needs *effective government*. The aspirations of the citizens are turned into practical reality by formal decisions implemented by means of various forms of public administration and the exercise of public authority. The political system must have economic and other kinds of resources at its disposal. Democracy also requires decision-making capability, including procedures and institutions that can mutually adjust various interests and requirements so as to arrive at clear decisions. Popularly elected politicians also need the support of an effective and professional organisation which can produce a sustainable basis for decision-making and which can implement the decisions that have been reached democratically.

It is in the nature of things that these three elements cannot always be combined in a harmonious fashion. The freedom of action of the majority is circumscribed by the safeguards that constitutional government affords minorities. The quickest and most effective solution in economic terms may conflict with the accountability required by popular government and the procedural requirements of constitutional government. Dilemmas and the weighing of pros and cons are part of the very nature of democracy. One of the components of a democratic form of government must therefore be a continuous dialogue on value conflicts.

Popular, constitutional and effective government are values that may in turn be given greater specificity. Every society has to discover the institutions and decision-making rules which best suit the general values of democracy at any one time. Within the SNS Democratic Audit of Sweden, we have made use of this concept of democracy as the basis for assessing not only national politics in Sweden but also the municipalities and the EU. The concept can also be applied to central and local government administrative agencies and is currently a keyword in official administrative policy.

However, not everyone agrees that popular, constitutional and effective government are generally applicable. The debate on the EU shows that effective government is frequently given priority. From such a standpoint, the EU would gain greater legitimacy by becoming more effective at delivering results to the citizens. Some of the contributions to the debate on the future of the Swedish municipalities also place great, not to say one-sided, emphasis on economic effectiveness. The requirements of popular government for oversight, participation and collective decision-making risk being neglected in consequence.

A similar line of thought is to be found in the debate on the Swedish regions. Studies of the experiments in setting up regions show that all models have significant shortcomings from the point of view of democracy. Research has failed to find any sign that the new metropolitan region of Västra Götaland has brought politics closer to the citizens, even subjecting the data to microscopic examination. Nor do the good citizens of the county of Kalmar seem to have experienced any form of democratic "boost".

The requirements of democracy have had on occasion to give way to inter-regional and inter-municipal "networks and partnerships". The advantages of such cooperative solutions are considered to lie in their success in creating an effective development strategy capable of countering the growth in external competitiveness. The same trend applies to the regional growth agreements. Negotiations between the municipalities, the county councils, county administrative boards and industry are improving the capacity of the regions to take matters into their own hands.

The culture of consensus makes it more difficult, however, for the citizen to discern identifiable political alternatives. Politics appears to vanish behind the closed doors of meeting-rooms. Accountability becomes more difficult to exercise. The trends favouring "a flexible distribution of responsibilities" and "incremental decentralisation" lead to neglect of the principles of popular and constitutional government.

There are many indications that the kind of negotiated democracy currently being developed within the experimental regional areas fails to meet the fundamental requirements of democracy. This could make it tempting to redefine democracy. Another option is either to abolish the regions entirely or to develop regional democracy in earnest.

LOCAL AUTONOMY

Multilevel democracy requires some form of distribution between the different levels of political organisation. It is by no means obvious, however, what exactly should be distributed between the levels. A distinction has to be drawn here between powers and resources.

A classification frequently used in political science takes the distribution of powers as it starting-point. This makes it possible to distinguish between confederations (where power is derived from below), federal states and unitary states (where power comes from above).

When economists refer to decentralisation they usually mean the distribution of resources, primarily economic ones. Powers and resources need not always go hand in hand. There are centralised federal states just as there are decentralised unitary states.

Another interesting aspect of multilevel democracies is the issue of who has the power to change the way power is allocated. In confederations the authority remains with the constituent member states; the powers delegated to the confederal level can be withdrawn with immediate effect.

Federal states constitute a half-way-house, a kind of compromise between the confederation and the unitary state. A federal model of this kind is based on several fundamental principles. There must be some form of vertical separation of powers. This form of allocation of authority means that political power is shared between the central and the regional level. Federalism also presupposes some degree of autonomy. Each level enjoys the power of self-determination within its own domain, the constituent states also have a constitutionally guaranteed power over their internal affairs. Federal states are also based on a principle of participation. The member states have the right to codetermination at the central level. As a result federal states usually have a bicameral parliament, in which one chamber represents the population of the entire federation and another chamber represents the member states. Usually there is also an arbitration process in place for the resolution of conflicts between the federation and the member states.

Unitary states are based on a different model. The competence to change the allocation of responsibilities rests in this case with the central state power. The state may of course delegate various tasks to local bodies but such delegation is always conditional. Where conflicts arise it is the state which has the final say.

Sweden cannot be placed unequivocally within any of these absolute models. Certain aspects of the Swedish polity clearly demonstrate that the country is a unitary state. It is parliament that passes local government legislation and the government that rules the realm. This is, however, not the whole picture; the municipalities are not simply local bodies for the administration of central government decisions. The Instrument of Government stipulates that local self-government is one of the cornerstones of Swedish democracy and that the municipalities may raise taxes in order to carry out their duties. Sweden is also a signatory to the European Convention on Local Self-Government.

Nor can the EU be characterised in terms of any one of the abstract models of political science. The EU lacks "authorising authority", i.e. the competence to change its own constitution, nor does it have the right to levy taxation. The EU, however, is far more than a confederation. The dimension of supranationality means that a member state can be forced to accept decisions against its will in those areas where majority voting applies. Community law also takes precedence over national law.

The aspiration to achieve a clearer division of areas of responsibility between the EU and its member states has been a principal theme in the debate of recent years. The Laeken Declaration devotes considerable attention to the problem. The European Council declared in Laeken that "the important thing is to clarify, simplify and adjust the division of competence between the Union and the Member States in the light of the new challenges facing the Union. This can lead both to restoring tasks to the Member States and to assigning new missions to the Union, or to the extension of existing powers."

The model referred to in the Laeken Declaration, and now being discussed in the European Convention, takes as its starting-point a clearer distinction of three sorts of competence: powers exclusive to the EU, the powers of the member states and powers shared between the Union and the member states.

Federal states have particular experience of ways of regulating the distribution of power between territorial levels. The allocation of authority can be arranged in several ways: by specification, by constitutional stipulations of principle or by contractual arrangements.

A common technique is to inscribe in the constitution which areas are the domain of the constituent states, which issues are the province of central government and in which areas responsibility may be shared. In the debate on the future of the EU, several contributors have proposed a similar arrangement based on an inventory of some kind, a catalogue of powers, listing who has the authority to decide about what.

Other contributors, however, warn that a legally binding document of this kind would prove too rigid and would hinder the dynamism and flexibility of the Union.

A different model, or possibly a complementary one, involves inserting a broad principle into the constitution as a guide to directing the allocation of tasks. Something of this kind would already seem to exist in the EU, namely the principle of subsidiarity. The Treaty of the European Community states: "In areas which do not fall within its exclusive competence, the Community shall take action, in accordance with the principle of subsidiarity, only if and in so far as the objectives of the proposed action cannot be sufficiently achieved by the Member States and can therefore, by reason of the scale or effects of the proposed action, be better achieved by the Community." This article may be broadly interpreted as a principle of decentralisation. The EU may not intervene if the member states are capable of dealing with the matter. But the wording is so general and vague that it rarely provides specific guidance as to whether an issue is the province of the EU or the member states.

A further method is to negotiate agreements. The various levels can agree to be bound by contracts with one another. Many areas of German politics are characterised by a cooperative federalism of this kind. In Sweden we have related experience of various forms of agreement between the government on the one side and representatives of local government bodies on the other, the Association of County Councils in particular.

As many contributors have indicated in the current debate on future developments, it is not enough to agree to a particular division of tasks once and for all. A dynamic perspective must also be incorporated which would allow for the possibility of reassigning responsibility among the levels.

This brings us to the issue of how the powers in question may be put into practice. Considering the matter from a more process-oriented perspective of this kind focuses attention on how the exercise of authority is to be monitored. Multilevel democracy requires a continuous process of scrutiny. A working group within the European Convention has proposed setting up an "early warning system" of a political nature, intended to reinforce the monitoring by national parliaments of compliance with the principle of subsidiarity. There would also be a broadened possibility of referral to the Court of Justice for non-compliance with the principle of subsidiarity.

The existence of various practical methods for achieving a more clearly-defined allocation of responsibility should not, however, obscure the fact that the problems of multilevel democracy in this context are actually concerned with a single, simple question. What should the EU do and what should member states do?

LINKS BETWEEN DEMOCRATIC GOVERNANCE AND LOCAL AUTONOMY

The two key problems of multilevel democracy, democratic governance and local autonomy, may be addressed separately, but there are also important interconnections between them.

Links of a causal nature are evident in the current process of transformation of the EU. The ongoing enlargement of the EU necessarily involves changes to the decision-making processes. An ever-increasing number of member states means that the unanimity rule will increase the likelihood of deadlock. Since it is enough for a single member state to oppose a measure for it to fail, the EU could soon end up in decision-making paralysis. Enlargement is therefore leading to an increased use of decisions based on qualified majority voting. This decision-making model means that member states run a greater risk of being brushed aside by the others. As a result member states are increasingly interested in defining in advance which matters the EU may, and may not, decide. Consequently the division of competence between the EU and the member states is becoming an increasingly vital issue.

The ideals of democratic governance can be made use of as the basis for a discussion of the various means of establishing local autonomy. It follows that the alternative models of local autonomy may also be evaluated from the perspective of democratic governance.

The requirement for popular government would favour maximising the possibilities of exerting influence and thus the number of levels. The local level also enjoys an advantage in terms of making possible direct participation by the citizens. However, the principle of popular government also imposes requirements for tolerance and political equality. Constitutional government makes demands on the organisation of the state in terms of predictability, due process and respect for rights and freedoms. When multilevel democracy is evaluated in terms of effective government on the other hand, it is qualities such as flexibility, decision-making capacity and efficiency that come to the fore.

Even this brief survey demonstrates that multilevel democracy encompasses several dilemmas with major implications. Each level within the organisation of political life must be characterised by democracy internally, while also being capable of effective functioning externally. On the one hand local government bodies insist on self-determination, and yet they also seek access to central government. Small bodies are closer at hand to the decisions they make whereas large bodies control greater resources. Adaptation to local conditions argues in favour of decentralisation, equal treatment calls for centralisation. The distribution of existing resources is facilitated by a centralised organisation, while innovation and dynamism are favoured by a decentralised environment.

As long as we want a democratic society capable of making a reality of several different ideals, value conflicts and dilemmas of this kind will be unavoidable. No expert can tell us how such conflicts should be managed. The task of finding the practical solutions is the province of democratically elected politicians and ultimately of the citizens themselves. (This chapter has no references.)

7

WHY FEDERALISM?

Dennis C. Mueller*

University of Vienna

INTRODUCTION

"If it ain't broke, don't fix it." This American adage, like many an adage, contains an important piece of advice. This paper attempts to provide answers for the question posed in the title. It also discusses the institutional structure that is needed to implement a proper federalist system, if one is desired. Thus, for any country like Sweden that does not already have a strong set of federalist institutions, it provides policy recommendations for the implementation of a strong federalist system. But before considering these recommendations, one must address the question raised by the adage. Is the current political structure broke? Is it sufficiently deficient in achieving its goals to warrant the constitutional and other institutional changes that would be required to create an effective federalism?

I shall assume that the objective in designing political institutions is to make them responsive to the wishes of the citizens, to make them produce the bundles of publicly provided goods and services that the citizens want. To achieve this objective a country's political institutions must satisfy two conditions: they must effectively supply the information concerning the bundles of goods and services that citizens want to those in the government, and they must provide incentives to ensure that those in government supply these public goods and services in the desired quantities and at the minimum cost. Thus, if a country's political institutions need fixing, they must be deficient in one or both of these tasks.

In this chapter I shall not attempt to demonstrate that Sweden's political institutions are deficient in accomplishing these tasks. By all measures of government size, Sweden has the largest public sector of any noncommunist country in the world. This could merely reflect a greater demand for publicly provided goods and services by Swedes than exists in any other noncommunist country, but it could also reflect a tendency for those in government to supply more goods and services than are demanded, or to supply them inefficiently.

Over the last two decades Sweden's income per capita has fallen from near the top in the world's ranking to the middle. Although there are probably several causes for this fall, certainly governmental policy failures cannot be ruled out.

Perhaps the best indicators of governmental failures, however, are the falling voter participation rates and survey evidence indicating declining support for political

* BWZ, Brünnerstrasse 72, A-1210 Vienna, Austria, dennis.mueller@univie.ac.at

parties and those in government that have been recorded over the last two decades. Although Sweden is not alone in the world in this respect, the fact that other countries' political institutions are failing — or at least are perceived by their citizens to be failing — is scant consolation for both those in government and those outside of it.

What might Sweden do to improve the performance of its political institutions? Although there are obviously many possible answers to this question, in this paper I shall take up only one of them — the introduction of a strong federalist system.[1] I shall also briefly discuss complementary institutional reforms involving the introduction of institutions of direct democracy and changes in electoral and parliamentary voting rules.

REVEALING CITIZEN PREFERENCES FOR PUBLIC GOODS

There are two essential conditions to justify introducing a federalist system to reveal citizen preferences for public goods.[2] First, there must exist public goods which provide benefits to only those living in specific parts of the country. We shall refer to these as *local* public goods. Second, the preferences of the citizens for one of these local public goods in one part of the country must differ from those in at least some other parts. The reasons why both of these conditions are necessary are rather obvious. If there are no local public goods, then one only needs political institutions that record citizen preferences across the entire nation for the national public goods. Even with local public goods, there is no need for local political institutions if the preferences for the local public goods are the same in all local communities. A single level of local public good provision will be optimal in all local communities and could be decided in the national parliament. Even with different preferences for local public goods across the local communities, it is conceivable that these preferences could be revealed in national elections. But as the number of local public goods and heterogeneity of preferences across local communities grows, the complexity of information required at the national level grows to such a level that local governments become optimal as institutions for revealing individual preferences for local public goods. Thus, the second necessary condition for introducing a federalist system is that the information needed to provide local public goods optimally can be obtained more accurately through a system of democratically elected local governments than through a democratic central government.

Our story could end here, if there were no spillovers across communities from the consumption of local public goods. Such spillovers are likely to be present, however. For example, the citizens of community *A* occasionally drive in *B*. They have, therefore, an interest in the quality of roads in *B*. If road construction and maintenance is treated as a local public good, then it creates an inter-jurisdictional

---

[1] Although the growing disenchantment with those in government might not be a direct result of some specific failure of Sweden's federalist system, increasing the transparency of the system and the strength of a citizen's voice in it might serve to reduce the level of disenchantment.

[2] I shall generally refer only to public goods, but by these I mean also public services, policies to correct for externalities, and so on.

externality. We turn now to a discussion of the issues raised by cross-community spillovers in a federalist system.

IMPOSING EXPENDITURE CONSTRAINTS

To simplify the discussion I shall continue to discuss the issues surrounding federalism as if they involved only two communities, *A* and *B*. Each community is responsible for the construction and maintenance of the roads in its territory. The citizens of *B* opt for a system of roads that is of lower quality than that in *A*, and this decision adversely affects the citizens of *A* when they travel in *B*. The population of *A* exceeds that of *B*, and *A* thus proposes at the central level of government minimum standards for road quality that match those in *A*. *A*'s population allows it to impose its level of standards on *B*. The externality is resolved.

There is no reason to expect that it is resolved optimally, however. The *A*s are better off, the *B*s, however, are worse off, since they must devote more resources to roads than they deem optimal. More resources for roads means less resources for other things. Either other local public goods, like education, must be cut back, or private consumption. In either case, the loss to the *B*s from this cut back could exceed the gains to the *A*s. The fact that the *A*s vote for minimum standards of road quality tells us that they are better off as a result of these standards, but it does not tell us by *how much* they are better off. Their gain could be large relative to the loss to the *B*s, or tiny. Allowing the central government to impose expenditure constraints on local governments is not the optimal way to deal with spillovers across communities caused by local public goods.

A second argument for centrally imposed expenditure constraints does not rely on the existence of spillovers, but rather citizen mobility and tax competition. The citizens of both *A* and *B* favor the same level of road quality and taxes to pay for it. If *B* decides to cut quality and taxes, however, citizens of *A* migrate to *B*, and *A* is forced to cut quality and taxes to stop the outward migration. This forces further cuts by *B* and a *race to the bottom* ensues with road quality along with taxes going to zero. By agreeing at the central level to impose minimum quality standards, this race to the bottom is avoided and the citizens of both communities are made better off.

Like all race-to-the-bottom arguments, this one presumes that the local public goods are not financed by benefit taxes. When benefit taxes are used, the race to the bottom disappears and with it the justification for centrally imposed expenditure constraints.

To see what is involved, consider the simple case of the local public good trash collection. Some people prefer one pick-up per week, others prefer two and are willing to pay the higher taxes that go with two pick-ups. Two hundred thousand people live in *A* and of these 110,000 prefer two pick-ups. Of the 100,000 residents of *B*, 45,000 prefer two pick-ups. If each community decides the number of trash pick-ups using the simple majority rule, there will be two pick-ups in *A*, and one in *B* (see Table 1).

Table 1: Initial Distribution of Population Across Two Communities

	Community A	Community B
Two pick-ups	110,000	45,000
One pick-up	90,000	55,000
Total	200,000	100,000

Following the usual race-to-the-bottom argument, if we now allow mobility between the two communities, migration from *A* to *B* will commence, and *A* will be forced to lower the quality of its trash pick-up service. But only the 90,000 residents of *A* who prefer one pick-up have an incentive to move. The 110,000 *A*s who are in the majority are receiving the exact level of services that they desire and have no incentive to move. Moreover, the 45,000 *B*s who would like two pick-ups a week have an incentive to move to *A*. With perfect mobility an equilibrium will be reached in which there are 155,000 people in *A* enjoying two pick-ups per week, and 145,000 in *B* enjoying one. Instead of a race to the bottom, we have a stable equilibrium with different levels of service provided in the two communities, we have the Pareto optimal outcome first described by Tiebout (1956).

If the level of services is decided at the central governmental level by say a simple majority vote across the two communities, there will be two pick-ups per week in both communities, since in aggregate 155,000 favor this outcome against the 145,000 favoring one. If the population is distributed as in Table 1, those living in *A* are neither better nor worse off under the centrally imposed level of service. In *B*, however, 55,000 citizens are made worse off as opposed to 45,000 who are made better off. If we assume that the net gain to someone from having the collective decision go her way is the same on average for members of each group — an assumption that would justify the use of the simple majority rule to make the collective decision[3] — then even when there is no mobility across communities, a centrally imposed level of service imposes a net welfare loss on society.[4]

We conclude that social welfare cannot be increased, and is likely to be reduced through the imposition of centrally imposed standards or minimum expenditure constraints. This conclusion rests on our assumption that local public goods and services are financed using benefit taxes. We discuss this option further below.[5]

---

[3] See May (1952), Rae (1969) and Mueller (2003, Ch. 6).

[4] Clayton Gillette (2001) has examined the arguments for centrally imposed expenditure constraints on local communities in the United States and concluded that they did not in general appear to resolve prisoners' dilemma problems among local communities.

[5] Our discussion has focussed only on individuals. Most race-to-the-bottom examples deal with immobile individuals and perfectly mobile capital. Perfect capital mobility does not suffice to create a race-to-the-bottom problem, however, *if* benefit taxes are used to tax capital. See, Oates and Schwab (1988).

INTER-JURISDICTIONAL EXTERNALITIES AND TRANSFERS

Let us return to our example of road expenditures. Assume that it would cost an additional 50m SK beyond what the citizens of *B* are willing to pay to raise the quality of its road system to that of *A*. Such an improvement in the quality of *B*'s roads would confer 50m SK in total benefits to citizens of *A*. *B*'s citizens would also benefit from the better roads, of course. Let us say that their benefits amounted to 30m SK. Since 30m is less than 50m, *B* is not willing to improve the quality of its roads out of its own money, but it would gain from an additional 50m SK expenditure on its roads if it, say, only had to finance half of this amount. A possible Pareto-improvement exists through a Coasian bribe from *A* to *B*. If *A* were to cover, say, half of the costs of the road improvements and *B* the other half, citizens in both communities would be better off.

When a cross-community spillover gives rise to such a Pareto-improving transaction between two or more communities, it will of course be the case that *both* communities benefit from the transaction. If a referendum were held in each community to approve the transaction, it would pass in each. Grants from central governments to local governments resemble the kind of Coasian transaction just described in so far as they involve efforts by the central government to induce local governments to spend more on specific local public goods, or perhaps just in general. Such grants differ from the example just given, however, in that they are not initiated by separate votes in each community. When a federal grant to a community *B* effectively involves a transfer from *A* to *B*, it is possible that the citizens of *A* would in fact not approve the transfer, if given a chance to vote on it as a separate item. If the transfer is decided at the central governmental level, such separate votes are not taken. The grant may come into existence because there are enough votes coming from *B* to offset the opposition from *A*. To ensure that intergovernmental grants do represent Pareto-improving responses to cross-community spillovers, they should not be decided by the central government using the simple majority rule, but should require approval of *all* local communities separately. Otherwise there is no way to differentiate between a Pareto-improving response to an inter-community externality and a simple redistributive transfer from one community to another.[6]

A consistent finding in the empirical literature on inter-governmental grants is the existence of a "flypaper effect." The amount spent by a local government out of a grant generally exceeds the amount one would expect to spent, *if the local government were maximizing the welfare of its citizens.*[7] One obvious explanation for this over expenditure is that the local government may not be trying to

---

[6] If the unanimity rule were used in the parliament of the central government, one could be sure that any decision it made was a Pareto improvement, and no additional ratification procedures would be needed. I assume, however, that the parliament uses the simple majority rule, and thus that a coalition of net-recipient communities may succeed in gaining parliamentary approval for a program of central government grants merely because of their redistributive properties.

[7] The welfare of its citizens is usually taken to mean the preferences of the median voter. For surveys of this literature, see Inman (1979), Heyndels and Smolders (1994, 1995), Hines and Thaler (1995), Becker (1996) and Bailey and Connolly (1998).

maximize the welfare of its citizens or of the median voter. The average, rationally ignorant voter may not be aware of the size of the transfer from the central government, or at least of its magnitude. She may, therefore, not realize that some of the money contained in the grant could have been transferred to her through a reduction in her taxes. This ignorance on the part of voters provides bureaucrats in the government who benefit from larger budgets to pursue their goals at the voters' expense. Such reasoning explains why government may be "too large" in a federalist system, when money is collected at the central level and then transferred to local levels.[8] The possibility of rational ignorance on the part of voters, and a potential principal-agent problem between voters and those in government provides further support for the recommendation that inter-governmental grants to eliminate inter-community externalities should be approved by the citizens of all communities separately. Such approval might be given through referenda in each community.

RAISING TAX REVENUE AT THE CENTER

Inter-governmental grants to eliminate inter-community externalities should be distinguished from a system in which local communities use the central government to raise their tax revenue, because the central government is more efficient at raising tax revenue. To see what is involved, assume that the central government is responsible for running a federal judicial system, local governments are responsible for local courts. Businesses are subject to both federal and local laws and make use of both sets of courts. The benefits a business obtains from the state provision of laws and a judicial system can be reasonably assumed to be proportional to its value added. If β_f is the proportional benefit to a business from the federal government's provision of laws and a judicial system, then the benefit tax charged by the federal government for this service obviously should be a value-added tax with a rate of β_f.[9] If β_l is the proportional benefit to a business from the local government's provision of its judicial system, then the benefit tax charged by the local government should be a value-added tax with a rate of β_l. Rather than have each local government and the federal government set up its own tax collection authority, it may be more efficient to have the federal government collect all of the value-added tax and transfer its share to each local government. If the costs of providing judicial services were identical across all local communities, a single value-added tax rate would apply to the entire country. If the costs of providing judicial services differ across local communities, perhaps because the quality of services provided differs, then each community might set a different value-added tax rate. A business' value-added tax would equal $\beta_f + \beta_l$, but β_l would now differ from one local community to another. If the benefits from other locally provided government services were also proportional to a business' value-added, β_l could be further increased to cover the costs for these services. Each local community would be responsible for setting its own level of services and taxes, but the federal government would be responsible for administering the value-added tax for all levels of government. The benefits from a

---

[8] For additional discussion and evidence, see Wilde (1968, 1971) and Grossman (1989a,b).

[9] Note also that this tax should be a value added tax based on the *production* of the business not on its consumption, as is the form of taxation in the European Union.

centralized tax administration can be enjoyed along with the benefits from a decentralized system of tax and expenditure policy.

Before closing this discussion of stacking taxes it is perhaps worth pausing to demonstrate that such stacking in a federalist system does not lead to economic inefficiencies, *if each level of government imposes benefit taxes.* To see why tax stacking might lead to inefficiencies consider the following example. Firm A produces 100 widgets per year and has a value added of 1000. The local government decides to levy a VAT of 10% on all firms in its territory. Firm A must raise its widget price to cover the tax, output falls to 90, value added falls to 900 and the local government collects 90 in tax revenue from A. Now suppose that the federal government decides to levy an additional value added tax of 10%. Output now falls to 80, value added falls to 800 and the federal government collects 80 in tax revenue from A, so too, however, does the local government. The imposition of an additional value added tax by the federal government reduces A's output and value added, and thereby the tax revenue going to the local government. The federal government's introduction of a value added tax imposes negative external costs on the local government in the form of lost tax revenue. As with all externalities, the optimal outcome can only be achieved if the two governments confer and agree on a single tax somewhere between 10 and 20%, and share the revenue.[10]

The optimality of such a negotiated common tax rate assumes, however, that the objective of the two governments is to maximize their collective tax revenue, or to collect a given amount of revenue while imposing the minimum "excess burden." That is, the analysis follows the standard practice in public finance of separating expenditures from taxes. The optimality of this outcome disappears if the taxes are benefit taxes. If the local government raises 90 in tax revenue from A, when it produces 90 units of output, and the tax is a benefit tax, by definition it must be providing services to A with costs of 90. If A's output falls to 80, the local government must provide fewer services and its costs fall from 90 to 80. The local government should be indifferent between supplying A services that cost it 90 and collecting tax revenue of 90, and supplying fewer services at a cost of 80 and collecting 80 in taxes. The same holds true for the federal government. With perfect competition in all markets, the Pareto optimal allocation of resources occurs when ratio of the price of X to the price of Y equals the ratio of their marginal costs of production. If the federal and local governments supply services to a firm, they should charge the firm the cost of supplying the services, and the firm's prices should reflect these costs, if resources are to be allocated optimally.

These considerations shed a different light on the familiar "assignment problem" in fiscal federalism: At what level of government should each public good and service be supplied? Which taxes should each level of government *be allowed* to levy? In an optimally constituted federal system, only the first question needs to be answered. Responsibility for the provision of particular public goods and services should be determined by the extent of their spillovers. Public goods whose spillovers are limited to small geographic areas can be provided optimally by local governments. Public goods whose spillovers blanket the entire country should be

[10] For a formal demonstration, see Sobel (1997).

provided by the federal government. Once the assignment problem for expenditures has been solved, the answer to the tax problem follows automatically. Each level of government should finance its expenditures using benefit taxes. These come in a variety of forms and no rigid assignment of taxes to different levels is likely to be optimal. It is quite likely that more than one level of government chooses to make use of the same tax base (value added, income, property), because the benefits from some public services at each level are closely related to this tax base. As the previous paragraph indicates, such multiple use of a tax base should not give rise to inefficiencies, if the benefit tax principle is adhered to. The efficiency gain from having a single government gather all of the revenue from a given tax base can be obtained without sacrificing the opportunity for each governmental unit to set its own tax rates.

REDISTRIBUTION

There are two ways to view redistribution, positively and normatively. The positive public choice theory of redistribution in a majoritarian democracy is relatively simple, those who succeed in forming a majority coalition take from the minority coalition. Any normative justification for this form of redistribution must lie in the normative case for the majority rule. But the assumptions one must make to defend the use of the simple majority rule *do not* characterize situations involving pure redistribution. The most important assumption one must make to justify redistribution normatively is that the gain to a winner when an issue passes equals the loss to a loser – a form of equal intensity assumption. But if this assumption is valid, redistribution becomes a zero sum game with net social welfare from it remaining unchanged.[11]

A normative justification for redistribution that is also consistent with the individualistic premises that justify democracy can be obtained, if the redistribution takes place under the unanimity rule. If *everyone* votes to transfer money from one group to another, everyone must be made better off by such a transfer, and the Pareto principle can be invoked to defend it.

Those from whom the money is transferred may still vote for the transfer, if they experience some altruistic pleasure from seeing the recipients made better off. Such redistribution is most likely to take the form of rich-to-poor redistribution.

Unanimity is also possible for some forms of publicly operated insurance programs, like unemployment insurance. At the time the program is introduced everyone is uncertain about whether they might someday become unemployed and benefit from the program, and experiences an ex ante utility gain from its introduction. Ex post the program results in transfers from the working population to the unemployed. One can also conceptualize rich-to-poor redistribution as a form of insurance program, if one assumes that individuals are willing to engage in Rawls's (1971) mental experiment of assuming that they are uncertain about their future positions in society.

[11] See again May (1952), Rae (1969) and Mueller (2003, Ch. 6).

When citizens write a constitution, they must select a set of institutions that will govern their lives for many years to come. The long-run nature of constitutional politics makes it a more natural setting for mental experiments in which one places oneself in the other person's shoes than everyday politics. Thus, an attractive option for dealing with redistribution is to address it in the constitution by establishing a set of rights or entitlements to minimum levels income and perhaps other basic services like medical care. The obvious tax base for financing minimum income entitlements is income or maybe wealth. If unemployment compensation were treated as an entitlement, then the natural source of finance for it would be a payroll tax.

If a country's redistribution programs were treated as constitutional entitlements with tax and payout formula adjusted for inflation written into the constitution, quasi-independent agencies to administer them could be introduced at the same time. Redistribution could then disappear from the political agenda, and the legislative bodies at each level of the federalist system would be left free to concentrate on supplying the bundles of public goods and services that the citizens demanded.[12]

THE OPTIMAL FEDERALIST STRUCTURE

Imagine the consequences of replacing the current system for acquiring groceries in which a consumer pays for each item at a supermarket check-out, with one where she would only pay a single fee to enter the store, and then was free to select and take home anything that she wanted — subject to the constraint that she could not resell any items under penalty of death. What would be the likely outcome of such a policy? First, there would obviously be some inefficiencies. A person who was indifferent between eating oranges and pineapple would select far more pineapple than she would have, if she saw the prices for the two fruits and had to pay for them herself. In general, people would select more expensive items than they would select if they had to pay the market-determined price for each item.

If the fee charged at the door was initially set to equal the average amount spent by a consumer under the system of paying for each item, the supermarket would find that it was running a huge deficit. It would have to raise the entrance fee. To this the consumers might object. If they could force the supermarket to hold its fees down, then the supermarket would have no choice but to take some of the higher priced items off the shelves. The eventual equilibrium would likely be one in which on average consumers were paying more per week for their groceries, and consuming groceries of lower quality.

The citizen-consumer of local public goods sees no prices when she shops. By supporting this party or that she can perhaps influence the quantities of certain public goods supplied, bring about more spending on police, less on education. In the same way, she can influence the *total bill* for the basket of local public goods. But she lacks the information needed to choose the optimal combination of local

---

[12] Buchanan and Tullock (1962, Ch. 8) propose treating redistribution in the constitution. See also Mueller (1996, Ch. 16).

public goods. She is in much the same position as the shopper who only needs to pay an entrance fee to the supermarket. The result is that she winds up paying more in taxes and consuming a bundle of public goods of lower quality than would occur if each public good was individually priced, and its quantity individually determined.

One of the reasons European citizens are dissatisfied with their democratically elected governments may be that they perceive that they are getting "too little value for their money," that they are not able to influence the outcomes of the democratic process. One way to rectify this problem would be to introduce a strong federalist system. The discussion here implies that it should have three main features:

1. Each level of government is directly responsible to its electorate.

2. Each level of government chooses the quantities of public goods and services that it will supply.

3. Each level of government selects the taxes to pay for these goods and services.

We have emphasized the importance of using benefit taxes to finance public goods in a federalist system. A major advantage of such taxes is that they increase the information available to the citizen-consumer. If police services are financed by a tax on property, then a proposal to increase spending on police must be coupled to an increase in the property tax. The consumer-citizen can easily decide if the benefits from greater spending on police are likely to exceed the rise in her property taxes.[13] Indeed, because citizens have so much information available to them under such a system, it becomes feasible to introduce citizen-initiated referenda as in Switzerland to give citizens even more control over government policies. If the local government voted to increase spending on police and the property tax rate, the citizens could call a referendum and reverse the policy, if a majority disapproved.

We have emphasized the importance of using benefit taxes in an ideal federalist system. It is often argued, however, that benefits from government policies are difficult to determine, and thus that benefit taxes are impractical. Although it is of course true that the benefits from government policies cannot be estimated with pinpoint accuracy, it is possible to match taxes and benefits to a reasonable approximation. I offer some examples.

The most obvious form of benefit tax is a user fee. Who benefits from a bridge, those who cross it. Who benefits from a museum, those who visit it. A variety of public goods can be financed through a system of user fees.

1. Roads — electronic road pricing, tolls, gasoline taxes

2. Airports and harbors — landing and dock fees

3. Museums, zoos, parks, etc. — entrance fees

4. Trash collection — fees based on amount of trash collected

[13] It is possible to construct examples in which such "earmarked taxes" lead to outcomes that are not Pareto optimal. The welfare gains from allowing citizens to make more informed choices seem far greater than the possible losses that might occur by using earmarked taxes, however.

5. Water and sewage — fees based on amount of water consumed
6. Hospitals — patient charges
7. Courts — client fees
8. Schools — tuition fees

The most controversial of these is, of course, tuition fees for schools, particularly at the elementary and secondary levels. A full discussion of this policy would take a paper in itself, so I shall make a few brief comments on it.

The first thing to note is that a shift from tax-financed education system to a fee-financed system would not place a tremendous economic burden of families with children, since their taxes could be reduced if all schools were financed by fees. Although the state could still operate schools under a fee-based system, private schools would now be in a position to compete with state schools. Parents in even medium sized communities would be able to choose among several schools offering different education programs at different prices. The resulting competition among schools should produce higher quality schools for the same level of expenditures.

The prediction that the quality of education would improve under a tuition fee system finds considerable support when one examines the university-level education systems in the United States and Western Europe. In most Western European countries universities charge token fees or none at all (e.g., Italy, Greece, Spain, Germany and Austria). In the United States tuition fees range up to some $20,000 per year at the most prestigious private schools, with even the state-funded universities charging fees of several thousand dollars per year. There is intense competition among US schools for students. The effect of this competition on quality is most visible at the doctoral level of instruction, where the US universities clearly dominate those of Europe (and the rest of the world), but can also be seen at the undergraduate level. At the private universities and liberal arts colleges of the United States, class sizes are much smaller on average than at Western European universities. Libraries are better stocked and open longer hours, computers are available in greater numbers, and so on. Although class sizes at the large state universities in the United States are probably comparable to those at Western European universities, they still offer superior library, computer and recreational facilities for students.

Less than 10 percent of the college age population in Austria attends a university. More than 20 percent of the college age population in the United States attends some form or college or university. Until this year Austrian universities have charged no fees. How can one explain this difference? A part of the answer lies in the fact that the introduction of tuition fees results in more than just a movement up a stationary demand schedule. The improvement in education quality produces a shift in the demand schedule. The same can be expected to follow the introduction of tuition fees at other levels of government.

User fees are infeasible for some publicly provided goods and services, like police protection. Police protection is a good example of a local public good. The beneficiaries of such local public goods can be easily identified — the people living in or visiting the local community. A property tax nicely targets these beneficiaries. The owner of an apartment worth 8m SK has more to protect than the owner of one worth 4m. Although the ratio of benefits from local police and fire protection, etc. may not be precisely two to one, a property tax that is proportional to value should be a reasonable approximation to a benefit tax for these local public goods. Since restaurants, theaters and hotels would also be subject to a property tax, it would indirectly fall upon those who do not reside in the community permanently, but still make use of its public services. Indeed, a property tax might by a reasonable form of benefit tax for all businesses in the community.

We conclude then that the selection of the proper set of benefit taxes to finance public expenditures in a federalist system is not an insurmountable task. This selection should not stand in the way of introducing the ideal federalist system.

CONCLUSIONS

In this paper I have tried to give an answer to the question posed in the title of the paper – why federalism? The answer I have given is that a federalist system can give citizens more control over their government, and thereby will make the state more responsive to the citizens' demands and more efficient. To achieve these advantages from federalism, however, it must be organized in such a way that the voter can make informed choices, and the government is responsive to the citizen's requests. This organizational structure requires: a constitutional assignment of responsibilities for different public goods to each level of government, tax authority granted to each level of government, a tax system that relies on earmarked/benefit taxes, the treatment of redistribution as a set of economic entitlements. To many this set of proposals will seem like a very radical departure from the status quo. Surely such radical reforms are unnecessary they will respond. If it ain't broke, don't fix it. If citizen alienation from government and apathy are serious problems in Sweden, then serious solutions are called for. If the problems are not serious, then tinkering on the margins might suffice. In writing this paper, I have started with the premise that the problems are serious.

Perhaps the most radical part of this paper is the emphasis it places on benefit taxes. When one looks at the tax structure of Sweden, or any other developed country for that matter, and tries to find a normative justification for each tax, one encounters a bewildering array of possible candidates. Some taxes, like a progressive income tax, might be justified under "the ability-to-pay" approach, others as attempts to minimize excess burdens, others as attempts to minimize collection costs, still others to penalize sin (smoking, drinking alcohol), and for some taxes — like those targeted toward tourists — there is absolutely no normative justification whatsoever. Their only justification is a cynically pragmatic one, tourists do not vote.

The natural reaction of someone who is charged more for a meal in a restaurant than the person at the next table is anger, a feeling of being unjustly treated. One consequence of paying for public services by using a bewildering array of taxes underpinned by a hodgepodge of normative justifications is that they wind up treating citizens unjustly. Two citizens who consume the same bundles of public goods and services pay different prices for them. Financing the provision of public goods and services through benefit taxes would eliminate this type of unjust treatment of citizens, and might thereby reduce their alienation from the political process.

Ironically this point was first made by a Swedish economist over 100 years ago. Sadly, Knut Wicksell's (1896) "New Principle of Just Taxation" has never been tried, and to many will seem just as new and radical as when he first proposed it. Perhaps the time has come for Sweden to follow its famous economist's advice.

REFERENCES

Becker, E. (1996) "The Illusion of Fiscal Illusion: Unsticking The Flypaper Effect," *Public Choice* 86, 85-102.

Bailey, Stephen J. and Stephen Connolly (1998) "The Flypaper Effect: Identifying Areas for Further Research," *Public Choice* 95, 335-61.

Buchanan, James M. and Tullock, Gordon (1962) *The Calculus of Consent*, Ann Arbor: The University of Michigan Press.

Gillette, Clayton P. (2001) "Funding Versus Control in Intergovernmental Relations," *Constitutional Political Economy* 12, 123-40.

Grossman, Philip J. (1989a) "Federalism and the Size of Government," *Southern Economic Journal* 55, 580-93.

Grossman, Philip J. (1989b) "Fiscal Decentralization and Government Size: An Extension," *Public Choice* 62, 63-70.

Heyndels, Bruno and Carine Smolders (1994) "Fiscal Illusion at the Local Level: Empirical Evidence for the Flemish Municipalities," *Public Choice* 80, 325-38.

Heyndels, Bruno and Carine Smolders (1995) "Tax Complexity and Fiscal Illusion," *Public Choice* 85, 127-41.

Hines, James R., Jr. and Richard H. Thaler (1995) "Anomalies: The Flypaper Effect," *Journal of Economic Perspectives* 9, 217-26.

Inman, Robert P. (1979) "The Fiscal Performance of Local Governments: An Interpretive Review," in Peter Mieszkowski and Mahlon Strazheim (eds.) *Current Issues in Urban Economics*, Baltimore: Johns Hopkins University Press, 270-321.

May, Kenneth O. (1952) "A Set of Independent, Necessary and Sufficient Conditions for Simple Majority Decision," *Econometrica* 20, 680-84.

Mueller, Dennis C. (1996) *Constitutional Democracy*, New York and Oxford: Oxford University Press.

Mueller, Dennis C. (2003) *Public Choice III*, Cambridge: Cambridge University Press.

Oates, Wallace E. and Robert M. Schwab (1988) "The Allocative and Distributive Implications of Local Fiscal Competition," *Journal of Public Economics* 35, 333-54.

Rae, Douglas W. (1969) "Decision-Rules and Individual Values in Constitutional Choice," *American Political Science Review* 63, 40-56.

Rawls, J.A. (1971) *A Theory of Justice*, Cambridge: The Belknap Press of Harvard University Press.

Sobel, Russell S. (1997) "Optimal Taxation in a Federal System of Governments," *Southern Economic Journal* 64, 468-85.

Tiebout, Charles M. (1956) "A Pure Theory of Local Expenditures," *Journal of Political Economy* 64, 416-24.

Wilde, James A. (1968) "The Expenditure Effects of Grants-in-Aid Programs," *National Tax Journal* 21, 340-48.

Wilde, James A. (1971) "Grants-in-Aid: The Analytics of Design and Response," *National Tax Journal* 24, 143-56.

8

STRENGTHENING FEDERALISM IN SWEDEN

Dennis C. Mueller* and Emil Uddhammar**

University of Vienna

The Johnson Foundation, Stockholm and the Department of Government, Uppsala University

INTRODUCTION

Two facts are famous in the Swedish debate on local self-government. The first is that the local self-government of municipalities is protected as a right in the first paragraph of the constitution. The second is that local self-government in Sweden has always to a large extent been constrained by the central government. In this chapter we discuss changes in the structure of government in Sweden that would allow its citizens to exercise their constitutional right to local self-government.

In chapter 2 the reasons why a federalist structure might improve the delivery of public goods and services were outlined. This discussion was rather general, however, and not directly linked to the structure of government in Sweden today. In this chapter we draw such a link.

Based on the arguments of chapter 7 we can identify five categories of structural reforms that might possibly be needed to achieve the full potential of a federalist system.

1. Political responsibility at each level of government. Citizens must be able to voice their approval or disapproval of the levels and scope of public services and taxes at each level of the federalist structure in such a way that the political system can be expected to respond in the appropriate way to these expressions.

2. Tax and expenditure authority are linked. Each level of the federalist structure must be able to levy the appropriate taxes to cover its assigned expenditures.

3. There exists a clear assignment of expenditure authority across the levels of federalist system. Such an assignment might be included in the constitution.

These three categories of institutions define the essential elements for an effective federalist structure. Chapter 7 contained two additional recommendations for creating a strong federalist system, however, and these will also be discussed in the Swedish context in this chapter.

---

* Professor Dennis C. Mueller, BWZ, Brünnerstrasse 72, A-1210 Vienna, Austria, dennis.mueller@univie.ac.at

** Elias Friesgatan 1, SE-752 31, Uppsala, Sweden; emil.uddhammar@swipnet.se

4. The main redistribution programs are assigned to the central government, and are perhaps treated as constitutional entitlements.

5. Maximum use of user fees and benefit taxes is made at all levels of government.[1]

These five areas cover what we believe to be the main components of a strong federalist system. They do not encompass all of the issues that arise under federalism, however. In particular, they do not include the important set of issues that arise when there are significant spillovers across communities, and when intergovernmental grants are used to deal with these spillovers. We shall only touch upon these issues in this chapter, since they are dealt with at length elsewhere in this volume.

The main objective of strengthening Sweden's federalist institutions would be to improve the accountability of government at each level, and thereby improve the allocation of resources. This improvement would come about for two reasons: (1) government would become more efficient at providing a given bundle of public goods and services, and (2) there would be a better match between the goods and services that citizens demanded from the state and the goods and services actually provided. Thus, much of this chapter focuses upon describing the institutions that would improve allocative efficiency. Redistribution programs are, of course, also an important part of government activity, and there is nowhere where this is more true than in Sweden, so we shall begin with these, so that the reader does not get the impression that we are proposing reforms that would eliminate all redistribution in Sweden. After discussion how redistribution might be dealt with in an ideal federalist system, we take up the other four major components of federalism listed above.

REDISTRIBUTION

A normative *raison d'être* for the state commonly invoked by public finance and public choice scholars is that the state exists to provide goods and services to its citizens that they cannot obtain in Pareto optimal quantities without the state. Any state-provided good or service must, therefore, have the *potential* of making *all* citizens better off. By implication any state redistribution programs must have the potential of making all citizens better off. Chapter 7 discussed two such normative arguments that have been put forward to justify state redistribution programs. We briefly review them here, and then take a look at the pattern of redistribution in Sweden to see how well it confirms to these justifications.

[1] Economists traditionally distinguished between two principles of taxation – the ability to pay principle, and the benefit principle. Under the benefit principle a tax is levied in such a way so that the benefits a consumer of a public service receives roughly match the taxes that she pays. Tax on gasoline used to finance the construction and maintenance of roads in obvious example. We discuss the possible use of property and value added taxes as benefit taxes below.

Redistribution as Altruism

Our normative criterion is that the state should undertake only those activities that potentially benefit all citizens. Redistribution from one group, say the *R*s, to another called the *P*s is consistent with this normative criterion only if the *R*s also benefit from the redistribution. One way in which this might come about is that the *R*s get utility out of seeing the *P*s made better off, and are willing to have their own incomes reduced to bring this about. This sort of *Pareto optimal redistribution* is quite plausible if the *R*s are richer than the *P*s, and have altruistic preference functions (Hochman and Rodgers, 1969). The rich will maximize their altruistic preference functions by transfer money to the poor until the marginal utility that a rich person gets from keeping an extra crown just equals the utility she gets from giving it to the poor.

One obvious question to ask is why the state must intervene to bring about these transfers? Why cannot the rich simply give money to the poor without the state? The usual answer given to this question is that a rich person does not want to see just one poor person made better off, but rather all poor persons. To accomplish this all rich persons must give to the poor and a potential free-rider problem arises. State intervention is needed to solve this free-rider problem.

It is reasonable to assume that a rich person gets more utility from giving to someone whose income is 1/10th of the rich person's income than to someone with half of her income. Giving to the poorest person in the community provides a rich person with the highest utility. These considerations lead to the following two predictions with respect to state-induced redistribution for altruistic purposes: (1) Both the rich and the poor benefit from and support such redistribution. (2) Transfers are first targeted to the lowest income people in the community. When their incomes have been raised to that of the second poorest group, transfers are made to both bottom level groups and so on until a level of income below that of the rich is reached such that the utility loss to a rich person from a transfer just equals her gain from seeing a poorer person made better off.[2]

Redistribution as Social Insurance

All insurance programs involve redistribution of one form or another. Individuals voluntarily enter such programs to avoid certain risks. When they do, they (unanimously) agree to engage in ex post redistribution. All purchasers of fire insurance agree to a redistribution from those who do not have fires to those who do.

Although the market is capable of providing many sorts of insurance – like that against fires – optimally, in some cases there may be market failures of one sort or another that justify state provision of the insurance. For example, if it were possible while we were still ensconced in the womb to purchase insurance against

---

[2] For further discussion and a demonstration of this proposition, see von Furstenberg and Mueller (1971).

our having future physical or mental handicaps that would cause us to be poor, we might all voluntarily sign the insurance contract. Such contracts are as yet infeasible, however, and by the time we are able to join such contracts our physical or mental handicaps are often already apparent, and those who need the insurance most cannot acquire it. Thus, state-run involuntary programs of redistribution can be justified on market failure grounds.

Rawls (1971) argued that every adult *ought* to undertake the *Gedankenexperiment* of pretending he might be rich or poor, and that the proper amount of redistribution in a society would be that amount that was unanimously agreed to behind such a veil of ignorance. Thus, we can again justify some forms of state-provided rich-to-poor redistribution as being consistent with the criterion that everyone is made better off by them. In addition to using income as a criterion for whether a person is bad off or not, we might also think of using other criteria. Blindness or other physical handicaps, mental deficiencies, sickness and unemployment are all obvious candidates. As with redistribution as altruism, redistribution as social insurance leads to the prediction that the recipients of state transfers are disadvantaged in some way.

Redistribution in Sweden

Table 1 presents figures from an OECD study on the patterns of transfers in several countries. The column on the far right reports average transfers in each country as a percent of median income and is thus a measure of the relative importance of transfers across countries. There are two figures for Sweden, 35.0 percent in 1981 and 35.5 percent in 1987. These two figures are higher than for any other country – more than three times the figures for some countries like Australia, Canada, Switzerland and the United States. The expectation that Sweden is a generous welfare state is confirmed in these figures.

The other figures in the table indicate where the transfers go. The column headed "bottom," for example, reports the fraction of transfers going to the bottom quintile of the income distribution. The figure for Sweden of 15.2 percent in 1987 is the *smallest* in that column. In both 1981 and 1987 a smaller fraction of transfers in Sweden went to the poorest 20 percent of the population as went to the richest 20 percent. These figures are difficult to reconcile with the normative arguments for redistribution presented above in which the recipients of transfers are expected to be poor or in some other way disadvantaged. These figures suggest that much redistribution in Sweden must be explained by the positive theories of redistribution developed in the public choice literature in which some groups succeed in getting the state to transfer funds from others to themselves.

Table 1: Distribution of Transfers by Quintile and Average Transfers as a Percent of Median Equivalent Income

		Bottom	2	3	4	Top	Total	Average Transfers as a Percent of Median Equivalent Income
Australia	1981	42.8	22.2	13.3	12.5	9.2	100.00	10.8
	1985	40.1	24.6	14.4	12.9	8.0	100.00	11.3
Belgium	1985	22.9	22.5	21.9	16.6	16.1	100.00	33.3
	1988	21.5	23.6	20.1	16.1	18.7	100.00	34.9
Switzerland	1982	38.5	19.2	15.6	13.3	13.3	100.00	7.3
Canada	1981	33.0	22.9	17.9	14.1	12.1	100.00	10.1
	1987	29.5	24.2	19.2	15.0	12.1	100.00	12.4
France	1979	19.7	21.2	18.8	17.7	22.6	100.00	22.2
	1984	17.5	21.8	18.4	17.7	24.7	100.00	25.0
Germany	1984	21.8	22.2	16.7	21.0	18.3	100.00	19.8
Ireland	1987	32.0	21.9	21.3	15.2	9.6	100.00	20.5
Italy	1986	15.6	16.4	19.7	20.7	27.6	100.00	21.4
Luxembourg	1985	17.3	18.3	19.5	22.5	22.4	100.00	23.7
Netherlands	1983	21.8	21.8	18.4	20.4	17.6	100.00	28.5
	1987	24.9	21.3	16.9	17.7	19.2	100.00	28.3
Norway	1979	34.0	20.9	16.4	13.6	15.1	100.00	13.5
Sweden	1981	18.0	23.9	19.8	19.5	18.7	100.00	35.0
	1987	15.2	25.8	21.7	19.9	17.4	100.00	35.5
UK	1979	30.6	20.0	17.4	17.0	15.0	100.00	18.5
	1986	26.7	25.9	19.4	16.1	11.9	100.00	24.3
US	1979	29.7	21.1	17.4	14.7	17.1	100.00	8.9
	1986	29.2	21.2	17.1	17.5	15.1	100.00	9.4
Finland	1987	25.9	22.6	18.2	15.8	17.6	100.00	27.7

Source: Atkinson, Rainwater and Smeeding (1995), Table 7.5, p. 107.

The reforms discussed below would eliminate much of this sort of zero-sum redistribution. Citizens would pay taxes to get particular public goods and services and the taxes paid would correspond to the benefits received. One must also recognize, however, that a wide consensus exists in Sweden that individuals should be ensured against certain risks like becoming unemployed or disabled, and that the state should ensure that no individual's income is so low that they cannot afford minimum levels of housing, food, clothing, etc. Both of these types of programs fit the normative criteria for redistribution discussed above, and we would see the state continuing to play a major role in providing this sort of redistribution. For reasons stated below, we think that these programs are best administered and funded by the central government. As discussed in chapter 7, one might even think of placing entitlements to certain forms of insurance like unemployment compensation, and to minimum levels of income into the constitution thereby removing them entirely from the day-to-day political agenda and freeing politicians to concentrate on those state activities that improve allocative efficiency. We shall not pursue these options here any further as the focus of our chapter is on federalist institutions and not redistribution, but the reader should keep in mind as proceed to discuss reforms that would dismantle certain portions of the Swedish tax and transfer system that we see basic rich-to-poor and insurance-type redistribution programs as having been "taken care of" at either the constitutional stage of the political process or by the central government. Local communities would, of course, be free to introduce additional redistribution programs if they so choose, but responsibility for the major redistribution programs would lie with the central government or national agencies.

POLITICAL RESPONSIBILITY IN A FEDERALIST SYSTEM

The first issue that must be addressed in designing a federalist system is the number of levels of government that it will contain. This choice depends on the size and heterogeneity of the polity. Consider, for example, the question of the optimal structure for the European Union, assuming that it would be organized as a federalism. At the top would be a central government elected by citizens from across the EU. Below it there might be various levels of regional governments designed to deal with public issues that go beyond national boundaries and at the same time do not concern every citizen of the EU (e.g., a Scandinavian government, a Mediterranean government, a British/Irish isles government, and so on). The existing nation states might constitute a third tier, regional governments within some nation states (e.g., the German Länder) a fourth tier, cities a fifth, and perhaps in the largest cities yet a sixth level of neighbourhood governments. For a polity as large and heterogeneous as the European Union, several layers of government would be needed to represent the preferences of its citizens accurately.

Such a multi-layered structure should not be necessary in a country as small and homogeneous as Sweden. Currently there are three types of governmental units in Sweden: central, county and municipal. With some important exceptions, as discussed in section IV, the assignment of responsibilities to the central and to the 290 municipal levels of government accords with the principles of a sound federalist system. The same cannot be said for the 18 county governments.[3] Their primary responsibility is over the provision of hospitals and health care. As argued below, hospitals are primary candidates for privatisation and the introduction of user fees. Health insurance to cover hospital costs could either be purchased directly by the citizen, or provided by the central government. Thus, the provision of health care would be taken away from the counties under a proper allocation and financing of health care in a federalist system. Once health is removed from the counties, the only other public good left in its budget is a miscellaneous category that includes some public transportation.[4] These activities could be assigned to either the central or the municipal levels of government. We conclude, therefore, that the county governments in Sweden could be abolished without any loss in efficiency of providing public services. Indeed, citizens would be net beneficiaries in that they would not have to pay the administrative costs associated with the county governments, and they would not have to participate in the selection of the county councils. This would be a gain for the citizen, because she would be freed from

---

[3] In addition to these there are two regional governments which do not serve any major function and could well be abolished. Some authors lump these in with the counties and refer to the existence of 21 counties in Sweden.

[4] See Figure 2 and discussion thereof in chapter 2.

participating in elections to select public officials who have little discretionary authority, because the criteria for providing health care are set at the central level. Participating in these sorts of elections is thus a pseudo-democratic activity, which quite possibly leads to alienation, as the citizen recognizes that her participation in the democratic process has little purpose.

Both the central and the municipal governments are elected. Thus, no fundamental changes are needed to make them potentially responsible to the citizens. Some changes might be made, however, to make the municipal governments *more responsive* to the citizens. Currently municipal councils *may* solicit the opinions of its citizens by calling a referendum. The council need not heed the outcome of the referendum, when making its decisions, however. Thus, citizens have a very limited scope for expressing their opinions about specific actions of the municipal councils. Their ability would be greatly enhanced by making referenda on particular actions by the councils mandatory, and/or be allowing citizen initiatives. With respect to the former, the constitution could stipulate that certain actions by municipal councils, as for example, changes in tax rates must be approved by the citizens in a referendum before their going into effect.

Many of the 290 municipalities in Sweden are sufficiently small that they could reasonably be organized as the most direct form of direct democracy – town meeting democracy. Instead of electing a council, which in turn elects an executive committee, the citizens could elect such a committee, or perhaps a single person, to deal with the suppliers of services to the municipality. The citizens could then meet together once or twice a year and vote on the main budget items, proposals for new ordinances, and so on. Studies comparing municipalities in Switzerland that employ some forms of direct democracy (town meetings or referenda) have revealed a closer correspondence between the wishes of the citizenry, as captured by the preferences of the median voter, and the municipality's policies, when institutions of direct democracy are present, with the closest correspondence present with town-meeting democracy.[5] Introducing elements of direct democracy at the municipal level is a feasible, and potentially powerful, device for increasing the responsiveness of government in Sweden. No special provisions would have to be included in the constitution to enable municipalities to opt for direct democracy. The reforms suggested here – better matching of taxes and expenditures at the local level – should make such an option more meaningful and attractive, however. Introducing referenda and initiatives to check the national government would also be feasible. Indeed, it would also be feasible to check the national government by calling referenda.

---

[5] See Pommerehne (1978), and Pommerehne and Schneider (1982). Mueller (1996, Chs. 7 and 12) and Kirchgässner, Feld and Savioz (1999) review the pros and cons for direct democracy and referenda. Kirchgässner, Feld and Savioz also discuss the experiences with direct democracy and referenda in Switzerland, Weimar Germany and the United States.

TAX AND EXPENDITURE AUTHORITY

For citizens to be able to hold their governments responsible for the levels of public services and taxes, they must know what these levels are and their representatives must have the authority to set both expenditures and taxes. By and large Swedish municipalities do possess authority over both expenditures and taxes, and so no major constitutional changes are needed in this respect. A number of tasks that municipalities carry out today are proscribed by laws passed at the central level, however. This practice makes it difficult for the citizen to assess whether a particular outcome at the local level is due to decisions by the local or by the central government. If the goal of having strong, local self-government is to be achieved, the lines of authority for the provision of each public good or service must be clearly drawn, and the level of government that has been assigned a particular public service must assume the responsibility for raising the revenue to provide it.

There are three governmental practices in Sweden that blur the lines of authority between the central and municipal levels of government and thereby weaken accountability at both the central and local governmental levels: (1) the central governments prescribing service levels for certain locally supplied public services, (2) the heavy use of block grants from the central to municipal levels of government, and (3) the freedom of municipal governments to run deficits and be bailed out by the central government when they do. We discuss each in turn.

Mandating Service Levels for Local Public Services

The essence of self-government is that a community is free to decide what it is that its government should do. This freedom is destroyed if a different level government can effectively override the preferences of the citizens in a municipality by effectively mandating that they spend more on a public service than they wish too. There is only one *normative* justification for allowing the central government to mandate that a given level of public services be provided in all local communities and this normative justification logically leads to the conclusion that the service should not be the responsibility of the local community at all, but rather belongs in the set of responsibilities assigned to the central level.

Imagine, for example, that a large majority of Swedes believes that any elderly person who is incapable of taking care of him- or herself is entitled to a minimum level of care in a home for the elderly. If providing care for the elderly is assigned to the municipalities, then this goal can be achieved by mandating the desired minimum level in all communities. A Swede living in Bjurholm obtains as much utility from knowing that an elderly person in Stockholm is receiving at least the minimum level of care as an elderly person in Bjurholm. But, this makes care for the elderly a form of national public good. The proper way to handle it in a well-designed federalist system is for care for the elderly to be financed by the central level of government out of taxes levied across the country. Such a fiscal structure is, of course, fully consistent with a highly decentralized government hierarchy for delivering the services.

Intergovernmental Grants

As discussed in chapter 2, intergovernmental grants can be justified on several grounds. One such justification relies on the existence of cross-community externalities. Communities A and B both sit on the banks of the same river. The outlays on sewage treatment that the citizens of A consider to be optimal are less than what citizens in the downstream community B deem that A should be spending. A potential Pareto improvement exists, which could take the form of a conditional grant from B to A that induces A to spend more on sewage treatment. To achieve its objective, B will clearly want to tie the grant to A's spending more on sewage treatment. There is no reason why it should want to subsidize more spending for libraries or a tax cut in A. Thus, the externality justification for grants leads to the prediction that they should be *conditional* grants.

Table 2 lists the percentages of the total revenues of Swedish municipalities from 1981 through 1999 that take the form of block or general grants and specific grants. Two things stand out from the table. (1) There has been a fivefold increase in the central government's use of general grants over the last 20 years. (2) By the end of the period block grants are a major source of the municipalities revenues.

Table 2: General and Specific Grants as Share of Total Revenues

Year	General grants	Specific grants
1981	0,04	0,21
1982	0,04	0,21
1983	0,04	0,22
1984	0,04	0,22
1985	0,04	0,22
1986	0,04	0,21
1987	0,04	0,21
1988	0,04	0,21
1989	0,04	0,21
1990	0,04	0,22
1991	0,04	0,22
1992	0,05	0,21
1993	0,14	0,08
1994	0,13	0,07
1995	0,13	0,05
1996	0,18	0,04
1997	0,19	0,03
1998	0,20	0,04
1999	0,19	0,03

Source: Statistical Yearbook of Sweden, 2000

The use of block grants to finance local government programs weakens governmental accountability at both levels of government. First of all, it is very difficult for the Swedish citizen to figure out what it is she is buying and where she is buying it, when her taxes paid to the central government are distributed to local governments in the form of block grants. As Clayton Gillette points out in chapter 5, the size and shape of grants in a federalist system can be thought of as the outcome of a bargaining process between the central and lower levels of government. Since the citizen has no way to observe this process enfold, or to judge the various alternative outcomes from the process, he cannot determine whether his representatives at either level made "a good bargain" for him. Second, a large literature studying the so-called "flypaper effect" of block grants reveals that they lead to a form of fiscal illusion. The citizens of a local community pay only a small fraction of the taxes used to provide it with a grant, and thus consider the grant as a sort of gift. They thus hold their elected representatives less accountable for how they spend this money, and a far larger fraction than is optimal winds up being spent by the local government.[6]

It should also perhaps be noted, that when grants are used to achieve Pareto optimality in the presence of externalities, these grants will never take the form of grants from the central to the local levels of government. Intergovernmental externalities will always take the form of activities in A, B and C impacting the welfare of citizens in D, E and F. The grant to correct this externality should obviously be from D, E and F on A, B, and C. Although one might rationalize involving the central government on transaction costs grounds, when there are 290 local governments as in Sweden costs of losing transparency by using the central government are likely to outweigh any transaction costs savings.[7] Grants administered by the central government today do not appear to be motivated to achieve allocative efficiency in the presence of the sorts of externalities just described, and thus eliminating these grants would not reduce allocative efficiency.

A somewhat different externality argument is sometimes used to justify central government grants to finance local public expenditures like education. Here the argument is that *everyone* in the country benefits from other citizens being educated and thus that there is a kind of generalized externality across all communities and the lowest cost way to achieve Pareto optimality is to have the central government subsidize education in all communities. Although this is a *possible* justification for government grants, in the case of education it is likely not to be valid, because the externalities caused by education are unlikely to be *Pareto relevant* (Buchanan and Stubblebine, 1969).

To see what is involved, consider a less controversial example of an externality. A community consists of 100 wooden houses. Individual *A* finds it personally optimal to paint her house once every 10 years. She feels, however, that the community looks shabby, if everyone only paints their houses once every 10 years. She is thus willing to vote for a tax/subsidy scheme that induces everyone to paint their houses once every 7 years. In doing so she of course winds up paying the same amount extra in taxes that she would have paid had she simply chosen to paint her own house every 7 years, but using the state to bring this outcome about solves the free-rider problem in this situation. Note that an implication of this argument is that, if *A* were given the option of not paying her tax and having to paint her house

---

6 See Inman and Rubinfeld (1997) and Mueller (2003, ch. 10) and references therein.

7 Another argument for central government grants is to achieve *fiscal equivalence* across communities. A superior alternative to this method that achieves the same normative goal is discussed in section V.

only every 10 years, while the state compelled everyone else to paint their houses every 7 years, she should accept this offer.

Now let us consider the analogous situation with respect to education. To simplify the argument, let us assume that everyone has the same income and each citizen has one child in school. The externality argument for central government subsidies must run like this. Individual A wants to spend only x in taxes for her own child's education, but because of the externalities from education, she wants people in other communities to spend y per child on education, $y > x$. She thus votes for a tax/subsidy scheme that involves her paying y-x in taxes to the central government and receiving back a grant from it of the same amount to be paid into the local school budget to finance her child's education. As with the house-painting example, if asked A should happily opt out of the tax/subsidy scheme for her own municipality so long as all 289 other municipalities stay in the program.

It would be rather easy to design a questionnaire to determine whether this example describes the situation in Sweden or not. Such a questionnaire might look like the following:

1. Would you be willing to see z Swedish Kronor less spent on your child's education per year and at the same time receive a tax reduction of z SKR, providing that the amount spent on education in all other communities does not change?

2. Would you like to see z SKR more spent on your child's education per year and at the same time pay z SKR more in taxes, providing that the amount spent on education in all other communities does not change?

If the externality-justification for central government taxes holds, every parent should choose 1 and state a positive value for z. We do not believe that this would happen, because most Swedes value the education of their own children highly enough, so that they would not choose to "free ride" by reducing expenditures on it. If we are correct, the case for central government transfers collapses as education is no longer a Pareto-relevant externality.

Another justification for intergovernmental grants is to achieve "fiscal equivalence" across communities. An individual's level of welfare depends not only upon his own income and his capacity to buy private goods, but also upon the public goods supplied to him, and thus indirectly on the incomes of other members of his community. If, for example, education is financed by a tax on income, a person with modest income will be able to "purchase" a higher level of education for his children with a given tax rate, if he lives in a wealthy community than if he lives in a poor community. There are two alternative ways to address this inequity, one by making *interpersonal transfers,* the other by making *intergovernmental transfers.*

Consider first the possibility of interpersonal transfers. Let us assume as recommended in the following section that the central government has the primary responsibility for redistribution in the country. Since being able to afford a decent education for your children is just as important as being able to afford decent food and clothing, the state should consider not only an individual's personal income and family situation when deciding whether she is eligible for an income transfer, but also the income/wealth of the local community in which she resides. More generally, the income taxes paid to or transfers received from the central government should depend on both the private income of a taxpayer and the income of her community in a federalist system in which local communities are responsible for funding local public goods out of their own tax revenue.

Such a program of taxes and subsidies would be fairly easy to implement. In Canada provinces use the federal government to collect their income taxes by simply setting a fraction of the taxable income reported to the federal government, which must be paid to the provincial government. Some counties in the United States use their state's definition of income to collect an income tax at the country level. Our proposal would merely reverse the procedure. When filling out her federal income tax form, the Swedish tax payer would not have a single table with tax rates for each income to consult, but several, each one specific to the municipality in which the taxpayer lives. Although it would be cumbersome to have 290 separate tax schedules, it should be feasible to group the municipalities by income and living costs levels and have five or ten tax schedules covering the 290 municipalities. Each individual would then know what her tax obligation is to the central government and could make her decisions on optimal expenditure levels at the local level accordingly. As with our other suggestions, this method for achieving fiscal equivalence would greatly improve the average citizen's ability to know what she is paying in taxes and for what her tax money is being spent.

The alternative to interpersonal grants to achieve fiscal equivalence is to introduce intergovernmental grants. This is the current practice in Sweden and is described in detail in chapter 4. Funds are transferred from communities with relatively high average incomes and low needs (for example, small numbers of elderly or children) to communities with low incomes and high needs. The formula are so designed that it should be possible after the transfers for a community to achieve the average level of spending on local public goods and services, if it is willing to impose the average tax burden upon itself. If the goal of the program is to *allow* poorer communities to achieve the spending levels of richer communities, rather than to *compel* them to do so, no additional mandates or conditions should be attached to the grants. Just as income transfers to individuals are superior to transfers in-kind because they allow the individual to achieve higher utility levels for the same money transfer, unconstrained equivalence grants to poorer local communities are superior to grants with strings attached, because they would allow local communities to use the funds in such a way as to maximize their citizens' welfare.

Sweden's current system of fiscal equivalence, conditional and block grants is filled with explicit and implicit constraints on the uses of the funds. Such constraints are often justified with claims that there is a "national interest" in the levels of certain local activities, as for example education spending. The existence of such "national interests" does not suffice, however, to justify spending mandates and similar constraints on local authorities. If the formula for the equivalence grant includes the number of children in a local community, as the one used in Sweden does, then every local community after it receives the grant can achieve the average spending level of education if it so chooses. If all Swedes agree that education is an important local governmental activity, then poorer local communities can be expected to spend the funds they receive from the richer communities on education. Thus, even if local spending on education has positive external effects on the rest of the country, forcing local communities to spend more on education may not be necessary, if they would spend the optimal amounts anyway. As in the example above, the positive external effects of local spending on education may not be Pareto relevant, once the fiscal capacity of poorer communities has been raised to equal that of the average community.

Arguments in favour of grants from richer to poorer communities are often framed in terms of wanting the poorer communities to be able to achieve *minimum acceptable* levels of public services in areas like trash collection, fire and police protection, and so on, and not necessarily *equivalent* levels as in richer communities. If this is the objective behind intergovernmental equalization grants, then one should expect them to decline in importance as average incomes increase in Sweden and more and more communities are able to provide generally accepted minimum levels of public services.[8]

Bailouts

When local governments run large deficits and are subsequently bailed out by the central government, the outcome resembles an ad hoc block grant. Since such bailouts also encourage a kind of moral hazard on the part of local politicians, they clearly should be avoided. Chapter 3 discusses the problems and potential for doing so.

THE DIVISION OF SPENDING AUTHORITY ACROSS DIFFERENT LEVELS OF GOVERNMENT

The logic of fiscal federalism requires that public goods that are consumed by all Swedish citizens regardless of where they live should be provided at the central level of government, public goods that benefit only citizens in a local community should be provided by that community. Table 3 provides a breakdown of expenditures per capita by municipalities in Sweden in 1999. Most items in the list fit one's usual perception of what local public goods are, as in particular the biggest item on the list – education. As we shall discuss in the next section, some items like preschool activities might be privatized and removed from the public sector entirely. The one item that clearly does not belong in the local municipality's budget is "elder and disabled care." Indeed, it is not clear that care for the elderly should be the responsibility of the state at all, since it fits neither of the two justifications for redistribution discussed above. Young-to-old redistribution of the type that one observes in Sweden and most other countries cannot be justified as a form of rich-to-poor altruism, because all elderly people are not poor, and all young people are

---

[8] Broadway and Johansson (in this volume) discuss a variety of national goals that might justify central governmental grants that go beyond fiscal equalization grants. To the extent that these national goals are Pareto relevant, our proposals differ from theirs in that we favour achieving greater transparency in the taxes and expenditures across the level of governments at the cost of under fulfilling some of these national goals.

not rich. Nor is it possible to justify redistribution from young to old as a form of insurance. Getting old is a natural process and every worker can consult life expectancy tables and calculate the likely length of time after she retires for which she will need a supplementary source of income. Personal savings and private pension systems can then be used to cover some or all of these needs.

Table 3: Municipal Expenditure per Inhabitant in 1999

	SEK
Political activities	497
Infrastructure, protective services etc	2 641
Recreation	997
Cultural affairs	870
Preschool, school-age child care	4 493
Education	10 635
Elderly and disabled care	10 220
Special care for individuals and families	2 703
Specially targeted programs	931
Total own activities	33 988
Business activities	2 242
Total	36 230

Source: Svenska Kommunförbundet

Switching from state-funded to at least partially privatized pension schemes is a politically difficult and controversial step, and thus one must recognize that the state is likely to play at least a residual role in providing care for the elderly for some time in the future in Sweden and many other countries.[9] Such a role for the state is usually rationalized with some sort of insurance argument – we all stand "the risk" of growing old and thus are willing to tax ourselves to insure against this risk. But this risk is borne by all Swedish citizens regardless of where they live, and thus implies a national pension/elderly care system not a local one. If the state is to provide care for the elderly, then this is clearly an activity that belongs in the central budget.

An additional reason for favouring the provision of elderly care at the national level is that this is an area where a "race to the bottom" can take place. Retired people are highly mobile. An elderly person who needs considerable care is likely to move to a municipality where she obtains high quality care. Any local community that provides high quality care out of its own tax revenue runs the danger of attracting more and more elderly people and needing higher and higher taxes to provide them with the care they require. These taxes in turn may drive those paying them to seek out other communities with lower taxes. The range of per capita spending on the elderly across municipalities illustrates that this is a potentially serious problem. Over the 1995-2000 period this range ran from a low of 2679 SKR to a high of

[9] There have been many proposals to privatize or partially privatize state pa-as-you-go pension systems. See, for example, Homburg (1997), Kotlikoff (1998) and Feldstein and Samwick (1998). Mueller (2002) discusses some of the normative and positive issues involved with more cites to the literature.

21291 SKR with the mean being 10101 SKR. Care for the elderly ranges from 11 percent of one municipality's budget to almost 45 percent of another's. This uneven burden on local taxpayers can to some extent be mitigated with grants from the central government to the municipalities that take into account the size of the elderly population in each municipality, as in fact occurs in Sweden. Such grants at best only offset the extra fiscal burdens on local communities with a lag, and may not fully offset them at all. Moreover, they are a cumbersome way to solve the problem. If the elderly are the fiscal responsibility of the central government, as implied by its policy of tailoring grants to local governments based on the number of elderly in the local community, then why does the central government not assume responsibility for them directly? Why place the burden on the local community and then lighten the burden through grants?

A similar logic implies that care for the disabled be funded and administrated by the central government.

Conspicuous by its absence from the list of locally funded public services is police protection. (Fire protection is included under "protective services," but not police protection.) In strong federalist systems, like those of Canada and the United States, both the central and local levels of government provide police services. Such an arrangement enables citizens to hold their local governments to better account for local crime. Several city governments in the United States have responded to citizen concerns about crime in their community by introducing reforms of police practices, increasing police budgets, and the like. Shifting some authority for police protection in Sweden to the municipal level is an obvious reform worth considering.

MAXIMUM USE OF USER FEES AND BENEFIT TAXES

As discussed in chapter 7 there are many advantages from replacing the rather arbitrary collection of taxes used to raise revenue in Sweden today with a greater use of user fees and benefit taxes. Although such a substitution would provide benefits even if no changes in the federalist structure of Sweden were undertaken, a greater use of user fees and benefit taxes carries with it the advantage in a federalist system of reducing or eliminating the potential costs of tax competition across local communities. When taxes and benefits are separated, anyone paying higher taxes in a community than the benefits that she receives has an incentive to move to another community where she is treated more fairly. When taxes and benefits are joined, this incentive disappears. The person receiving large benefits from living in a particular community has no incentive to leave it to avoid the high taxes levied to finance these benefits, since she will lose the benefits as well as the taxes when she leaves. Although there are incentives for different communities to provide different levels of benefits, these incentives arise because citizens have different preferences for public goods. Once each citizen has found the community, which comes closest to providing the level of benefits and taxes that he most prefers, he has no incentive to move other than for the usual personal reasons (change of job, change of family status, etc.).

But how do we measure the benefits a citizen receives from publicly provided roads, police and fire protection, and so on? How do we identify the beneficiaries of the publicly provided goods and services by the city of Lund? As a first approximation, these beneficiaries are the people living, working or visiting Lund. Moreover, the extent of their benefits is likely to be proportional to the time that they spend in Lund. Someone who lives in Lund benefits far more from the public services provided by the municipal government than someone who visits the city for a week. Trying to capture these different benefits with an income tax will be difficult. A property tax comes much closer. If it is levied on businesses and individuals, it will also be paid in part by those who only visit the city, assuming that they eat in its restaurants, stay in its hotels, frequent its theatres, etc. And the total taxes a person pays will be directly proportional to the time and money spent in the city.

Property taxes have several other advantages over income taxes. Property is, for example, far less mobile than capital and far more difficult to conceal. While it is possible that someone earns 10 million Sk on investments abroad, but only declares and pays taxes on the 1 million she earns in Stockholm, if she chooses to live in an apartment that matches her income, she will be taxed the equivalent of someone earning 11 million Sk, and not like someone earning only one million.

Second of all, the benefits from several publicly provided goods and services *are* reasonably approximated by the value of their property. The loss from fire to someone owning an apartment worth 10 million Sk is likely to be roughly double that of someone owning an apartment worth 5 million Sk, and the same can probably be said of the likely value of any goods protected from theft by the police.

Revenues from property taxes are far more stabile than are revenues from income taxes, and thus the dangers of municipalities running deficits and needing bailouts are smaller with property taxes as a main source of revenue (see discussion in chapter 3).

Property taxes also generate strong incentive effects for local politicians to undertake policies that stimulate development and raise property values. Jørn Rattsø (2001) has found that the use of property taxes in Norway has lowered the costs of local governments by as much as 14 percent.

Probably the biggest advantage of replacing the income tax with a property tax at the local level would come, however, through the important incentive effects on the individual taxpayer that such a change would bring about. The high marginal income tax rates in Sweden today produce significant "deadweight losses" and have important negative incentive effects, which make part-time jobs relatively more attractive as opposed to full time work, one job more attractive than two, early retirement more attractive than continuing to work. If the municipal proportional income tax were replaced by a fixed property tax that raised the same amount of revenue, there would be an important incentive for Swedes to work more than they do today. The property tax on an apartment must be paid so long as one lives in the apartment. The income effect of a property tax coupled with the substitution effect of a reduction in the income tax would give all Swedes a greater incentive to work longer and harder, and this in turn would have long-run positive effects on Sweden's national income.[10]

In 2000 the average municipal tax rate was 21.2 percent, and the average county tax on income was 10.1 percent. Anyone with an income above 255,000 Sk paid an additional 20 percent of her income to the central government and if she earned more than 399,000 Sk she paid another 5 percent upon that. Thus the marginal tax rate in Sweden in 2000 varied on average from between 31.3 percent of income to 56.3 percent. If the municipal tax on income were entirely replaced and the other taxes on income remained unchanged, these marginal tax rates would fall to between 10.1 and 35.1 percent. Given that the deadweight losses from taxation increase exponentially with the marginal tax rate, these reductions imply substantial savings in deadweight losses and substantial incentive effects on the margin.

As reported in Table 2, the mean per capita municipal outlays in Sweden in 1999 were roughly 36,000 Sk. Of these roughly half are financed out of municipal tax revenue. Assuming that this tax revenue came entirely from a property tax, it would amount to some 18,000 Sk per year – the equivalent of roughly a 1,500 Sk increase in a taxpayer's monthly rent. A hefty sum, but not one that should induce most people to live on the street once one takes into account that their income taxes have been cut, and their net of tax income has been left unchanged.

In addition to replacing the income tax as the major source of tax revenue for municipalities with the property tax, we propose a much greater use of user fees. To see the potential for this source of revenue, consider the figures in Table 4. Per capita budget figures for 2001 are presented for three municipalities. Bräcke is a small rural community, which has experienced a long recession and high unemployment; Värnamo is a thriving small-business community with a lot of entrepreneurs and manufacturing, and almost no unemployment; Stockholm is Stockholm. The first columns for each community present the per capita outlays that cannot be funded with user taxes, because the beneficiaries are too poor (children with needs), or the beneficiaries cannot be directly charged a fee (fire protection). The second column for each municipality lists the per capita user fees that would need to be levied where feasible to cover each activity. In total roughly 3/4ths of each community's budget could in principle be covered by user fees.

[10] The property tax has some disadvantages relative to an income tax. Perhaps the most serious of these is that a person suffering a permanent income fall might be forced to move to a cheaper, smaller apartment or house to lower his property tax obligation.
The tax rates on property needed to replace the income tax would, of course, differ across communities being low in communities with high property values, and high where property has low values. All taxes distort behaviour. Just as high market values for property induce people to buy smaller houses and rent smaller apartments, high property tax rates in communities with low property values would over time distort the selection of housing toward smaller living units.

Table 4: Net per Capita Expenditures and Main Revenues in Three Different Types of Swedish Municipalities, and Suggestions for User-fee Financed Activities, Alternate Tax Levels and Property Tax

	Bräcke		Värnamo		Stockholm	
Proposed base of finance	Taxes	Per capita fees	Taxes	Per capita fees	Taxes	Per capita fees
Political superstructure	791		479		307	
Infrastructure	2 971		2 317		1 662	
Sports & leisure		1 323		951		676
Cultural activities		726		664		848
Preschooling, school day care		3 958		3 930		4 364
Per child cost (1-12 yrs)		*130 837*		*89 488*		*100 878*
Education		13 964		10 663		9 227
Per child cos.						
basic education (7-15)		*69 289*		*54 052*		*70 980*
education (16-18)		*91 226*		*68 357*		*71 706*
Elderly *		11 217		7 610		7 706
Per elderly care cos.						
home		*267 025*		*74 368*		*71 459*
institution		*291 326*		*306 899*		*323 277*
Disabled	2804		1903		1927	
Social allowance, indiv. care	1 392		1 345		4 108	
Need-based subsidies	300		620		-84	
Total costs	8 140	31 188	7 048	23 818	7 901	22 821
Sum total net costs		39 328		30 866		30 722
Tax revenues		23 895		25 780		26 520
Central gov transfers		15 392		4 307		2 373
Population 2000		7 577		32 256		750 348
Average income		150 000		177 000		201 0005,4
Average local tax level **		15,9%		14,6%		17,6%
Av tax IF NO GOV TRANS		26,2%		17,0%		14,4%
Av tax level IF FEES		5,4%		4,0%		3,9%
Property tax base per capita		270 000		220 000		300 000
Property tax rate with presen costs		14,6%		14,0%		10,2%
Property tax rate IF FEES		3,0%		3,2%		2,6%

Note: The figures are based on the fiscal year 2000. Please observe, that the fees for care and education do not correspond to the real fees people would pay; they are average per capita costs. Also included (in bold italics) are the actual costs per child/elder. The figures indicate considerable variations in costs across municipalities – more than 50 per cent. Differences in demography as well as efficiency makes it impossible to exactly predict what the costs would amount to if some services were privatized.

*) According to the propositions in this chapter, costs and responsibilities for care of elderly should be transferred to the central, state level.
**) Note that this is not equivalent to the actual tax levels; it is calculated on the per capita costs and mean incomes presented here. The figures are only rough estimates and should be related to the average tax rate for Swedish communities that is 20,1 per cent.
SOURCE: SCB. Kommunal Fastighetsskatt, Skattebasberedningen, Svenska Kommunförbundet. Sid 15.

Some of the items that we have included in the potential-user-fee category, like care for the elderly and some items in the category covered by local taxes, like care for the disabled, should as argued above be part of the central government's budget and not the local governments' budgets and would disappear from the latter no matter how they were funded. Police protection would, on the other hand, be added into local budgets, and this expenditure item would have to be covered by taxes.

The bottom rows reveal the level of tax burden of the present system, and the levels that would exist if greater use were made of property taxes and user fees. At the current levels of expenditures, the tax dividend in the two smaller communities amount to roughly 15 percent of average incomes given the current levels of government transfers, in Stockholm the figure is 18 percent. Abolishing grants from the central government and at the same time shifting care for the elderly and the disabled to the central budget would raise the average tax burden in Bräcke by about one percent, lower it in Värnamo by about 2.5 percent, and lower it in Stockholm by about 4 percent.

To cover current outlays entirely out of a property tax, it would have to be set at roughly 14 percent of property values in the two small communities, at 10 percent in Stockholm. Maximum use of user fees reduces the levels of property taxes in all three communities to only about three percent of property values.

One argument that has been put forward in support of public financing of day-care centres is that the community gains from children attending day-care centres, because they do better later in school than children who remain at home (see discussion and evidence cited in chapter 2). This argument seems to assume that parents are not interested in how well their children do in school, and thus that parents will not take into account the effects of day-care centres on their children's subsequent performance in school, when deciding whether or not to send them to day-care. If this assumption is false, if parents are concerned about how well their children do in school, then this externality from day-care centres is internalised. This first argument fails to distinguish between Pareto-relevant and infra-marginal externalities.

A second argument for public financing of day-care centres rests on the assumption that it leads to a substantial increase in (mostly female) labour participation and thus to enhanced state revenues from income taxation. Female participation rates have been rising in all of the highly developed countries, however, regardless of whether child day-care is publicly or privately financed. In 1999 the female participation rate in the United States reached 60 percent, a figure not that far off from the level Sweden, even though the state plays little or no role in providing day-care services in the United States.[11] One must recognize, therefore, that a large fraction of the subsidies for day-care provided by the state go to families which would have paid the full costs themselves if need be. Thus, a large component of day-care programs consists of a pure redistribution with no effects on allocative efficiency whatsoever. This redistribution is from those without children to those with, *and* from those with children who do not utilize day-care facilities to those who do. On the assumption that two-income families have higher incomes on average than one-income families, this latter form of redistribution is from the bottom toward the top. The existence of programs like state-financed day-care is one explanation for why so much redistribution in Sweden is "targeted" on middle and upper income groups. Financing such programs through full-cost user fees would increase both the efficiency and the fairness of the system.

We wish to stress that we are not proposing that Sweden abandon all forms of redistribution programs that favour families with children. As discussed in Section I, we see the brunt of redistribution based on altruistic and similar criteria to fall onto the central government. When determining who is eligible for an income transfer or a tax reduction the central government should certainly take into account the number and age of a family's children. Once sufficient tax reductions and transfers have been granted so that all parents are able to take care of themselves and their children properly, we believe that it should be their choice and not the state's as to whether they put their children into preschool programs and the like. And fairness demands that they pay the full costs for these programs, if they choose to take advantage of them.

User fees are, of course, the most direct way of informing a citizen about the costs of a particular government service and then letting the citizen decide how much of the service she wants to consume. A greater link between costs and price can also be achieved even where user fees are impracticable, however, through the use of earmarked takes. Returning to our example of a property tax, for example, one could choose to finance the fire department with a tax of x percent of property values, police protection through a tax of y percent, and so on. Anyone wishing to see more spent on police protection would then know that y would have to be increased, and could calculate exactly what this improvement in public services would cost. Such reforms cannot help but make citizens better informed and thereby improve the quality of the collective decision process.

RECOMMENDATIONS

The discussion of this chapter leads logically to a set of institutional changes that would improve the accountability and performance of Sweden's democratic system. Some of these changes could and ideally would be written into the constitution. Others would be reforms that could be implemented by the national parliament or by the municipal governments. To crystallize thinking and sharpen debate we offer the following lists of constitutional and institutional changes for consideration.

---

11 Council of Economic Advisors (2001, p. Sherwin Rosen (1996) contrasts the experiences of Sweden and the United States with respect to women's entering the labor force.

Constitutional Changes

1. The work of government is divided into two levels – the central and the municipal levels.

2. The constitution provides for citizen-initiated referenda at both the central and municipal levels, with referenda perhaps mandated for some types of decisions. These referenda are binding on the level of government in question.

3. The constitution assigns authority over certain expenditures to each level of government. For example, national security, care for the elderly and disabled, healthcare, and unemployment insurance are the responsibilities of the central government, primary and secondary education, sanitation, fire and local police protection are the responsibility of the municipalities.

Institutional Changes Outside of the Constitution

1. Direct, town-meeting democracy is adopted in communities of fewer than 10,000 inhabitants.

2. Reduce or eliminate central government prescriptions of performance levels for activities assigned to the municipalities.

3. Reduce or eliminate entirely general grants from the central to the municipal levels.

4. Replace taxes with user fees for financing the provision of publicly goods and services wherever feasible.

5. Replace the income-based municipal tax with a fixed property tax on both residential and business property.

6. Employ earmarked taxes where feasible.

Discussion

All of our proposals are, of course, merely suggestions to think about in the context of constitutional reform in Sweden. Although some of our proposals – like the elimination of central government mandates – might be written into the constitution, we do not recommend that this be done for fear that it would unduly constrain future government actions. The ability to call referenda and reverse governmental policies would be a check against such infringements by the central government on local autonomy.

For similar reasons we do not recommend that the constitution require that local communities of less than 10,000 inhabitants be organized as direct democracies, or that they rely on the property tax as their main source of income. Our goal is merely to demonstrate the potential for such reforms, it should be for each community to decide which of these it wishes to adopt.

CONCLUSIONS

A major problem for the citizens of Sweden is that the political and administrative systems devised for welfare and services on the local level are almost incomprehensible. No ordinary person can know to what extent the taxes that she pays correspond to the public services that she receives. To a large extent this system was created through cooperation between local and central government politicians and reflects a political consensus that evolved over the 20th century in favour of creating a fair system for all. But the result has been that Swedes pay way too high of a price for services that could be provided more fairly and effectively in other ways.

A major obstacle in the way of the changes that we propose lies in the political rhetoric about "the right for equal treatment across all of Sweden," and "the right to equal services regardless of where one lives." Our proposals would allow citizens to receive the same level of benefits over the entire country, but would also provide the citizen with the power to decide exactly what kind of benefits and at what levels she wished to receive them at the municipal level. It would also give the citizen considerably more power to determine the amount of her own money that is spent on local services.

Our proposals would give Sweden a clearer federalist structure, and thereby would enhance political responsibility and expenditure authority at both levels of government. The enhanced transparency arising out of linking local expenditures and taxes would increase the citizen's ability to understand the local political process and the decisions it makes. Reforms like the introduction of direct democracy would also increase the citizen's ability to affect outcomes of the political process at the local level. Together these changes would negate the second fact about local self-government in Sweden, stated at the beginning of our chapter, by creating real and effective local government. In so doing these reforms would add meaning to the right to local self-government proclaimed in the first paragraph of the Swedish Constitution.

REFERENCES

Atkinson, Anthony B., Rainwater, Lee and Smeeding, Timothy M. (1995) *Income Distribution in OECD Countries,* Paris: OECD.

Buchanan, James M. and William C. Stubblebine (1969) "Externality" *Economica* 29, November, 371-84.

Council of Economic Advisors (2001) *Economic Report of the President,* Washington, D.C.: Government Printing Office.

Feldstein, Martin and Andrew Samwick (1998) "The Transition Path in Privatizing Social Security" in Martin Feldstein (ed.) *Privatizing Social Security,* Chicago: University of Chicago Press, 215-60.

Furstenberg, George M. von and Dennis C. Mueller (1971) "The Pareto Optimal Approach to Income Redistribution: A Fiscal Application," *American Economic Review* 61, September, 628-37.

Hochman, Harold M. and James D. Rodgers (1969) "Pareto Optimal Redistribution," *American Economic Review* 59, September, 542-57.

Homburg, Stefan (1997) "Old-Age Pension Systems: A Theoretical Evaluation," in H. Giersch (ed.) *Reforming the Welfare State*, Berlin: Springer, 233-46

Inman, Robert P. and Daniel L. Rubinfeld (1997) "The Political Economy of Federalism," in Dennis C. Mueller (ed.) *Perspectives on Public Choice,* Cambridge: Cambridge University Press, 73-105.

Kirchgässner, G., Feld, L.P. und Savioz, M. (1999) *Die direkte Demokratie. Modern, erfolgreich, entwicklungs- und exportfähig,* Basel: Helbig und Lichtenhahn.

Kotlikoff, L. J. (1998) "Simulating the Privatization of Social Security in General Equilibrium," in Martin Feldstein (ed.) *Privatizing Social Security*, Chicago: University of Chicago Press, 265-306.

Mueller, Dennis C. (1996) *Constitutional Democracy*, New York: Oxford University Press.

Mueller, Dennis C. (1997) "Federalism and the European Union: A Constitutional Perspective," *Public Choice* 90, 255-80.

Mueller, Dennis C. (2002) "The Political Economy of Aging Societies," in Horst Siebert (ed.) *Economic Policy for Aging Societies,* Berlin: Springer, 269-284.

Mueller, Dennis C. (2003) *Public Choice III*, Cambridge: Cambridge University Press.

Pommerehne, Werner W. (1978) "Institutional Approaches to Public Expenditures: Empirical Evidence from Swiss Municipalities," *Journal of Public Economics* 9, April, 163- 201.

Pommerehne, Werner W. and Friedrich Schneider (1982) "Unbalanced Growth between Public and Private Sectors: An Empirical Examination," in R. H. Haveman (ed.) *Public Finance and Public Employment*, Detroit MI: Wayne State University Press, 309-26.

Rattsø, Jørn (2001) "Productivity and Costs in Public Production of Services," mimeo, Norwegian University of Science and Technology, Oslo.

Rawls, John A. (1971) *A Theory of Justice*, Cambridge, Mass.: Belknap Press.

Rosen, Sherwin (1996) "Public Employment and the Welfare State in Sweden," *Journal of Economic Literature*, 34 (June), 729-40.

Uddhammar, Emil (2000) *Conflict, Consensus and the Influence of Political Parties: The Swedish Case 1900-1999, with a Reference to the United Kingdom.* Working Paper, City University of Stockholm.

9

A SUMMARY, AND FOUR THESES ON STATE-LOCAL RELATIONSHIPS

Per Molander*

Mapsec, Stockholm

INTRODUCTION

Conditions in the municipal sector and the relationships between the state and the municipalities have been analysed in a number of different perspectives by the contributors to this book – economical, democratic, and legal. In this concluding chapter, we summarise some of the findings and present a handful of theses on state-local relationships. These theses to some extent draw upon the earlier chapters but are also based on the international literature.

BY WAY OF SUMMARY

In their closing discussion, Boadway and Johansson summarise a number of points that could possibly qualify for being included in the constitution. The first of these points serve to stress the common interest that national and local government are intended to serve: social justice and nationwide redistributive equity, equality of opportunity and the efficient functioning of the national economy. Second, the constitution could include a section outlining the responsibilities of local government, both exclusive and shared. There is also the problem of residual power, which according to the authors is most naturally assigned to the national level in unitary states. But no matter what is finally decided in these respects, there is a need for permanent re-interpretation, and disputes will never be fully eliminated.

Von Hagen and Dahlberg, in their detailed analysis of the bailout problem, conclude that a moral hazard mechanism is in fact at work, but that the main problem at least in Sweden seems to lie on the supply side. A tradition of high ambitions in welfare policy, ambiguity and discretion in dealing with local financial difficulties, and a strong commitment to macroeconomic stabilisation are all factors that favour bailouts. By contrast, the relatively high degree of financial autonomy at the local level reduces this risk. In an isolated bailout perspective, there is thus a strong case for a high degree of local autonomy. But the final division of powers, financial and other, of course needs to take other aspects into account as well.

Equalisation is a contentious issue. In countries where the state assigns a large number of costly tasks to the local level, some sort of equalisation of resources is necessary, either via explicit equalisation systems, or by state grants, or both.

* per.molander@mapsec.com

According to Chernick, the present design has its pros and cons. Equalisation acts as an insurance against economic shocks and reduces the incentives for potentially costly beggar-thy-neighbour policies, but it may also reduce the incentive for each municipality to stimulate economic growth, more specifically per-capita labour supply. At present, it is not possible to judge which of these effects dominates. Nonetheless, there may be reasons for considering alternative designs of the equalisation system.

Grants represent a carrot rather than a stick, but as Gillette points out in his chapter, the use of grants does not put an end to the discussion about state interventions and local autonomy. By tying more or less specific conditions to grants, the state may impose restrictions that are in reality as far-reaching as if they were imposed by legislation. Thus, even in an ideal world of positive stimuli, there is a need for some sort of mechanism for conflict resolution.

Mueller and Uddhammar draw attention to the fact that state-local issues are in fact a subset of a wider collection of problems pertaining to freedom and resource allocation in general in society. A strengthened federalist system requires both democratically elected governments at the local level, and a clear link in the citizens' eyes between the taxes that they pay and the services that they receive from government. Whether fees or taxes are chosen as sources of financing for public services affects the borderline between public and private, and therefore indirectly also the need for equalisation and state transfers. On the other hand, extensive use of fees as advocated by the authors calls for risk polling via insurances or taxes and consequently leads to other design problems.

The creation of the European Union, as Olof Petersson stresses, has added another layer to an already complex structure of interdependencies. There is a need for a permanent development of mechanisms of accountability in order to counter the downside effects of this increasing complexity. But even so – and here several of the authors join in their conclusions – there is no "solution" that will eliminate the problems under investigation.

It is because of this absence of a definite solution that so many authors, irrespectively of their point of departure, reach the conclusion that there is need for an ongoing debate and that dispute solving has to be formalised. In order to ensure some reasonable degree of rule of law, accountability and predictability, as much as possible of the division of powers should be specified in the constitution. But no lawmaker can foresee all situations that will emerge and all trade-offs between conflicting goals that will have to be made. This is why the constitution should also delineate a formal legal procedure for solving disputes between the various levels (see section 9.4).

ON THE FUNCTIONING OF THE PUBLIC SECTOR

The literature on multi-level democracy is voluminous, and a large part of it is devoted to the search for a division of powers and responsibilities that is in some sense optimal. The *principle of subsidiarity* epitomises the idea that responsibility should be as far down the hierarchy as possible. The motives may be based on democracy theory, as in the European Charter of Self-Governance[1], in the treaty of the European Union or in chapters 7 and 8 of this book, or largely economical, as when Brennan and Buchanan claim that low-level decisions lead to lower expenditure levels allegedly more in accordance with voter preferences[2]. Irrespectively of the motives put forward, there is an implicit hypothesis about a best solution.

A different hypothesis, presented by Scharpf[3], is that it is precisely in the interaction between the various levels that problems arise. According to Scharpf, public decision-making functions less well both in Germany and in the European Union because the central level is dependent on lower level for its decisions and, further, that unanimity or almost full unanimity is required by the decision-making framework. The deadlocks that arise, in Scharpf's view, lead to irrational decisions and to institutional sclerosis that make institutional reforms impossible.

Hypotheses of this kind are of course neither comprehensive nor unambiguous. As is clear from the discussion in chapter 2, general principles seldom admit of clear-cut conclusions. Both the European Charter and the Amsterdam treaty have escape clauses from the principle of subsidiarity, implying that it often remains an open question what is in a concrete situation the solution to be preferred[4]. Further, the complete veto power that Scharpf assumes in his argument is seldom or never at hand. What is common to the two modes of explanation is that the functioning of the system is assumed to depend mainly the division of power and resources at the macro-level.

An alternative view would be that the functioning of the public sector is to a considerable extent decided at the level where the activity is located.

***Thesis no. 1**: How well the public sector works at a certain level depends more by control and audit mechanisms at the level in question than by the general division of powers or the interaction between the levels. A basic requirement is that a reasonably clear division of responsibilities actually obtains.*

In order to justify this proposition, let us start from the essence of the democratic mission. Political decision-makers face the electorate in general elections and, more informally and with varying intensity, between elections. In order for the electorate to be able to judge how the task is handled during the election period, information about what is happening in the public sector is required – how various activities develop, if the total expenditure level is under control, if actual decisions are in line with political priorities, and if service production is efficient. In general terms, we know what is necessary for this to be accomplished – a well-functioning budget process, reliable accounts, autonomous audit, and, for the most complicated problems, resources for qualified evaluation and research. This is true whether

---

[1] European Council (1985).
[2] Brennan and Buchanan (1980).
[3] Scharpf (1985).
[4] The European Charter has the formulation, " Allocation of responsibility to another authority should weigh up the extent and nature of the task and requirements of efficiency and economy"; the phrasing of the Amsterdam treaty is similar.

activities are run at the municipal, state, or supranational level. *A certain division of powers cannot replace these basic requirements on control of activities and financial flows.*

For the sake of clarity it is necessary to underline the need for a clear definition of responsibilities as a basis for this process. In order for standard instruments of economic control (in a wide sense) to be efficient, a clearly defined task is necessary. This is far from a trivial requirement; many of the problems currently encountered in the public sector stem from unclear interfaces between the state on the one hand and municipality or county council on the other.

International experiences point in the same direction. For a number of years, a wave of decentralisation has swept across the administration in many countries. This process of decentralisation has both a geographic dimension – in the sense of devolution of power to regions and local governments – and within the central administration, by the creation of agencies. The experience from these experiments is mixed. As pointed out by Allen Schick[5], new forms of governance based on contracts assume norms and modes of thinking that cannot be taken for granted in all environments. In a study of decentralisation of financial power in 78 countries, De Mello and Barenstein[6] show that the quality of governance (measured for instance by corruption indices or efficiency) does not correlate in any simple way with the degree of decentralisation. In fact the quality of governance tends to deteriorate when the revenue from local taxes pass a certain threshold, which the authors explain by the difficulties of maintaining accountability at the local level. Similar conclusions have been drawn from studies made at the initiative of the World Bank[7]. In addition, the ability of the state to live up to its responsibility for macroeconomic management can be undermined if financial policy at the local or regional level is not sufficiently disciplined[8].

Against this background it is clear that a basic condition for successful decentralisation is that mechanisms quality control and financial control that are standard at the national level are maintained also the local level[9]. Concerning audit, there is room for substantial improvement in the municipal sector, but it must be stressed that the situation is highly variable[10]. Also the sources of revenue may be if importance. Empirical tax research indicates that the visibility may be of importance. Rattsö's analysis of Norwegian municipalities indicate that a municipal property tax can lead to higher efficiency in local government[11]; a likely explanation is that capitalisation creates an incentive for local politicians to manage well. A stronger role for fees as a source of revenue, as argued in chapters 7 and 8 in this book, can be expected to have similar effects. Yet another mechanism that strengthens the position of the citizen in the encounter with local service producers is the possibility to choose among the producers of for instance child-care or care for

[5] Schick (1998).
[6] De Mello and Barenstein (2001).
[7] See Kahkonen (2001) with further references.
[8] Ter-Minassian and Craig (1997).
[9] Molander (1999), Rattsö (2002).
[10] Lundin (1999), Cassel (2000).
[11] Rattsö (2002).

the elderly[12]. The source of financing is of less importance in this context, given that it is the possibility to choose that is important.

What could be perceived as a counterexample to the thesis presented is the bailout problem analysed in chapter 3. The origin of this problem is precisely the interaction between two levels of the public hierarchy and the risk of irresponsible behaviour that goes with expectations on the state level. But it is important to notice in this context that bailout situations do not emerge automatically as soon as multilevel uncertainties of this kind prevail; the source of the problem is rather inadequate economic control at the lower level. As shown by von Hagen and Dahlberg, it is not the poorest municipalities that run the greatest risk of failing. The main antidote against bailouts is by consequence improvement of the control function, and the responsibility of the state in this context is to maintain and develop the regulatory framework.

Economic control mechanisms in a narrow sense are of course not the only ones that are important. Democratic, legal, and mass media routines and institutions are needless to say of vital importance to the functioning of the public sector.

Summarising, the search for the final ideal division of powers and responsibilities between the various levels of the public sector appears somewhat misdirected. The development and systematic strengthening of mechanisms of economic control must be pursued, irrespectively of the division of responsibilities chosen. This is not to say that the basic division of powers is uninteresting; there are obviously highly unpractical solutions to be avoided. But within the spectrum of reasonable divisions of responsibilities, the success of the democratic system to a considerable extent is determined by other factors than precisely which activities have been assigned to one or the other level.

ON STATE RESPONSIBILITIES

In order for the public sector to function properly a comprehensive regulatory framework is required. Further, a continuous flow of information is necessary – information about activities, quality, finances – and part of the regulatory framework is devoted precisely to specifying the requirements on this flow of information. Only the state can in the final instance assume responsibility for maintaining and developing this framework.

Thesis no. 2*: The state is responsible for maintaining and developing the regulatory framework for municipal activities necessary for their proper functioning. The requirements on the local government budget process should be strengthened.*

In the context of fundamental human rights guaranteed by the constitution, the above proposition is not an issue, not even in federal states with far-reaching autonomy for its member states. At a more down-to-earth level, the Swedish law on local government stipulates the conditions for local government activities

[12] See the report from the SNS economic Policy Group (2000) with further references.

concerning mandates, administration, the basics of the budget process and a range of other aspects. Sector legislation likewise regulates conditions for the activities that municipalities and county councils are responsible for. This is quite natural, just as private-sector activities, by definition autonomous, must conform to general requirements such as formulated in corporate law, legislation on working conditions, etc.

There is similarly a strong case for state as regulator of the requirements on information about local government conditions. Information is obviously a key resource in the principal-agent relationship that citizens and decision-makers are involved in. Information is collective good, not only in the municipality that it concerns directly but also more generally when aggregated with information about other municipalities, as a basis for comparison between different solutions or more qualified evaluation efforts. The Council for Municipal Analyses and Comparisons, created by the Swedish parliament in 2002, illustrates the collective nature of this sort of information, and how the coordination problem can be handled.

It is sometimes claimed that nationally regulated requirements on information about local government would imply a threat to local autonomy. This seems hard to defend, given that collection and aggregation of information falls well within the boundaries suggested by the European Charter of what can be justified in order to secure efficiency[13]. Nor is it an argument that the information about a municipality concerns only the members of that municipality. Such an argument presumes that each and every municipality be self-sufficient concerning knowledge about the partly very complicated issues that public-sector governance gives rise to. The typical (median) Swedish municipality has a population of about 16.000 inhabitants and cannot be assumed to possess all the expertise needed to maintain the control mechanisms necessary for quality and efficiency requirements to be satisfied.

Another objection sometimes heard – and one that to some extent runs counter to the previous one – is that information about the various activities can only be understood by representatives of the profession involved. Thus, for instance, statistical information about educational results could only be understood by people with pedagogical training. Within the health care system, certain clinics may specialise in difficult cases, something that would bias the statistical record. But this does not appear to be a legitimate objection. One could for instance compare with another security-related activity such as the Swedish mandatory regular motor vehicle inspection. The state-owned company in charge of this service publishes annual data from these tests, including detailed information about the results for various car brands. Also in this case it is reasonable to imagine that certain types of cars are owned and run by persons with typical manners of driving that bias the result, but this is something that the manufacturers have to live with, and it is certainly not considered as an argument for handing over the responsibility for the inspections to the manufacturers, including the right to decide what results should be published.

---

[13] ”requirements on efficiency and economy”.

The Association of Local Authorities and the Federation of County Councils have for a number of years been involved in developing key indicators for the activities that their members are responsible for. As mentioned above, a new agency was created in 2002 with the task of coordinating the work on data bases, standardisation etc.[14] It is important that this work takes into account not only the interests of the producers but above all defends the perspective of the citizens. A national, comprehensive database has the potential of becoming a powerful instrument for quality and efficiency control in the local government sector.

The financial area is of course central; the bailout problematique is, as was shown in chapter 3, a most real one. In a country with a well-developed welfare state it is difficult to imagine that the state would *not* intervene if a municipality finds itself in a financial quandary. Even if the state support that has been granted in recent years has to some extent been coupled to tangible restrictions on the municipal administrations involved, there is no guarantee against the repetition of the same patterns of behaviour in the future. That the financial well-being of every municipality is carefully monitored can only be seen as a necessary component of the implicit insurance relationship that exists between the state and the local government sector.

In the local government act the state formulates some basic requirements on both the budget process and the substance of the decisions involved. The latter part concerns in particular the requirement on a balanced budget, coupled to a requirement on recuperation of unintended deficits within (in principle) two years. It can be questioned whether this is sufficient in municipalities suffering from a long-term financial deterioration, quite apart form the fact that the condition in itself has been criticised for being too rigidly formulated. It should be noted that the paragraph in question has an escape clause ("very strong reasons").

In view of what has been said it would be natural for the state to formulate more far-reaching requirements on the municipal budget process. The requirements should have the same character as are currently maintained at the state level, with due adaptations to the special conditions of the municipal sector. This route also has the advantage of being less authoritarian, given that the conditions are formulated for the process rather than its outcomes[15].

ON DISPUTE SOLVING

An economic analysis of what may be a reasonable division of responsibilities between state and local government gives certain indications but in most cases no definite answer (chapter 2). That the military defence of the territory and the legal system belong to the state level and that public parks and sports grounds to the

---

[14] Ds 2000:48, SOU 2001:75, Dir. 2002:91.

[15] There are certain parallels here to the EU stability and growth pact, the conditions of which are formulated for measurable entities such as the deficit, accumulated debt etc. A protocol to the Maastricht agreement contains conditions also on national procedures in the budgetary area, but these conditions have not been operationalised, nor have they been used in the implementation of the treaty.

local is easy to justify, but beside such clear-cut cases there is a broad spectrum of tasks for which there are arguments in both directions.

In all important policy areas the state codifies ends and to a considerable extent also means. Areas such as basic education and health care are characterised by high ambitions, partly materialised in documents such as national curricula. In these cases, we are dealing with delegation of production responsibilities to the local level, not with activities that are the result of local initiatives. In order for delegation to function, a clearly defined task is required, as well a continuous flow of information that is processed at the state level, and a repertoire of sanctions to be used when the nationally defined level of ambition is not reached or restrictions of various kinds are violated. Unfortunately, central agencies such as the National School Board or the national Board of Health and Welfare are to some extent circumscribed in their efforts by the idea of local autonomy, something that must be taken into account when responsibilities are divided between the levels. Agencies such as these often lack in evaluative capacity, even if important progress has been made in recent years.

There is a natural expansive drive in most administrations, including local government. But the main point of dispute between the state and local government is in most cases not about the fundamental issue who should be responsible for a given task but rather how this responsibility should be exercised once it has been assigned to the local level. There is a strong feeling at the local level that the state, once it has delegated responsibility downwards, must also allow this delegation to find its true expression. If the state delegates a major task but arrogates to itself the power to intervene in details, many of the potential gains to be reaped from delegation risk being lost, both with respect to economic efficiency and sense of autonomy. Assistance to the handicapped and the supply of library services are some recent cases in point from the Swedish scene.

If the requirement on accountability is pushed very hard, the conclusion will be full state responsibility both for production and financing, the reason being that legislation is national by origin. But this requirement on accountability must be balanced against other requirements, and a certain lack of clarity will always prevail. There seems to be no way of solving this conflict once and for all by some form of legal invention. It is noteworthy that the European Court of Justice has so far not in any of its cases relied exclusively upon the principle of subsidiarity, in spite of its inclusion into the Treaty and a rather expansive policy on the part of the Court. Discussions in the EU convention on an extended role for the principle and the possibility indicate that it can form the basis for developing legal practice in this area[16]. It is likely that the application of the principle be limited to severe infringements on lower-level autonomy (see further the discussion by Gillette in chapter 5).

The situation for the principle of financing – the requirement that new state initiatives be fully financed – is in a sense easier. Even though the application in practice of this principle sometimes calls for rather intricate economic analysis, it is

[16] european.convention.eu.int

in most cases easier to give a relatively precise answer to the question what compensation is necessary.

***Thesis no. 3**: If a dispute arises between the state and a municipality or a group of municipalities concerning the application of the principle of subsidiarity or the principle of financing, the conflict should be solved by a legal procedure of arbitration.*

That higher levels in the public hierarchy assign tasks to lower levels without guaranteeing proper financing is a universal problem. In the United States and Canada for instance, there is a lively debate on unfounded mandates. The principle of financing laid down in Sweden in 1993 requires that the state compensate the municipalities for increased costs stemming from new legislation, and in reverse, that state grants can be adjusted downwards if costs are reduced. New legislation that affects municipalities or county councils generally, for instance in their role as employers, is not taken into account. In practice only parliamentary decisions have been affected, but also regulations and ordinances decided and enforced by agencies may of course have economic implications for local government.

When the principle of financing was introduced, the government in office claimed that there was no need for legislation[17]. The period during which the system of annual negotiations has been in operation has however been marred by recurrent conflicts about the application of the principle in practice. The fact that the government has the last word when it comes to the interpretation of the principle in concrete situations threatens the legitimacy of the system. The discussion is about decision-making with economic consequences for legal entities outside the state, and it is not conformal to the constitution that such decision-making does not occur "under the laws". There is consequently a strong case for codifying the principle. A codification would require a formula that is unambiguous enough to be used in normal legal practice. If the conflicts that may arise are considered to be so complicated that they require special competence, it is possible to create a special court of arbitration for this purpose. It would be appropriate for such a court to deal also with conflicts concerning the division of responsibilities, restrictions on state grants etc. that Gillette analyses in his contribution (chapter 5).

ON A MODIFIED SYSTEM OF EQUALISATION

As noted in the European Charter of Self-Government (art. 9), some sort of equalisation procedure compensating for differences in expenditures and revenue sources is necessary. Equalisation may be accomplished in more than one way, however, and the level of ambition also varies between countries.

Equalisation is an important topic on the political agenda, mostly in relation to individuals and households, and the central issue is what level of equality should be accomplished using taxes and benefits. It is well known that such equalisation sometimes, though far from always, leads to socio-economic costs. Arthur Okun has used the metaphor of a leaky bucket; the more one carries, the more is lost, but the

[17] Gov. bill 1991/92:150, p. 24-25

desire to equalise makes most people prepared to accept a certain cost[18]. The core problem of redistribution is consequently a trade-off between equality and efficiency.

Against this background it seems necessary to stress that equalisation between municipalities in order to finance public-service production has a totally different character than equalisation of disposable incomes at the individual or household level. In the absence of intra-municipal equalisation, inhabitants of a high-income municipality would pay lower taxes than inhabitants of a low-income ditto, even if service levels and underlying cost structures were the same. This would create an incentive to move to the high-income municipality that, unlike classical Tiebout migration, would *not* be socio-economically efficient. A certain equalisation of tax bases and compensation for differences in cost structures is by consequence economically justified.

Equalisation of tax bases has another beneficial effect: it reduces incentives to potentially costly competition for industrial location. If the revenue source of the single municipality depends strongly on its own tax base, there is a strong temptation to attract industries via various forms of subsidies – in the form of subsidised land prices or even tax rebates. The risk of ending up in an inefficient equilibrium characterised by large industrial subsidies is substantial, and international experience shows that such apprehensions are well grounded.

This is not to say that all equalisation can be justified by reference to socio-economic efficiency arguments; if this were the case, the differences in equalising ambitions would be smaller than is currently the case. Even within the group of Nordic countries that have a common tradition of ambitious welfare policies, there are noticeable differences in the systems of equalisation. What is common to the Nordic systems is the desire to raise the poorest municipalities to a level that makes it possible to deliver public services at the decided minimal level with reasonable economic sacrifice. What differs is the policy towards high-income municipalities, where the Swedish system to a higher extent absorbs the part of the tax base above the mean.

As noted by Chernick (chapter 4), it is difficult to verify in practice what are the actual costs of the system of equalisation. Critics of the system claim it affects the incentives to work and growth significantly. Some care must be exercised in this discussion, however. Taxes, benefits and income-dependent fees affect the labour supply and saving behaviour of single individuals in a way that can be assumed to imply socio-economic costs. This is not a contentious issue, although economists differ in their appreciation of the precise size of the effects. But the choices of individuals or households in these respects are not affected by the inter-municipal system of equalisation, because what the municipality (indirectly, its members) gets or contributes is independent of these choices.

Critics of the system then claim that there is an analogy with the classical debate on the excess burden of taxation in the sense that inter-municipal equalisation would affect the incentives in the municipal leadership to stimulate per capita labour supply. This is possible but to our knowledge has not been tested empirically.

[18] Okun (1975).

First, it is uncertain to what extent municipalities actually affect per-capita labour supply. Econometric studies indicate that female labour supply is somewhat elastic and can be affected by policy. The most important measures in this context are well functioning child-care and a generous system of parental leave. Of these measures, the first is mostly and the second fully decided by the state. There is of course also a possibility that municipalities decide on measures that affect labour supply positively irrespectively of the direct economic incentives involved, because there are other effects on prosperity.

There is probably more substance to the criticism that the Swedish system is overly ambitious, in the sense that it compensates for differences that are not based on the mandatory part of municipal expenditures. Given that equalisation affects total revenues and expenditures, compensation will be made also for the part of public services that municipalities have decided on voluntarily. It is of course possible to defend equalisation also for this category of public expenditures, but the case is obviously stronger for the mandatory part.

What estimates can be given for the socio-economic cost of equalisation? As long as the system is based on the principle that the net contribution to the single municipality is independent of decisions made in that municipality, the costs are probably moderate. Nonetheless, it is likely that budget constraints, because of equalisation, are perceived as softer than they would otherwise be, and that leads to a weaker pressure for rationalisation than would prevail if equalisation were less ambitious.

Independently of the level of ambition, there is reason to discuss the technique of equalisation.

***Thesis no. 4**: There is reason to consider replacing the present system of inter-municipal equalisation by a system of state grants in which the levels are adapted to the revenue bases and expenditure structures of the municipalities.*

The Nordic method of equalisation is unusual, both by international comparison and in relation to equalisation within the systems of welfare policy in general. The normal route followed is a system of state grants that is adapted to the own resources of the recipient and its burden of expenditures. The Swedish system – the "Robin Hood system" in colloquial language – instead creates an explicit zero-sum game between the municipalities, in which a limited number of municipalities carry the financial burden. Down to the last dollar it is possible to see how much each average inhabitant gets or contributes.

The method contrasts starkly with the policy style developed in welfare policy at large. The Scandinavian model is based on relatively large gross flows aimed at integrating the overwhelming majority of citizens into one and the same system – a principle that consciously or unconsciously makes it very difficult for the single household to find out what the net flow from the system actually is.

The Robin Hood system generates conflict because of its focus on details in net flows – a level of detail that significantly exaggerates the actual degree of precision and redistributive justice embedded in the system. Statistical estimates are in fact highly uncertain; it is difficult or impossible to know whether the "right" explanatory factors have been used in the estimates, and a stochastic element always remains. The models do not recognise effects of crowding in large municipalities. Revenues from other sources than taxes are not taken into account; a municipality may for instance be a large owner of hydropower production facilities while still being a large net recipient of equalisation transfers. As in the case of individual taxation it is difficult to decide what should be weighed into the equation.

The mode of presentation invites a winner/loser perspective. When the public commission on inter-municipal equalisation published its report[19] in 1998, 90 per cent of the mass media reports and comments had a winner/loser perspective[20]. This concentration on the redistributive effect in the debate stands in no reasonable relation to the actual effect. In fact, differences in standards of living stemming from differences in price levels, housing costs, state transfers to households, and differences in municipal service production not compensated for in the inter-municipal system are much greater.

It is possible to achieve approximately the same type of redistribution as in the current system via a system of state transfers, with levels adapted to local conditions. A condition is that the state takes care of a larger part of personal income taxation than today, so that all municipalities become net recipients of transfers. This implies a tax-sharing model of a kind that is frequently used abroad. The state would in that case levy perhaps one third or half of personal income taxation instead of just the progressive part. The excess burden would not be different from that of the present system. The distribution of transfers would of course have to take into account local or regional differences in conditions – related to demography, population density etc. Given that the revenues of the system would come from individuals and not municipalities, it would not be possible as it is today to compute net flows at the municipal level. The public debate would focus less on the counterproductive winner/loser perspective and instead concentrate on what is actually accomplished.

A potential downside – that may have played a role in the design of the current system – is that all the municipalities would end up on the same side of the negotiation table facing the government, something that could in the long run affect the total expenditure level. If a court of arbitration of the kind sketched in previous paragraph were created, this would be a manageable difficulty.

CONSTITUTIONAL REGULATION

Many of the measures presented above or in earlier chapters do not call for constitutional change. In some instances they do, and in other cases it may be wise to codify changes even when, strictly speaking, it is not necessary to do so. Some of the candidates for constitutional regulation are:

---

[19] SOU 1998:151.

[20] Own calculations on the basis of a synthesis made by Stockholm-based mass media consultant Observer.

- The principle of subsidiarity, possibly with some concrete examples of what would be considered national and local responsibilities, respectively.
- The principle of financing, requiring economic compensation at the municipal level for national legislation or other binding regulations that affect the general cost level.
- The principles of a court of arbitration, with the task of resolving disputes between the state and municipalities or groups of municipalities concerning the interpretation of the principles of subsidiarity and financing.

The European Convention[21] discussion of the principle of subsidiarity allows for a truly dynamic perspective. The proposal put forward includes both a legal test maintained by the European Court and a political control function to be exercised by the member states parliaments. This is a model that might be of relevance also to the national/sub-national level.

A reformed system of equalisation does not in itself call for any amendment to the constitution. What may be appropriate is:

- A general paragraph establishing that the same principle of efficient use of public resources as holds for the state is valid for the municipal sector. Special reference should be made to a municipal budget act (organic law) specifying basic requirements on the budget process, accounting for finances and results, and external audit.

REFERENCES

Brennan, G., Buchanan, J. (1980) *The Power to Tax: Analytical Foundations of a Fiscal Constitution*. Cambridge University Press, Cambridge.

Cassel, F. (2000) *Behovet av kommunal externrevision*. (The need for external audit in the municipal sector) SNS Förlag, Stockholm.

De Mello, L., Barenstein, M. (2001) *Fiscal Decentralization and Governance: A Cross-Country Analysis*. IMF WP/01/71, Washington D.C.

Dir. 2002:91. *Rådet för kommunala analyser och jämförelser*. (Directives for the council on municipal analyses and comparisons).

Ds 2000:48. *Snabbt och riktigt, utvalt och viktigt*. (Fast, correct, selected, and important. Requirements on data for inter-municipal comparisons).

Ekonomirådet (2000) *Politisk makt med oklart ansvar*. (Power and accountability in Swedish politics) Report from the SNS Economic Policy Group 2000. SNS Förlag, Stockholm.

European Council (1985) *European Charter of Local Self-Government*. European Treaty Series No. 122, Council of Europe, Strasbourg.

Kahkonen, S. (2001) "Decentralization and Governance: Does Decentralization Improve Public Service Delivery?", *PREM Notes* 55 (June 2001), World Bank, Washington D.C.

---

[21] european-convention.eu.int.

Lundin, O: (1999) *Kommunal revision: En rättslig analys.* (Municipal audit. A legal analysis) Iustus, Uppsala.

Molander, P. (1999) "Reforming Budgetary Institutions: Swedish Experiences", in R. Strauch and J. von Hagen (eds.) *Institutions, Politics and Fiscal Policy.* Kluwer, Boston.

Okun, A. (1975) *Equality and Efficiency. The Big Trade-Off.* The Brookings Institution, Washington, D.C.

Rattsö, J. (2002) Chapter 5 in T.M. Andersen and P. Molander, *Alternatives for Welfare Policy.* to be published by the Cambridge University Press in 2003.

Scharpf, F.W. (1985) "Die Politikverflechtungsfalle: Europäische Integration und deutscher Föderalismus im Vergleich", *Politische Vierteljahresschrift* 26, 323-356.

Schick, A. (1998) "Why Most Developing Countries Should Not Try New Zealand Reforms", *World Bank Research Observer* 13(1), 123-31.

SOU 1998:151. *Kostnadsutjämning för kommuner och landsting. En översyn av statsbidrags- och utjämningssystemet.* (Cost equalisation for municipalities and county councils).

SOU 2001:75. *www.kommunadatabas.nu.*

Ter-Minassian, T., Craig, J. (1997) "Control of Subnational Government Borrowing", i Ter-Minassian, T. (ed.) *Fiscal Federalism in Theory and Practice.* International Monetary Fund, Washington D.C.

INDEX

R

S

U

Kolibri 360 GmbH
Ferdinand-Jühlke-Straße 7
99095 Erfurt, Deutschland
produktsicherheit@kolibri360.de